DEPARTMENT OF EDUCATION AND SCIENCE

WELSH OFFICE

A NEW PARTNERSHIP FOR OUR SCHOOLS

...ort of the Committee of Enquiry appointed jointly ... ...ecretary of State for Education and Science ... the Secretary of State for Wales under the chairmanship of Mr. Tom Taylor, CBE

LONDON
HER MAJESTY'S STATIONERY OFFICE

i

ISBN 011 270457 3

The Rt. Hon. Shirley Williams MP
Secretary of State for Education and Science
Elizabeth House
York Road
LONDON SE1 7PH

The Rt. Hon. John Morris QC MP
Secretary of State for Wales
Welsh Office
Cathays Park
CARDIFF CF1 3NQ

Dear Secretaries of State

We were appointed by the then Secretary of State for Education and Science and the Secretary of State for Wales in April 1975 with the following terms of reference:

"To review the arrangements for the management and government of maintained primary and secondary schools in England and Wales, including the composition and functions of bodies of managers and governors, and their relationships with local education authorities, with head teachers and staffs of schools, with parents of pupils and with the local community at large; and to make recommendations".

I would like to place on record our most sincere thanks to the secretariat and the assessors for their help and advice given so readily.

I now have the honour to submit our report to you both.

T TAYLOR
Chairman

FROM

THE SECRETARY OF STATE FOR EDUCATION AND SCIENCE
AND THE
SECRETARY OF STATE FOR WALES

6 *July* 1977

T Taylor Esq
34 Tower Road
Feniscliffe
Blackburn
Lancs

Thank you for your letter of 24 June enclosing the report of your Committee. Arrangements are being made for it to be published in September. We now look forward to studying the report and its recommendations carefully since, in our view, it concerns an area of central importance to the effective future operation of our schools systems. Your Committee's conclusions will call for wide-ranging discussions amongst all those involved in the provision of education and particularly amongst local education authorities, teachers and parents. It is, we believe, particularly timely for the report to become available at a point when many aspects of the education service are the subject of debate. We are sure that your report will be a valuable addition to these discussions, and wish to express our gratitude to you and to all the members of your Committee for your work.

SHIRLEY WILLIAMS

JOHN MORRIS

THE COMMITTEE

Appointments shown are those held by members at the time the Committee was constituted.

Chairman:

Councillor T Taylor CBE, JP,
Leader of Blackburn Council

Members:

Professor G Baron,
Professor of Educational
  Administration, in the University
  of London

Miss J Barrow OBE,
Senior Lecturer, Furzedown College,
  London

Mrs M B Broadley,
Headmistress, Dick Sheppard School,
  London

Mr D P J Browning,
Chief Education Officer, Bedfordshire

Councillor E Currie-Jones CBE,
Chairman, South Glamorgan County
  Council

Mrs A E Edwards,
Parent

Mr F D Flower MBE,
Principal, Kingsway Princeton
  College, London

Councillor P O Fulton JP,
Chairman of Education Committee,
  Cleveland County Council

Mr J E Hale MBE, JP,
Headmaster, Shears Green County
  Primary Junior School, Kent

Mr G M A Harrison,
Chief Education Officer, Sheffield

Mr R N Heaton CB,
formerly Deputy Secretary, Ministry
of Education

Councillor E G Hett,
Member of Clywd County Council

Councillor J R Horrell TD, DL,
Chairman, Cambridgeshire County
Council

*Mr J A R Kay,
former director of various industrial
concerns

Miss B Lynn,
Teacher, Beech Hill Primary School,
Calderdale

Mr J Macgougan,
General Secretary, National Union
of Tailors and Garment Workers

Miss A C Millett,
Deputy Headteacher, Tile Hill Wood
School, Coventry

Mr M J Moore, OBE, JP,
Deputy Chairman, Electricity
Consultative Council for Merseyside
and North Wales

The Rev P J Reilly,
Secretary, Birmingham Diocesan
Schools Commission

Mrs J Sallis,
Parent

Mrs J Stone,
Parent

Mr K J Turner,
Headmaster, Foxhayes Combined
County Primary School, Devon

Canon R Waddington,
Bishops' Adviser for Education,
Diocese of Carlisle

---

*Resigned 24 September 1975

vii

Assessors:

Mr M W Hodges,
Department of Education and Science

Mr C A Norman,
HM Inspectorate of Schools (from
Nov 1976)

Mr S K Bateman,
Welsh Office (until Sept 1975)

Mr J B Davies,
Welsh Office (from Jan 1976)

Secretary:

Mr J K Sawtell

Assistant Secretaries:

Mr C R Appleby (until 31 December
1975)

Mr D A Wilkinson (from 9 February
1976)

The estimated cost of the production of the Report is £99,261, of which £9,261 represents the estimated cost of printing and publication, £66,000 the cost of administration, and £24,000 the travelling and other expenses of members.

viii

CONTENTS

PREFACE

1. The report which follows is the distillation of more than two years' enquiry and discussion. The relevant law, the history of school government, and the development in recent years of a bewildering variety of practice and opinion combine to make our study a complex one.

2. Nevertheless, the essential issues which emerge from this study seem to us to be very simple, and we think they are well understood by the public, whose interest in our schools has surely never been greater. Our task was threefold. First we had to identify those areas of decision-making which ought to be school-based, given that on the one hand we have traditionally set great store in this country by the variety and individuality of our schools, and that on the other people are increasingly and properly concerned to ensure that the quality of education available to *all* our children is as high as we can make it. Second, we had to determine which were the interested groups with a keen and legitimate concern with the success of an individual school. Finally, we had to find a way in which these interests could combine to bring that concern to bear on the running of that individual school, ensuring that in every aspect of its life and work it reached the highest possible standards, was run both co-operatively and responsibly, and was sensitive to the needs and wishes of the community it served. Our goal was a school with enough independence to ensure its responsive and distinctive character, taking its place in an efficient local administration of an effective national service.

3. We were pleased to have been given wide terms of reference in this task, since we were able to apply ourselves to it with few constraints on our freedom of thought. In chapter 1 we describe how we set about our work and the assumptions we made. In chapter 2 we look at the existing framework for the management and government of schools which derives from the 1944 Education Act and at the development of the system as we found it within that framework, adding at Appendix B a historical note on the period preceding the 1944 Act.

4. In chapter 3 we consider the various alternative courses of action, ranging from the retention of the present system unchanged to the complete abolition of managing and governing bodies as we know them. This chapter argues the case for a revitalising of the present system, with one governing body for each school and a clear line of delegated power running from the local education authority through the governing body to the head and staff of the school. This new-style governing body would be an equal partnership of all the interests concerned.

5. Chapter 4 is concerned with the composition of the governing body while chapter 5 sets out its vital role in promoting communication and co-operation within the school and between the school and the local education authority, the parents of its children and the wider community. Chapters 6–9 examine in detail the functions of the new body in relation to the curriculum, finance, staff appointments and other matters. Chapters 10 and 11 deal with the training of the new governors and the procedures by which they should work. Voluntary schools, insofar as their management and government derives from their voluntary character, were outside our terms of reference, but in chapter 12 we consider the implications for voluntary schools of our recommendations for county schools.

Chapter 13 deals with the means by which our recommendations should be implemented, and we conclude the report with a full summary of its recommendations.

6. What the reader will seek, in following our statements of our findings and our thoughts, is evidence of a recognisable guiding philosophy, relating it particularly to the objectives of our study as set out in paragraph 2 of this Preface. The principles which seemed to us important after studying all the evidence, listening to hundreds of people concerned with the education system up and down the country, and discussing the matter among ourselves were these:

i. within the framework of national and local policies, however these may change with time, the special character of the individual school is precious to most people and should be protected;

ii. that character is essentially a product of *local* considerations and of the skill, support and concern of all those on the spot who care about its success;

iii. one body should have delegated responsiblity for running the school, and in forming that body no one interest should be dominant—it should be an equal partnership of all those with a legitimate concern, local education authority, staff, parents, where appropriate pupils, and the community;

iv. the governing body thus formed should be responsible for the life and work of the school as a whole: we did not consider that a school's activity could be divided, and neither could accountability for its success;

v. the decision-making role of the governing body is only part of its functions: equally important is its responsiblity for promoting and protecting good relationships both within the school and between the school and its parents and the wider community: where we recommend particular measures to achieve effective communication and harmonious relationships, we therefore charge the governors with the task of ensuring their satisfactory operation;

vi. while the detail of the new arrangements which we recommend should be left to a considerable extent to local discretion, the essential features should be universal.

7. This statement of the fundamental elements in our thinking is necessarily brief and general. In the chapters which follow we examine these matters in greater depth and set out the reasons for our conclusions. We believe that many people will welcome a new approach based on the principles of equal partnership, clear and indivisible authority and responsibility for good relationships. We hope so, since whatever measures are taken by central and local government to implement our recommendations, success will depend essentially on the will of all those concerned at school level to achieve it.

CONTENTS OF THE MAIN REPORT

Page

Chapter 6 Curriculum (contd.)

Appendices *Page*

CHAPTER 1—INTRODUCTION

Formation and mode of operation of the Committee

1.1. In the House of Commons on 27 January 1975, the then Secretary of State for Education and Science, Mr Reg Prentice, announced the Government's intention to establish an independent enquiry into the management and government of schools in England and Wales. In a further announcement on 27 February, Mr Prentice and the Secretary of State for Wales, Mr John Morris, set out our terms of reference:

"To review the arrangements for the management and government of maintained primary and secondary schools in England and Wales, including the composition and functions of bodies of managers and governors, and their relationships with local education authorities, with head teachers and staffs of schools, with parents of pupils and with the local community at large; and to make recommendations".

1.2. These terms refer specifically to primary and secondary schools and so we have not been concerned with the management of nursery schools, for which no arrangements are at present prescribed, or the government of special schools. So far as the latter are concerned, it was explained in the House of Commons on 4 August 1975 that the Secretaries of State had taken the view that the considerations affecting the government of special schools were different from those which concerned ordinary schools and could best be reviewed by the committee, under the chairmanship of Mrs Warnock, which had already been established to consider the education of handicapped pupils; any of our conclusions and recommendations which appeared relevant to special schools would be referred to the Warnock Committee for consideration. We therefore provided that committee, in the latter stages of our work, with a statement setting out our general approach and describing in broad terms the developments in school government for which we looked.

1.3. In a supplementary letter to the Chairman on 5 May 1975, Mr Prentice, who was writing also for Mr Morris, suggested that we should not concern ourselves with those aspects of voluntary school management and government which reflected the present structure of the "dual system" of county and voluntary schools. The relevant part of the letter is quoted in chapter 12 where we consider the position of the voluntary schools. In the first eleven chapters we concentrate on the management and government of county schools.

1.4. In the same letter Mr Prentice also referred to the question whether the arrangements for the management and government of schools should impose an obligation on the head teacher to consult his staff on matters relating to the internal organisation, management and discipline of the school. We deal with this matter in chapter 5.

1.5. We held our first meeting in May 1975 and in July of that year invited evidence from interested organisations and individuals and from the general

1

public. Over 400 submissions were received. A full list of witnesses is given in Appendix A. Their evidence has been of great assistance to us and we have taken it fully into account in formulating our recommendations.

1.6. We thought that those reading our report might find it helpful to be reminded of some of the more important developments in the development of the concept of school managing and governing bodies. We therefore invited one of our number, who was personally involved in some of the events that led up to the introduction of the present arrangements for school management and government, to prepare an account of the period prior to 1945. His account is reproduced in Appendix B.

1.7. We decided at an early stage that a wholesale survey of current school managing and governing practice, authority by authority, would not be helpful, especially in view of the reorganisation of local government in the previous year. In any event a comprehensive study, financed by the Department of Education and Science, had been undertaken by the Department of Educational Administration of the University of London Institute of Education from September 1965 to April 1969*. We decided to use this study as a starting point and to obtain up to date information, which would throw light on more recent developments as well as supplement the considerable amount of information likely to emerge from written evidence, by carrying out a programme of visits to selected areas (details are given in Appendix C). We greatly valued the opportunity of seeing at first hand something of the arrangements in these areas and of discussing their effectiveness with those concerned. The names of all those who took part in these discussions have not been listed but the Committee is grateful for the contribution they made to its work. The Committee's thanks are also due to the local education authorities who organised the meetings.

1.8. For comparative purposes we took a number of opportunities to examine relevant aspects of the government of further education colleges and also different approaches to school government in countries other than England and Wales. The Scottish Education Department, the Foreign and Commonwealth Office and the British Council provided us with up-to-date factual information about the arrangements in Scotland and a number of other countries. We were also able to discuss arrangements in Scotland and in France, Germany, Norway, Sweden and the United States of America with experts from these countries.

1.9. In addition to the discussions in the course of our visits we have held 21 full meetings, some extending over two days and two residential week-end conferences.

The William Tyndale Schools Inquiry

1.10. Our deliberations have coincided with a further growth of public interest in school management. To some extent this can be attributed to the wide publicity given to the events at the William Tyndale Junior School. When

---

*Baron George and Howell D.A., The Government and Management of Schools. Athlone Press, 1974.

2

Mr Auld's report* appeared in July 1976, we were enjoined in numerous articles in the press to take full account of the lessons of Tyndale. By that time we had been sitting for over a year and the particular basic issues highlighted in Mr Auld's report had already been put before us both in written evidence and in the course of our area visits. We had not, however, previously found such a concentration of so many of these issues in a single school over such a relatively short period. These factors invested Mr Auld's report with a special interest for us and though, obviously, care must be exercised in drawing lessons of general applicability from such a concentration of incidents in a single school, which we are satisfied was in many ways exceptional, we have nevertheless taken full account of Mr Auld's report.

Assumptions underlying the report

1.11. We have made a number of assumptions which should be clearly stated at the outset since they underlie our recommendations. These assumptions relate to three main areas—the roles of central and local government in the provision of education, the current debate about devolution of central government functions and the need to avoid unjustifiable public expenditure.

1.12. We assumed at the outset that the roles of central and local government as specified in the 1944 Education Act would remain unchanged. When subsequently national attention was drawn to the topic by the Prime Minister's speech at Ruskin College in October 1976 we had already considered some of the issues that he opened up for general discussion. We were aware that the specific questions for discussion in this context would be fundamental and would cover the school curriculum, the assessment of standards, the education and training of teachers and school and working life. We were concerned lest basic changes in the relationship between central and local government might result that would radically affect our work. We were therefore glad to be reassured on this point by the present Secretary of State for Education and Science, who stated in a letter to the Chairman on 5 November 1976:

" . . . There is no question of the government contemplating the introduction of a detailed central control of the school curriculum which would deny teachers reasonable flexibility or diminish the contribution which local education authorities and the managers or governors should make to the conduct of the schools".

1.13. We were concerned about the possible implications for our work of changes in local government in England and Wales which might follow from ideas about devolution that have been under consideration. We sought Ministerial advice and in a letter to the Chairman on 28 June 1976, the then Secretary of State for Education and Science, Mr Fred Mulley, told us:

"I have consulted the Secretary of State for Wales on this matter and it seems to us that, while an indefinite continuation of the present structure of local government cannot be assumed, the Committee would be facing an impossible task if it sought to devise arrangements for school management and government that would not need review in the light of possible future changes in local

---

*Inner London Education Authority. William Tyndale Junior and Infants School Public Inquiry conducted by Robin Auld Q.C., I.L.E.A. 1976.

government structure. We are sure that the Committee's recommendations will be heavily influenced by the need to ensure that any arrangements for school government and management ought to be flexible and capable of adaptation to different circumstances. If and when the need arises, the position can be reviewed by the Government".

We have proceeded on the basis of this advice.

1.14. Finally, we have assumed that the country's present economic circumstances required us to make proposals which are realistic and which, in particular, involve the maximum use of existing facilities and resources. Where our recommendations involve additional expenditure we are convinced of the value which will be derived from their implementation. In such cases we have where possible provided an estimate of the cost and in chapter 13 we set out our recommendations in a way which indicates our views on their order of importance and how their phased implementation might best be achieved. In this way we hope that a new and improved system of school government can be brought into being smoothly without any large, sudden increase in public expenditure.

CHAPTER 2—PRESENT ARRANGEMENTS FOR SCHOOL GOVERNMENT

2.1. In this chapter we examine the existing arrangements for the management and government of county schools. We begin by setting out the present position in law and go on to consider school government in practice, briefly reviewing the evolution of managing and governing bodies since 1945* and analysing their present performance.

The legal background

2.2. The Education Act 1944† requires every maintained school to have a body of governors (in the case of a secondary school) or managers in the case of a primary school. The Act provides for the constitution of these bodies to be prescribed in an instrument of government or management and for the functions of the governors or managers, the local education authority (LEA) and the head teacher to be set out in articles of government or rules of management. It allocates responsibility for the making of instruments and articles or rules between the Secretary of State and the local education authority and lays down certain requirements to be met in all cases. In May 1944 the then Board of Education issued a White Paper entitled Principles of Government in Maintained Secondary Schools (Cmnd 6523). On 26 January 1945 there were issued, with Administrative Memorandum No 25, a model instrument and model articles of government for a county secondary school.‡ (Hereafter these documents will be referred to as the 1944 White Paper and the 1945 model.) Generally, over the past 30 years it has been the practice of successive Secretaries of State to uphold the principles set out in the 1944 White Paper and to expect local education authorities to do the same.

2.3. Local education authorities possess a wide discretion in the matter of the constitution of county school managing and governing bodies. Apart from a provision concerned with minor authorities§, the Education Acts do not stipulate what interests should be represented on these bodies; their constitution is thus a matter for decision by local education authorities who have been able to introduce such elements as they consider right for their own schools. Further-

---

*Developments prior to 1945 are dealt with in Appendix B.
†Relevant extracts of the Act are given in Appendix D.
‡The administrative memorandum and the model are reproduced in Appendix E.
§Where a county primary school serves an area in which there is a minor authority, Section 18 of the Education Act 1944 requires that two-thirds of the managers shall be appointed by the local education authority and one-third by the minor authority. The definition of 'minor authority' given in Section 114(1) of the Education Act 1944 was amended by Section 192(4) of the Local Government Act 1972. As from 1 April 1974 a 'minor authority' is, in England, a parish council (or the parish meeting where there is no such council) and, in Wales, a community council; or, where in either country there is no parish or community council, a non-metropolitan district council. Where the area served by a school takes in any combination of such councils the expression 'minor authority' has to be construed as referring to all of these authorities acting jointly. Section 31(10) of the London Government Act 1963 provides that in relation to any school maintained by the Inner London Education Authority, the expression "minor authority" shall be construed as a reference to the councils of the inner London boroughs and the Common Council.

more local education authorities are empowered to make arrangements for the grouping of any two or more county schools under a single governing body.

2.4. As regards the powers of these bodies, a distinction is drawn in the 1944 Education Act between primary and secondary schools. The functions of the managing bodies of county primary schools are determined solely by the local education authority which make the rules of management; the functions of secondary school governing bodies must be set out by the local education authority in articles of government which have to be approved by the Secretary of State. The responsibilities allocated to governors cover all or some aspects of the appointment and dismissal of teachers and other staff; the admission of pupils; internal organisation and curriculum; finance; the care and upkeep of the premises; and the fixing of certain school holidays.

County school government in practice

2.5. In turning to the actual development of governing bodies of county schools within this legal framework it is useful to summarise the impression likely to have been gained from a study of official reports and parliamentary debates on this subject and the common connotations of a term such as "governing body". It might have been expected from such a study that each school would have associated with it a body of interested and informed men and women, concerned with it as an individual institution rather than as a unit within a system. It would have been reasonable to assume that among these men and women there would be some representing the local education authority (whether elected members or not), some appointed or co-opted by reason of their educational or other qualifications, and some who could represent the interests of parents, of teachers and of the community in general. It would also have been reasonable to assume that a governing body so constituted would share with the local education authority and its officers, and with the head of the school, responsibility for the making of appointments, for the general direction of the conduct and curriculum of the school, for the preparation of estimates and for representing the school in issues of importance.

The reality in 1965-69

2.6. Such expectations would have been very far from being met at the time of the research study carried out by Baron and Howell between 1965 and 1969*. This showed that of the 78 county boroughs in existence at that time in England (the study did not deal with Wales) only 21 had governing bodies for each of their schools; 25 had governing bodies for groups of 2 or 3 schools; 12 had governing bodies for 4 or more schools; and in 20 cases the borough council simply nominated a single governing body to act for all its schools. In one county borough for example, there was a single body of managers for all primary schools and a single body of governors for all secondary schools; both bodies were composed of the same persons and both were identical with the primary and secondary schools sub-committee of the borough education committee. In the counties the grouping of secondary schools for governing purposes was less frequent, 22 out of 45 counties having individual governing bodies throughout, 20 having a mixture of governing bodies for individual schools and for groups

---

*Cf. Baron and Howell, pages 3 and 4 (see paragraph 1.7 footnote).

of schools and 3 having only the latter. A similar pattern was found in the counties in respect of the management of primary schools; but in the county boroughs these were still more likely than secondary schools to be governed in very large groups.

2.7. A feature of very many areas, especially county boroughs, was the close control by the local education authority, and within it by the dominant political party, of the composition of managing and governing bodies. The justification put forward for this was an argument that elective local government required not only that the local education authority, but also all its subordinate bodies, must reflect the people's elective will in their composition. In many cases membership was virtually confined to councillors, each governing body worked to tightly controlled agendas and reports and minutes were kept to a bare minimum. In other cases, the membership of governing bodies (and also managing bodies) was extended to take in members of the rank and file of political parties or other people of known sympathy with their policies.

2.8. The 1965–69 research study, in enquiring into the functions performed by managing and governing bodies, paid particular attention to three major aspects of school government: appointment of staff, curriculum and finance. In virtually all areas governors were involved in some way in the appointment of heads of schools, most frequently by taking part in interviewing procedures, either as a body or through representation on a joint committee whose other members were drawn from the authority's education committee. But the true extent of their involvement depended upon a variety of factors, including their part in the drawing up of the short list, the range of information regarding the candidates made available to them, the part played by officers and inspectors or advisers in questioning candidates and the capacities, degree of interest and above all the self assurance of individual governors. In most counties and in a substantial proportion of county boroughs governors took some part in other major appointments. Junior appointments and especially first appointments were often left to the head and the authority's advisory staff.

2.9. There was little evidence to show that, at the time of the study, the standard provision in the articles that "the governors shall have the general direction of the conduct and curriculum of the school" was taken seriously. Heads invariably maintained that they were entirely responsible for deciding what was taught, although they kept governors informed of any changes of note. Similarly, the most frequent response from governors was that they felt that the curriculum should be left to the head and his staff. There were instances, however, of reports being made by heads of departments or other teachers on aspects of teaching in the school.

2.10. Involvement in financial matters was very slight indeed and seldom went beyond receiving and formally approving estimates drawn up elsewhere. It was argued that the time factor, the administrative discretion needed by officers and heads, the provision by the local education authorities of equipment and for repairs and maintenance, and above all the pre-determined nature of the bulk of school expenditure, all combined to leave governing bodies no role in purely financial matters. There were two or three authorities which had introduced

7

arrangements designed, in the main, to give heads rather than governing bodies greater discretion in respect of minor expenditure.

2.11. In short, the extent to which managing and governing bodies carried out the functions assigned to them in rules and articles was slight. In many areas they did not, in any real sense, exist at all. The formulation of instruments, rules and articles and the approval of the latter by the Secretary of State were no guarantee that managing and governing bodies would play the role originally intended for them.

2.12. This state of affairs was due in large measure to developments many years ago which reduced the effectiveness of forms of management and government, themselves inherited from the mid-nineteenth century. As a result of the 1902 Act local education authorities took over the managerial functions which the School Boards had hitherto performed, and could delegate to managers, in respect of "provided" elementary schools. These included the responsibilities for the care of premises, the making of appointments and all financial matters which in voluntary schools continued to rest with the managers. Like the School Boards, the local education authorities were empowered to delegate their functions to managing bodies but, except in the county areas, were not required to establish such bodies. Provision for secondary schools to have governing bodies was essential when secondary education became a responsibility of local education authorities after the Education Act 1902, because schools which came under local education authority control then received grants directly from the Board of Education and had to have a responsible body to which such grants could be paid. But the need later disappeared when, save in the case of voluntary and direct grant schools, the local education authorities became, for all intents and purposes, the financing agencies.

2.13. Efforts were made before and after the passing of the Education Act 1944, to breathe new life into managing and governing bodies but these efforts were largely ineffective. Shortages of money and teachers in the post-war period led to the need to determine priorities and a greater degree of central control became necessary; centralised budgeting techniques were being developed and local education authorities' financial time-tables were affected by rate-support grant considerations. Governing and managing bodies consequently found that they had no indispensable role to perform within the executive structures set up by local education authorities. Moreover, in certain county areas the authorities had to delegate certain functions in the sphere of primary and secondary education to the councils of "excepted districts" and to other divisional executives. The consequence was that any functions assigned to managing and governing bodies were shared by other and more powerful partners, themselves increasingly limited in their freedom by national policies and agreements. The increasing emphasis on party politics in local government also had its effect. Party control of appointments extended to places on governing bodies, and the majority of them were filled by party nominees.

Events since 1969

2.14. During the eight years since the research study was completed there have been very significant changes in the context and atmosphere of school government. Many of the practices described are still to be found, but they are being modified by new forces which were only beginning to emerge during the 60s. These forces derive on the one hand from the reorganisation of local government and the reorganisation of secondary education and on the other from a demand for broader participation in educational decision-making which has come from lay and professional people alike.

2.15. The reorganisation of local government in 1974 has had a number of consequences. It has brought about, first, a reduction in the number of authorities and an increase in the size of many local education authority areas, which in turn has created a demand for greater involvement in decision making at school level. This foreseeable consequence was one of the reasons for the attention paid to governing bodies by the Royal Commission on Local Government* in 1969. The point was re-emphasised in the Second Report of the Public Schools Commission† in 1970. Second, it has often brought under one administration localities in which governing and managing bodies have had some real purpose and others in which they have received only perfunctory attention. This has resulted in the loosening of older traditions in favour of practices more in accord with the times. Third, the coming of "corporate management" in its various forms has fostered awareness of the value of the governing body as a distinctive means of ensuring proper consideration for the education interest in local government.

2.16. The reorganisation of secondary education on comprehensive lines has been significant in stimulating interest in what is happening in the school system among many who otherwise would have left the running of the school to local education authorities and teachers. Familiar scenes have changed, new and challenging opportunities have been announced and campaigns and counter-campaigns have both reflected and attracted widespread public interest. Active public opinion concerning the schools has become an element in the national and the local political situation of which parties, administrators and teachers have had to take account.

2.17. Concern expressed itself during the 1960s in the establishment of a number of voluntary organisations, notably the Advisory Centre for Education (with its periodical "Where") and the local associations for the Advancement of State Education, brought together in a national Confederation (CASE) which publishes a quarterly newsletter, "Parents and Schools". Both bodies early saw managing and governing bodies as one of the means by which they could achieve the ends they had set themselves. Similar interest was shown by the National Confederation of Parent/Teacher Associations with its journal, "Parent/Teacher". Towards the end of the '60s there came into being the National Association of Governors and Managers, with its publication "NAGM News", specifically for the purpose of revitalising school management and government. The results of the activities of these bodies affected other and much longer established organisations. Managing and governing bodies came to be mentioned

---

*Royal Commission on Local Government in England 1966-1969 (Cmnd. 4040) HMSO 1969.

†Public Schools Commission. Second Report HMSO 1970.

more frequently, after long years of neglect, in the proceedings of major teacher and local authority associations. Moreover, they came to be discussed not only in the educational press but also in the general press and to claim the attention of parliamentarians.

The position in 1975

2.18. The situation which we found when we began our work in May 1975 was one of transition. The formal framework of instruments, rules and articles was the same as six years earlier when the Baron-Howell study was completed and many of the practices then noted still continued. Thus one large authority we visited still grouped together as many as 26 primary and secondary schools under one governing body and attached so little importance to this aspect of its administration that minutes were not circulated to members. In another there was a transition to individual governing bodies from a single managing body for all primary schools and a single governing body for all secondary schools. In some other areas we visited, where there was a tradition of each school or small group of schools having their own governing bodies, their part in the making of appointments, in the discussion of school matters and in relating the schools to the communities they served, was minimal.

2.19. But there were significant differences to be noted. Several authorities had set out to institute carefully planned and effective systems of managing and governing bodies where these had not existed before. Their emergence was something not to be observed in the mid 1960s.

2.20. Another difference and one of likely great significance was the widespread acceptance of parental representation. The research study revealed formal provision for parental representation in only 9 counties and 11 county boroughs, though, of course, many of those appointed as councillors or as other representative or co-opted managers or governors were parents. A survey published by the National Association of Governors and Managers showed that in May 1975 provision was made for parents to be represented on governing and managing bodies by 70 out of the 82 local education authorities which provided information.

2.21. At the time of the research study in 1965–69 teacher representation was still more infrequent than parental representation; only a few authorities allowed teachers, whether in their own service or not, to serve on managing or governing bodies. The survey by the National Association of Governors and Managers showed, however, that 62 of the 82 authorities had set aside places for teachers.

2.22. Two other groups with claims for representation had hardly asserted themselves at all in 1969 when the research study was completed. These were the pupils in secondary schools and non-teaching staff. Now, although the practice is not widespread, a number of authorities make provision for pupils over the age of 18 to serve on governing bodies and in some cases a lower age limit may have been set. Some authorities arrange for pupils to have observer status only. There are also authorities which provide for non-teaching staff (secretaries, caretakers, groundsmen, technicians) to appoint members of managing and governing bodies.

2.23. By and large it is in the structure and composition of managing and governing bodies that change has been most marked in recent years. Redefinition of function has not proceeded at the same pace, possibly because the changes in structure and composition are, in many cases, only very recent. It would seem that where individual governing bodies have replaced large groups there is greater involvement by governors in the making of appointments, and necessarily the affairs of each school receive more detailed attention. But there are few indications that governors have gained any real financial powers. In those areas where there is some freedom of resource allocation at school level, it is the head rather than the governors who makes the effective decisions. There is little evidence that governors have in the last ten years exercised a significant influence on what is taught in the schools or on the methods used, and the governors' power over the direction of the school curriculum remains in general a dead letter. Certainly in the course of our visits there was rarely any challenge to the convention that, with few exceptions, these territories are the preserve of heads and teachers alone. The Tyndale case* may be a notable exception, but the recent growth in some areas of short training courses for managers and governors which are likely to lead to a questioning of constraints hitherto unquestioned, could be an important new factor. The following chapters spell out the way in which a positive contribution could be made by parents and others, without undue interruption of the school's daily activity, by careful definition of the possible area of debate and discussion and the forum in which it is to be conducted.

---

*See paragraph 1.10.

CHAPTER 3—A NEW APPROACH TO SCHOOL GOVERNMENT

3.1. In this chapter we consider possible approaches to the management and government of county* schools in England and Wales in the future and set out our general conclusions.

The range of options

3.2. Four possible courses were open for consideration:

i.   to retain the existing arrangements for school management and government unchanged;

ii.   to reform, to a greater or lesser extent, present practice and procedures within the existing arrangements;

iii.   to replace the existing arrangements with an alternative system of school government;

iv.   to abolish the existing arrangements putting nothing in their place.

3.3. The first option is included for logical completeness. It was not advocated by any of our witnesses and we share their unanimous opinion that the existing arrangements should not be preserved completely unchanged. Thus, the effective choice lay between reforming, replacing and abolishing them.

Evidence

3.4. Very few witnesses urged the abolition of managing and governing bodies. The National Association of Schoolmasters/Union of Women Teachers (NAS/UWT) and the National Association of the Teachers of Wales (NATW) considered such bodies to be superfluous to the proper conduct of a school's affairs. This, they argued, could and should be left to the local education authority (as the elected body responsible for the running of the schools in its area) and the headteacher and his colleagues (as the professionally trained and qualified people appointed to teach in the schools). Both associations believed that provision would have to be made to facilitate communication between members of the community served by the school and its teachers and the local education authority. For this purpose the NAS/UWT recommended the formation of community consultative committees, the NATW the election of parent advisory bodies.

3.5. Very similar conclusions were reached by the small number of witnesses who argued that managing and governing bodies should lose their executive functions and have a purely advisory or consultative role. Proponents of this view included the Association of Education Committees, the Welsh Joint Education Committee, the National Association for Multi-racial Education and the Professional Association of Teachers. Apart from these proposals in favour

---

*Voluntary schools are considered in chapter 12.

of advisory or consultative bodies, we received very few submissions suggesting alternative approaches to school government. Most of these turned out to be little more than new names for old concepts.

3.6. The overwhelming majority of witnesses agreed that the present pattern of school government should be continued. They recognised—explicitly or implicitly—a need for county schools to have associated with them bodies of interested persons concerned for their welfare. Whilst differing in their views about the membership, responsibilities, powers and even the basic purpose of such bodies, these witnesses placed their varied proposals for reform and improvement within the context of the existing framework of school management and government. Indeed many of their proposals are already established practice in different parts of England and Wales. Drawing attention to this and to the wide scope for advance and development under existing arrangements, the Advisory Centre for Education argued "for an extension throughout the system of the good practice which is already established in some parts of it". Although rarely stated so explicitly, this belief in the potential of today's managing and governing bodies underlay the bulk of our evidence in favour of reforming (or perhaps, more correctly, revitalising) the present arrangements.

The Committee's views

3.7. In examining the evidence and considering possible approaches to school government in the future, our starting point was to establish whether there is a need, over and above those which can be met by the local education authority and by the headteacher and his staff, to be satisfied by a body entrusted with specific responsibility for a particular school.

3.8. We believe that there is such a need, namely to ensure that the school is run with as full an awareness as possible of the wishes and feeling of the parents and the local community and, conversely, to ensure that these groups are, in their turn, better informed of the needs of the school and the policies and constraints within which the local education authority operates and the head and other teachers work.

3.9. To meet this need we believe that all the parties concerned for a school's success—the local education authority, the staff, the parents and the local community—should be brought together so that they can discuss, debate and justify the proposals which anyone of them may seek to implement. We recognise that co-operation for the good of the school can and does take place between these interests both formally and informally on both an advisory and a consultative basis. We consider it necessary to go beyond this and propose that all the parties should share in making decisions on the organisation and running of the school since, in our view, this is the best way of ensuring that every aspect of the life and work of the school comes within the purview of all the interests acting together. The specific functions to be undertaken by our proposed partnership are considered in detail in chapters 6 to 9.

3.10. We believe that present managing and governing bodies could be reshaped and adapted to act as the means of conducting our proposed partnership. The remainder of this chapter sets out the basic changes we consider necessary if they are to be able to do this effectively.

Powers and responsibilities

3.11. The first such change, which will set the framework within which we wish the new bodies to operate, is designed to eliminate confusion about the general basis on which the exercise of decision-making powers is distributed between local education authorities, governing bodies and headteachers.

3.12. The present arrangements for the distribution of power and responsibility have been widely criticised as imprecise and unrealistic. To some extent these criticisms relate to the forms of words employed in articles of government, but they also stem from the difficulty in some respects of reconciling the apparent intentions of the 1944–45 arrangements with the practical realities of running a maintained school. Section 17(3)(b) of the Act, in providing for every secondary school to be conducted in accordance with articles of government, allows for some powers, in relation to county secondary schools at least, to be conferred directly and absolutely on both the governing body and the headteacher: the provisions of the 1945 model articles were intended to give effect to this. It was always accepted that such powers are not, and cannot properly be, exercised without regard to the responsibilities of the local education authority. It follows that the divisions of responsibility laid down in the articles could never be hard and fast. As a consequence there was in practice a blurring of responsibilities and over the thirty or more years that have elapsed since 1944 this blurring of responsibilities was aggravated, to some extent, by the imprecision of the language of certain of the articles but even more by the factors which we have noted in chapter 2.

3.13. Mr Auld, in the Tyndale report*, pointed to a similar blurring of responsibilities in the case of primary schools, where the managers are given certain powers and responsibilities by the rules of management. But, as Mr Auld pointed out, notwithstanding the popular confusion which this seems to have caused about where the ultimate power and the final responsibility lie, the rules themselves are made—and can be unmade and remade—at the will of the local education authority.

3.14. We do not think this position is satisfactory. As a basis for considering the major functions which we should wish to see undertaken by governing bodies in the future, we have accepted two general propositions. The first is based on a recognition that the general statutory duties of the local education authority with regard to the provision of education in its area—duties which it has not been open to us to question—place upon the local education authority the ultimate responsibility for the running of the schools in its area. This proposition is in three parts:

a. the local education authority is responsible for the provision and efficient conduct of county schools and so must be empowered to prescribe general policies and issue general directions, and must have, if it thinks fit, the final word on any matter affecting the exercise of its statutory duties for such schools;

---

*See paragraph 1.10.

b. subject to the overriding functions of the local education authority, the governing body should be in a position to determine the lines on which the particular school is organised and run;

c. many day-to-day decisions must in practice be made by the head and staff of the school.

3.15. The second proposition which we have accepted is that the governing body should stand in the direct line of formal responsibility between the local education authority and the head of the school. We have considered alternative concepts but, as we make clear later in chapter 6 on the curriculum, we take the view that the life and work of the school are indivisible: there is no area of the school's activities in respect of which the governing body should have no responsibility nor one on which the head and staff should be accountable only to themselves or to the local education authority. These considerations have led us to the conclusion and *RECOMMENDATION that, in order to ensure that decision making-powers are not only appropriately distributed but are clearly seen to be so, all the powers relevant to school government should be formally vested in the local education authority.*

3.16 There should be provision for appropriate delegation of these powers by the local education authority to the governing body. The latter would expect the headteacher to run the school on a day-to-day basis, normally dealing directly with the LEA's officers but aware, especially when the need for a critical decision arose, that his powers derived from the local education authority through the governing body. This approach should facilitate the definition of a clear and straightforward line of responsibility and authority running from the local education authority through the governing body and the head to every person engaged in the running of the school. It does not follow that the local education authority and its officers should make, or be concerned in, or even know about every decision made in the school. The governing body and the headteacher must clearly be given, on a formal and secure basis, a substantial measure of discretion if proper respect is to be had to their position and potentialities and if the school is to be run efficiently and satisfactorily.

3.17. We cannot lay down, in terms which would be both precise and generally valid, the extent of delegation which would be appropriate in any particular field. As a guiding principle we *RECOMMEND that there should be as much dele-gation by the local education authority to the governing body as is compatible with the LEA's ultimate responsibility for the running of the schools in its area, and as much discretion in turn granted to the headteacher by the governing body as is compatible with the latter's responsibility for the success of the school in all its activities.* As we make clear in chapters 6 to 9, when we consider in detail the functions of governing bodies, this general principle should in certain respects be expressly reinforced, while in a few other respects its application should be limited.

3.18 Our recommendations on these matters will involve substantial changes in the law and the present apparatus of rules, articles and instruments of government and management, and in the role to be played in the future by the Secretaries of State. These issues are discussed in chapter 13.

Separate bodies for each school

3.19. Section 20 of the Education Act 1944 empowers local education authorities to group any two or more county or voluntary schools (subject in the latter case to the managers' or governors' agreement) under a single governing body.

3.20. The 1944 White Paper explained some of the circumstances in which it was felt that the grouping of schools under a single governing body would be necessary. There had been an increase in the number of secondary schools and it could be convenient to link together schools of a particular foundation or denominational character. There were advantages in grouping schools on a geographical basis, with schools of all types finding a place in the group. It was hoped that the problems of self-government in the (then) newer types of secondary schools would benefit from shared experience and community of interest and that sharing of teaching staff and transfer of pupils between the various types of school would be facilitated. Over the years other reasons for grouping arrangements have emerged. It has sometimes been found convenient for one group of governors to take responsibility for two or three very small schools in a rural community or for two schools which share the same site. More recently there has been a tendency in some areas to constitute a single governing body for a comprehensive secondary school and its feeder primary schools, or to appoint a joint body for a two-tier secondary school where compatiblity of syllabuses is regarded as particularly important.

3.21. There are however, disadvantages in such arrangements. When a number of schools are grouped together it is often necessary, in order to provide for a wide variety of interests, for very large governing bodies to be established; these can be cumbersome and impersonal. The White Paper recognised the danger that grouping arrangements might tend to blur the individual character of each type of school. It has been argued strongly that the members of a group governing body cannot give proper consideration to the interests of any particular schools under their aegis, because they inevitably lack a personal identification with the school, a knowledge of its special needs in depth and a close understanding of its links with the local community. We recognise that the arguments in favour of grouping arrangements may have had some validity in the past but we are convinced and we are strongly supported in this by the evidence, that they no longer hold good.

3.22. Our aim is to foster a working partnership which would give staff, parents and community an equal part with the local education authority in the government of their own schools. To be effective this partnership must operate in relation to individual schools; it must not be diffused by grouping arrangements. It is an essential feature of our proposals therefore that each school should have its own individual governing body.

3.23. We hope that grouping arrangements already made will be replaced as soon as possible by arrangements for separate governing bodies. We recognise, however, that local education authorities may need to ensure that there are opportunities for collaboration between the governing bodies of schools that are educationally linked (ie lower and upper secondary schools or secondary schools and feeder primary schools) so as to allow matters of common interest such as complementary courses to be considered. Ways and means of achieving this are considered in chapter 5.

3.24. *We RECOMMEND that Section 20 of the Education Act 1944 should be repealed as soon as possible and that, from a date to be fixed by the Secretaries of State every school should have its own separate governing body.*

The new governing bodies

3.25. The distinction between the "management" of primary schools and the "government" of secondary schools is rooted to a considerable extent in history and in an older view of primary school education. In recent years, especially in the light of the Plowden* and Gittings Reports†, there has been a much greater appreciation of its significance and a corresponding increase in the sophistication of its approach and methods. Moreover, the introduction of middle schools, spanning part of the primary and part of the secondary age range, has tended to blur the traditional distinction. For all these reasons we think it is not appropriate that the distinction should be preserved by general differences in the arrangements for the administration of primary and secondary schools. We are aware that on many particular points there remain important differences, but we believe that our recommendations take these fully into account and can be applied in general terms in schools of all age ranges without inhibiting differentiation of approach and emphasis where this is appropriate.

3.26. To reflect this approach we think, as did many of our witnesses, that an end should be made to the distinction between the "management" of primary schools and the "government" of secondary schools. We have given careful consideration to a number of alternative titles which some witnesses thought more appropriate for the responsible bodies, but we concluded that "governing body", because of its long usage and wide acceptance, remains the most appropriate title. *We therefore RECOMMEND its retention and its application by law to all bodies whether they serve primary or secondary schools.‡*

3.27. The new governing bodies should, like the existing managing and governing bodies, act as corporate bodies. Under our proposals in chapter 11 it will be for a governing body to decide upon its own procedures and standing orders. It might, at a properly constituted meeting, choose to delegate certain of

---

*Central Advisory Council for Education (England). Children and their Primary Schools. Chairman Lady Plowden J.P. HMSO 1967.

†Central Advisory Council for Education (Wales). Primary Education in Wales. Chairman Professor C. E. Gittins. HMSO 1967.

‡In the rest of this report, when we look to the future, the term governing body is used in respect of both primary and secondary schools.

its functions to one or more of its members but in performing those functions the individual governors would be acting on behalf of the governing body as a whole. We mention this expressly in view of the problems caused at the William Tyndale Junior School by managers acting individually and in factions.* In the rest of this report all reference to the rights and responsibilities of the governing body should be read literally. It is the governors as a body that we have in mind.

---

*We endorse Mr. Auld's conclusion, "Whatever the managers decide to do, they should decide together, and by vote if necessary, at a properly constituted managers' meeting. There should be no decision taken by factions of the managing body. Nor should there be meetings between members of the managing body with the Authority's representatives to discuss the problem in the absence and without the knowledge of the chairman of the managers, or of the headteacher or the teacher-manager".—para 834(i) of the report on the WILLIAM TYNDALE JUNIOR AND INFANTS SCHOOLS PUBLIC INQUIRY.

CHAPTER 4—MEMBERSHIP OF THE NEW GOVERNING BODIES

4.1. We have referred in the opening paragraphs of Chapter 2 to the wide variety of practice which has developed in relation to the composition of school governing bodies. It is not surprising that no single pattern of school government should have developed because the statutory framework of the Education Act 1944 was deliberately drawn up in broad general terms to allow for variety. The Secretary of State's approval is required for the articles of government of county secondary schools but, apart from making provision for the representation of minor authorities* on the managing bodies of primary schools, the Act did not stipulate what interests should be represented on managing and governing bodies. With this limited exception, local education authorities have complete discretion to make the instruments of management and government for all county schools, although they were expected by the Minister to have regard to the views expressed in the 1944 White Paper and in the 1945 model. It may assist the assessment of our own proposals to quote here those sections of the White Paper relating to the constitution, composition and size of governing bodies:

"Constitution—All secondary schools are to be governed by governing bodies specially constituted for the purpose. In the case of county schools the governing body is to consist of such number of persons appointed in such manner as the local education authority may determine; in the case of voluntary schools the governing body is to consist of such number of persons as the Minister may determine, subject to compliance with the prescribed proportions of foundation governors and of governors appointed by the local education authority.

Composition—In all schools it may be assumed that the governing body will include:—

i. Adequate representation of the local education authority †
ii. Other persons whose qualifications are such as to enable them to play a useful part in the government of a secondary school.

The practice of allowing a limited number of co-opted members nominated by the governing body has proved of advantage and might be continued in appropriate cases.

In the case of girls' and mixed secondary schools a proportion of women should be included on the governing bodies.

Among the persons referred to under ii. above it would be appropriate to appoint a representative of a University or University College—particularly of the local University where one exists; and the inclusion of one or more persons associated with the commercial and industrial life of the district is desirable.

There is general agreement that the interests of the teaching staff of the school or schools, as well as of parents and old scholars, should be reflected in

---

*A definition of 'minor authority' is given in the footnote to paragraph 2.3.
†The authority's representatives will not necessarily be in all cases members of the authority.

the composition of the governing body. The majority of bodies consulted hold that this can be secured without the staff or parents' and old scholars' associations having the right to nominate governors for the purpose.†

Size—No precise guidance as to the size of the governing body can be given. In the past governing bodies have sometimes tended to be too large and in consequence their transactions have in some cases been formal and stereotyped. The governing body should be large enough to ensure that the various interests are adequately represented, but small enough for the effective conduct of business in such a way that all members can play an active part."

4.2. The model instrument provided for both representative governors (appointed by the local education authority) and co-opted governors (to be appointed by the governing body itself). It excluded from membership teachers and "other persons employed for the purposes of the school". This exclusion was of long standing—see for example paragraph 122 of Appendix B. It doubtless reflected a feeling that teacher representation might create conflicts of loyalties and interests or might place the headteacher in a difficult position. Certainly the representation of teachers on the governing bodies of schools in which they are employed is not ruled out by the Education Acts and the White Paper noted that there was one section of opinion among the bodies consulted which thought that there should be governors specially nominated by the teaching staff. In any event, the restrictions on staff membership suggested in the model instrument have in recent years been decreasingly reflected in the instruments made by local education authorities. Many have made provision for heads and other teachers to serve as managers and governors. Moreover in several areas members of the school's supporting staff have been appointed. In many areas the composition of governing bodies has been broadened not only in this way but also by the inclusion of parents; pupils also have been brought into membership in some cases. Nevertheless there remain local education authorities which have taken very little action to widen the range of representation and governing bodies very commonly continue to have a majority of LEA elected members or at least of LEA nominees. This tendency, already referred to in chapter 2, for local education authorities to want the majority of the places on governing bodies may be due to a belief by the local political parties that central control through elected representatives is a valid and necessary means of ensuring that individual schools do not depart too far from the overall policies of the local education authority.

4.3. Some authorities who hold this view have grouped all their primary schools under the schools sub-committees of their Education Committees and established governing bodies, with a majority of political appointees, for groups of secondary schools. The general question of the grouping of schools for purposes of management and government has already been considered in chapter 3. Here it is sufficient to note that even where grouping arrangements are in force it is sometimes difficult for local education authorities to find elected members to appoint to all their governing bodies. The increasing number of authorities with a separate governing body for each school have discovered that

---

† "One section holds that governors should be specially nominated by the teaching staff and by parents' and old scholars' associations."

there are not enough elected members to serve on all of them. To achieve political control they have to rely on the appointment of additional nominees on a political basis.

4.4. It is clear from our written evidence and from our visits that there is widespread dissatisfaction with the dominance of governing bodies by political parties—a feeling which is reinforced by the fact that not all the LEA representatives turn up regularly at meetings. There is dissatisfaction too, with the failure of some governing bodies to exercise any effective control over the way in which their schools are run.

4.5. Our visits included several to areas where the composition of governing bodies had been broadened to provide representation of a wide range of interest. The opportunities we were given to study the experience of these local education authorities, added to the weight of the written evidence, has enabled us to assess the benefits which can result from securing the involvement of all interested parties. We are convinced that if the revised system of school government which we advocate is to operate effectively, provision must be made to ensure that the local education authorities, the staff, the parents of the children attending the school, and the local community have adequate representation on the governing body. The first three were frequently identified by witnesses as the most important of the interests which need to be considered for membership of the bodies. The main differences between witnesses on this issue related to the proportions in which the various interests should be represented. There were differing views on the need for having representatives of all interest groups on the governing body and there were some who did not see the need for any precise pattern of membership to be laid down but preferred this to be settled locally, where the claims of particular groups might most readily be assessed. Some witnesses envisaged the establishment of bodies (with a mainly advisory function) whose membership would be drawn both from local authorities and from teachers, parents, pupils and other interested bodies. Others suggested a general widening of membership, designed to make governing bodies "more democratic" and involving many different interest groups (teachers, parents, pupils, non-academic staff, parishes and district councils, local community organisations etc); but such submissions often left unspecified the proportion of places to be assigned to these various elements.

4.6. It seems to us that any consideration given to the means by which governing bodies could be made more representative should be based on the recognition first and foremost that each of the four main interest groups can contribute towards the establishment of a partnership based on their common interest in the welfare of the school; second, that no one interest group should play a dominant role; and, third, that between them, the members of the body should be able to speak with knowledge and experience over the whole range of matters which are likely to come up for discussion. We have concluded that within these terms such a partnership is most likely to work effectively if each of the four main interest groups receives the same proportion of the places available on the governing body. *We RECOMMEND therefore, that as a matter* *of principle, the membership of governing bodies should consist of equal numbers of local education authority representatives, school staff, parents with, where appropriate, pupils and representatives of the local community.**

4.7. We do not believe that implementation of this "four equal shares principle" need involve complete uniformity of practice throughout England and Wales but in the following paragraphs we have set out the basis on which the main interest groups should in our view be represented on the governing body and, where appropriate, have indicated the manner in which appointments in each of these categories might best be made. The table at the end of this chapter gives examples of the detailed composition of governing bodies on the basis we have suggested. Of course, the size of the governing body will need to vary with the size of the school. Local education authorities will have to consider this question of size in the light of the circumstances of each school but in our opinion, *and we so RECOMMEND, there should never be less than two members in any one category—a minimum of eight for a governing body—and twenty four members should normally be regarded as the maximum for efficient operation. The examples given in the table are based on these principles.*

Local education authorities

4.8. We have referred above to the fairly widespread criticism of the political control of managing and governing bodies. Grouping arrangements have sometimes been made to secure this control but even where individual school governing bodies have been established and authorities have claimed to introduce reforms by widening the membership of these bodies efforts have often been made at the same time to strengthen the political grip. It seems to us very doubtful whether it has ever been of much benefit to local education authorities to attempt to achieve political control of governing bodies or indeed that any principal of democracy or good administration makes it necessary for them to do so. We do not believe that an LEA's ability to meet its responsibilities for the provision of primary and secondary education will be weakened significantly if its representation is reduced within the revised framework we propose.

4.9. This does not mean that we wish in any way to minimise the importance of the part which local authority representatives will need to play in the work of the governing body. Many of our witnesses attached considerable importance to the link with the local education authority which the latter's representatives provide. It has also been suggested to us that their presence helps to ensure that the governing body does not develop a sense of remoteness from the authority. Much of the work of the future governing bodies will, we envisage, be concerned with issues relating to the allocation of resources, both human and financial, and here a well-informed representative of the local education authority will

---

*We recommend in paragraph 4.30 how people representative of the local community should be identified and selected. The legislative implications of this and other recommendations relating to the composition of the governing body are considered in chapter 13.

be able to play a valuable part by explaining the policy background to education committee decisions. A further factor, of less importance but one which should not be underestimated, is that many LEA representatives will have had experience of working in committee, a useful asset to a governing body some of whose members may have no previous experience of school management and government or the way in which meetings of public bodies are normally conducted.

4.10. Obviously the local education authority should decide who should represent it on the governing bodies of the schools in its area. In making their decision we suggest that local education authorities give careful consideration to the possibility of including, where appropriate, representatives of district and parish councils, the statutory community councils which in Wales are the equivalent of the latter and the inner London authorities which are not local education authorities. At present, representation of such councils as "minor authorities" is required only in the case of primary school managing bodies. It is clear that this provision in the Education Act 1944 was designed to ensure the participation in school management of the communities served by the schools. Under our proposals one-quarter of the governing body will consist of members specifically chosen to represent local community interests. We consider it unnecessary, therefore, to have a statutory requirement for the appointment of minor authority representatives and *RECOMMEND the repeal of the relevant provisions of Section 18 of the Education Act 1944.*

4.11. At the same time we accept that statutory local authorities of the kind referred to are in general well equipped to make available to governing bodies members with experience in local affairs and knowledge of the opinions and aspirations of the local community. *We RECOMMEND, therefore, that any elected member of a local authority in the area served by the school should be eligible for appointment to a school governing body in either the "local education authority" or the "community" category.*

4.12. Not only will this enable the local education authority to take such a person into consideration when filling its "quota" on the governing body; it will also be possible, when individuals are being chosen to fill the "community" places (see paragraph 4.30) for any authority, of which he is a member, in the area served by the school to put forward his name for consideration in the "community" category if that council is not already represented in the "local education authority"group. His claims can then be weighed against those of other candidates for appointment as "community" governors.

The school staff

4.13. *The headteacher*

No consideration of the composition of a governing body can properly be undertaken without a clear understanding of the essential role of the headteacher in all its activities. We suspect that few, if any, would dispute the truth of the claim made by the National Association of Head Teachers (NAHT) that "the success of schools depends very much upon the calibre of leadership as projected by headteachers whose first duty must always be towards their pupils". It seems to us equally true that the success of the new governing bodies will also depend to a large extent on the effectiveness of the head's contribution to their deliberations and actions.

4.14. We have given careful consideration to the view put forward by the NAHT and others that the head should not be a member of the governing body. It has been argued that the head's position should largely be advisory and for this purpose he needs a measure of independence which cannot be maintained if he is a member of the governing body. It has also been suggested that it is not necessary for the head to be a governor in order to build up a good relationship with his governing body, and that he would be better able to report in an objective way on matters under consideration if his role was solely that of an officer serving the governors.

4.15. It is, however, fundamental to our conception of the governing body that so far as possible those with a direct interest in the running of the school should participate fully not only in its deliberations but also in its decisions. The governing body's overall responsibilities for the life and welfare of the school will generally, on a day-to-day basis, be discharged through the head and we do not believe that it would be sufficient for these joint responsibilities to be exercised on the basis of a relationship between the head and the governing body which enabled him to take part in discussions but fell short of involving him fully, through membership, in all the important decisions taken by the governing body. We recognise that some head teachers might initially be reluctant to exercise the right to vote which would result from appointment to the governing body in case they became involved in local political arguments. We respect these feelings and acknowledge that occasions could arise when a head, like a governor in any other category of membership, would either find it necessary to withdraw entirely from discussion because of a special interest, or might prefer to abstain from voting on a particular issue for personal reasons. Situations of this kind have been dealt with successfully in those areas where headteachers already serve on school governing bodies and we are confident that in general a head's exercise of his right to vote will not in any way prejudice his professional objectivity or result in difficulties with other members of the governing body which would adversely affect his professional status. We believe that the greater involvement of the head in the work of the governing body will be a community service of lasting benefit to the school and its pupils.

4.16. *We therefore RECOMMEND that the headteacher of a school should always by a member of its governing body and that he be included ex officio in the group of members representing the school staff.*

4.17 *Other staff*

Of the places on the governing body allocated to the staff of the school, one would be reserved for the headteacher. The allocation of the remaining places within this category will depend on the size and character of the school. For example, large schools have, in addition to teachers, many supporting staff in a wide range of occupations with different conditions of service, both full- and part-time. We believe that the expertise and knowledge of all members of staff—teachers and ancillaries—should be deployed through membership of the governing body. Obviously it would not be right for representation on the governing body as between teaching and supporting staff to be based purely on numerical strength. The role of the teacher is fundamental to the success of the school. *We therefore RECOMMEND that priority in the allocation of places within the school staff group on the governing body should be given to teachers, the opportunity being taken to add representatives of the supporting staff where size permits.* In schools whose governing bodies consist of eight members, it will be impossible for the supporting staff to be directly represented. In such cases we regard it as important that the views of these members of the staff are obtained by the governing body through arrangements of the kind considered in chapter 5.

4.18. The places available for the staff group should in our view be filled through elections in which the teachers and, where relevant the members of the supporting staff would vote separately for those of their own number who had declared their willingness to serve on the governing body. The precise procedures to be used in the elections should in our view be settled by the local education authority in consultation with all the interests concerned.

Parents and pupils

4.19. *Parents*

We have stated our view that the new governing bodies should be representative of all those with a major interest in the running of a particular school. It follows that the governing body should include representatives of the parents. We do not believe, however, that parent membership of the governing body is sufficient in itself to achieve the full involvement of all parents in the life and activities of the school. Parent governors are an important means of developing a closer relationship between homes and schools but additional measures will certainly be needed to develop and strengthen this relationship. Our views on what might be done in this direction are given in chapter 5.

4.20. We have considered whether parent membership should be limited to parents of pupils currently at the school or should be extended to parents of former pupils. Parents with children currently attending the school have, of course, an immediate and direct interest in its efficient conduct and well-being. This is, in our view, a compelling reason for concluding that only they should be eligible for appointment to the governing body in this category. Parents of former pupils might well be eligible in a different category.

4.21. We have given a good deal of attention to the means by which parent representatives should be chosen. The widespread appointment of parents to school governing bodies is a comparatively recent development and there has been a wide variety of practice among those authorities which have appointed them. For example they may have been chosen by the headteacher or by the local education authority, nominated by the parent teachers association or co-opted by the governing body. We recognise the good work which has been done by parent governors appointed by such methods. However, not having offered themselves for election, such governors could never be sure of the extent to which they were speaking for the general body of parents; nor indeed might they have had much opportunity to make the acquaintance of other parents. Both factors have undoubtedly contributed to the sense of uncertainty and isolation which has affected some non-elected parent governors. We believe, moreover, that in keeping with the normal democratic processes of our society in general. parents can properly expect to be allowed to choose their own representatives,

4.22. We recognise that in the past, when parent governors have been elected, some very low polls have been recorded. To those who would use this as an argument against the general introduction of parent elections, we would make the following points. First, the limited interest shown in elections to governing bodies in the past should not be projected into the future when these bodies, under our proposals, will play a central role in the school's life and development. Second, many of the electoral procedures used in the past (eg a single, little-publicised meeting combining the nomination of candidates, electoral addresses and the ballot itself) will, we hope, be eliminated and replaced by improved practices. Third, many elections in the past have been isolated events. If, however, they are to have real significance for the general body of parents they must in our view take place in an environment of regular contact and co-operation between parents and between parents and the school. (We discuss the means of promoting such an environment in chapter 5). *We accordingly RECOMMEND that those to be appointed as the school's parent governors should be elected by the parents of the children attending that school.*

4.23. *We RECOMMEND that the local education authority be made respons-ible for drawing up the rules and procedures for the election of parent governors in its area, and for ensuring that they are put into effect.* Whilst acknowledging that the local education authority is best placed to work out detailed schemes suited to local conditions, *we RECOMMEND that all elections be school-based, and combine meetings and other procedures to ensure maximum participation given the circumstances of the area concerned; and that these procedures should satisfy the following broad criteria:*

i. *communications with parents should be in plain words;**

---

*In some areas it may be necessary to send out notices in more than one language.

ii. every parent* with a child at the school should be eligible to nominate candidates, to stand for election, and to cast one vote;

iii. nomination and voting papers should be sent to every eligible parent;

iv. the results of the election should be communicated to all eligible parents.

4.24. Pupils

It has been suggested to us from a number of sources that provision should be made for a school's pupils, or at least some of them, to play a part in the government of the school. We have been advised by the legal advisers of the Department of Education and Science that in their view the office of school governor is a public office and so cannot be held lawfully by a person under the age of 18. Thus the scope for pupil membership of the governing body, in the proper sense, is at present severely limited: only very few pupils, in the minority of schools which cater for pupils over 16, can lawfully be appointed as governors and their tenure of office must be short.

4.25. We are in no doubt that every effort should be made to draw on pupils' knowledge and ideas for the benefit of the governing body, and we have carefully considered several arguments to the effect that service on governing bodies should be seen as a special exception to the principle set out above and that legislation ought expressly to permit pupils below the age of 18—perhaps those aged 16 or more—to serve as members of school governing bodies in future.

4.26. It is unclear to us whether it would be possible by a single legislative act to extend full membership of governing bodies to pupils between the ages of 16-18, which a majority of us would wish to see, or whether the whole law in respect of minors holding public office would need to be changed. The latter question we consider falls outside our terms of reference. *We RECOMMEND that the Secretaries of State should take definitive advice on whether it is possible to change the law to enable pupils to serve as governors at 16 without opening the whole question of the age of majority and the holding of public office.* In the light of that advice they should consider, as soon as practicable, whether the law should be amended or whether the question should be raised in its wider context. *Meanwhile we RECOMMEND that secondary school pupils should participate in school government to the fullest extent allowed by law until they are eligible for membership.* Where the circumstances of the school make it a practical possibility, the local education authority should consider making provision for the appointment of pupils, on election by at least the upper classes of the school, to one or more of the places available for parents. Where this is not considered practicable, every effort should be made to involve pupils in the work of the governing body to the utmost extent compatible with the law. We see no reason why one or two elected pupils should not, for example, receive the papers of the governing body, attend its meetings and take part in the discussion of any matter. Where age permits, experience of this kind could well precede, and merge almost imperceptibly into, a short period of service as a

---

*If any difficulty arises in identifying the persons entitled to vote the local education authority should determine who should be regarded as the parents for this purpose.

member, in the proper sense, of the governing body. In addition to the pupils who will be able to play a direct part in the work of the governing body in the ways outlined above, a much greater number should in our view be able to make a contribution towards the consideration of matters which are the responsibility of the governing body; we develop our views on this in chapter 5.

The wider community

4.27. Our recommendations are intended to lead to the establishment of governing bodies representing a wide cross-section of local opinion about education and the conduct of a school. This will partly be achieved by the inclusion in the governing body of representatives of the local authorities, the school staff and parents. But if the governing body is to take due account of the expectations of the local community and of all the various external pressures and demands made on the school (such as those of employers, examining bodies or institutions of further and higher education) it is essential that its members include people with experience of the external forces and influences at work on the school.

4.28. In most localities there will be a number of organisations able to suggest the names of individuals with relevant knowledge and experience who might make a valuable contribution if appointed to membership of a school governing body. We do not believe it would be practicable or desirable for us to attempt to list them: different areas and schools, will have differing needs; but, certainly in the case of secondary schools examples of the kind of body we have in mind are local employers' (or business) organisations, trade unions and institutions of further and higher education. In accordance with our recommendation in paragraph 4.10, invitations to submit nominations should always be extended to statutory local authorities in the area served by the school where representation of any such authority has not already been included in the group representing the local education authority on the governing body. Finally, there may well be individuals, not members of any particular organisation, whose background and qualifications merit consideration in this category.

4.29. There is one aspect of the community representation which deserves specific mention. The importance of ensuring representation on the governing body of ethnic groups in areas where there is a concentration of minority groups was stressed in evidence submitted by the Community Relations Commission and the National Association for Multi-racial Education. The latter put forward the view that as a general principle minorities should be represented in proportion to the size of such groups in the catchment area of the school concerned. After careful consideration we see no need to make specific provision for the representation of particular interests because this would not be compatible with the procedures we have recommended below whereby the community governors will be chosen by those who will be filling the places on the governing body in the three other categories of membership. We are satisfied that our overall proposals will result in a significant increase in direct local participation in school government and ethnic minorities should thus in future receive greater opportunities for participating in this service.

4.30. *We RECOMMEND that the procedures for the appointment of community representatives should be based on the principle that the individuals concerned should be co-opted by the governors representing the three other interest groups.* Thus when a governing body is being newly formed the individuals designated for appointment to represent the local education authority, the staff of the school and the parents should meet to decide who, as nominees of local organisations or as individuals, are to be invited to join the body as community representatives. To carry out this task the individuals representing the three other interest groups will need to have before them a list of organisations willing to propose nominees and of individuals willing to serve· *We RECOMMEND that the task of drawing up these lists should be the responsibility of the local education authority.* In view of the need for secondary schools to establish close relationships with interests representing the world of work, we further *RECOMMEND that in compiling these lists the local education authority should always invite both local employers' (or business) organisations and trade unions to submit nominations.*

4.31. We do not wish to lay down any detailed procedures for this operation but the following suggestions may be of assistance. Not less than one month before the other governors-designate are to meet, the local education authority might invite applications by advertising in newspapers circulating in the area served by the school and by giving publicity to the notice in any manner which may be thought desirable. It should be open to the other governors-designate to approach any individual or organisation not on the local education authority's list with a view to their making a nomination for membership of the community group. Nominations might be put forward by organisations acting alone or jointly with one or more other organisations.

Boarding schools

4.32. The application of the principles set out above to the governing bodies of boarding schools maintained by local education authorities* presents some difficulties, first because such schools do not serve a defined locality or other community, and also because in some cases the school is situated outside the maintaining authority's area. Nonetheless, we believe that the arguments we have put forward for the representation of the four main interest groups on the governing bodies of day schools also hold for boarding schools.

4.33 The appointment of representatives of the local education authority and the election of staff members to serve on the governing body should not present any special problems. Schools with only a few boarders will need to keep the parents of these children in touch with the activities of the parent body and to give them good notice of arrangements for the election of parent representatives on the governing body. In the case of schools that are wholly or mainly boarding the timing and organisation of parent elections will need special consideration

---

*At 1 January 1977 there were 92 county secondary and 4 county primary schools with a total of 5,807 boarders. These included 12 wholly boarding schools with a total of 2,441 pupils.

but we are confident that local education authorities will be able to make arrangements for these which satisfy the general principles of our proposals even though it may not be possible to meet all the criteria we have recommended in paragraph 4.23.

4.34. We see the appointment of community representatives on the governing body as a particularly useful way of linking a boarding school with all the various interests in its immediate surroundings and counteracting any tendency to isolation. The choice of the individuals best suited to represent these interests, as in the case of the appointment of the community group on all other governing bodies, will be a matter for decision by the individuals designated for appointment as representatives of the local education authority, the parents and the staff of the boarding school.

Community Schools

4.35. We have proceeded on the basis that a separate governing body will be needed for the "school" side of a community school* and that, as at present, some additional arrangements will be necessary for the management of the other facilities provided at the institution.

4.36. The interests of the governing body of a community school are likely to be very much wider than those of the ordinary primary or secondary school but will vary considerably depending on the additional facilities available at the institution and the arrangements for their administration that have been locally decided. The special position of the school in a community complex makes it particularly important to ensure a full range of interests on the governing body. In our view it should be possible to achieve this without any departure from the principles we have recommended for the constitution of governing bodies in general. The local education authority will need to give careful consideration to the value of including representatives, within the "local authorities" group on the body, not only of any district and parish councils (or community councils in Wales) who may have an interest because the school serves their area but also of any such councils who may be involved in the provision of other facilities in the community complex. At the same time special attention will need to be given to the provision of places within the community group on the governing body for representatives of the various activities which take place in the premises of which the school forms a part. These are considerations which can be properly assessed only at the local level. We accept that in order to cater on a reasonable basis for all interests, the governing bodies of community schools may in some cases need to be larger than the maximum of twenty four recommended in paragraph 4.7.

Disqualification

4.37. There will of course be a need to ensure that persons who ought not, in

---

*The nature of community schools, the responsibilities of the governing bodies of such institutions in relation to the school premises, and the implications for the exercise of their functions in general, are discussed in paragraphs 9.35 – 9.39. We are concerned here only with the composition of the governing body for the "school" side of an institution which provides facilities for a wide variety of activities.

the general public interest, to hold office as governors are debarred from doing so. *We RECOMMEND that:—*

i. *a person should be disqualified if he is an undischarged bankrupt, has been convicted of a serious offence (such as is referred to in section 80(1)(d) of the Local Government Act 1972) or if, having been appointed he has not attended an ordinary governors' meeting for a year or is incapacitated from acting as a governor.*

ii. *any person who, holding office as a governor, ceases to be qualified for appointment as a governor, either in one of the respects mentioned above or in respect of the capacity in which he was appointed, should forthwith cease to be a governor.*

Constitutional position of the Local Education Authority

4.38. It will be desirable for the local education authority to have the formal responsibility for making and terminating the appointment of all governors irrespective of the category into which they fall. Authorities will need to ensure that their discharge of this responsibility is, and is seen to be, independent both of their power to choose the persons who are to be appointed as LEA representatives and of their decisions on matters of policy within a governing body's field. If, given the new relation between local education authorities and governing bodies envisaged in chapter 3, an authority finds that the actions of a governing body are unreasonable, the authority's remedy will be to override the latter's decisions—and in the last resort to withdraw temporarily from the governing body the functions delegated to it. The governing body should be given back its functions as soon as the difficulties necessitating their withdrawal have been resolved. In the event of its being suggested that a local education authority had acted unreasonably in withdrawing or withholding such functions, the governing body could have recourse to the Secretary of State who already has power to intervene if satisfied that an authority is in default of a duty or is acting (or proposes to act) unreasonably.

Term of office

4.39. The increased responsibilities which, under our proposals, will fall on governors make the need for continuity in the governing body a matter of considerable importance, if only because frequent changes of membership would seriously inhibit the development of a sense of corporate identity and responsibility. After a transitional period during the 1970s all local councillors will be elected for a term of four years. In our view a term of office of comparable length for governors is called for. *We therefore RECOMMEND that the term of office for governors should in general be within a four year framework.*

4.40. In our view governors should not be seen as delegates nominated to serve the interests of particular groups. We accordingly do not consider it would be right, in general, for a group to be able to bring about the dismissal of a governor appointed on its nomination following a properly conducted election. We recognise, however, that a rapid turnover of teaching staff, such as that experienced in many schools in recent years, could give rise to legitimate demands for more frequent elections. Thus in some areas it may be considered right for teacher members of the governing body to be appointed for periods of only two years at a time. We regard this as an appropriate matter for local decision provided there has been full consultation with the relevant teacher associations.

4.41. Exceptions would also, in our view, be justified in the LEA's category in circumstances where council elections had led to changes in the balance of political parties, with the consequence that a governor might no longer be regarded as truly representative of the council. We consider therefore that where there has been such a change. the local education authority as appointing body should have the power to dismiss a governor appointed to represent it, whether or not he is a member of the authority.

Limit to the number of governing bodies on which any person should serve

4.42. We have referred elsewhere in this report to the need for governing bodies to develop a sense of collective identity and responsibility. This will be possible only through a high level of personal commitment and involvement, which cannot in our view be properly achieved if an individual serves simultaneously on a large number of governing bodies, as commonly happens at present. We accept that it would not be desirable to limit governors to experience of a single stage of education: their contribution could be enhanced by knowledge of schools covering between them the whole primary and secondary age range. There is widespread overlapping between the age groups served by particular kinds of school even within the same LEA area (eg infant and first schools, junior and middle, 11–16 and 11–18 secondary schools, sixth form colleges). In order to prevent an individual's being appointed to the governing bodies of a number of schools serving different, but overlapping age groups, *we RECOM-MEND that no person should be eligible to serve on the governing body of a school catering in an age group served by any other school of which he is already a governor**.

Retirement age of governors

4.43. We have considered whether it would be desirable to set an upper age limit for school governors or to limit governors to a specific number of terms. In our view these are matters to be considered by each of the interests concerned when choosing its own nominees. We do not therefore make any recommendation about them.

---

*In our view a primary or secondary school governor should be able to serve also as governor of a special school, whatever the age group of the children attending that school.

ANNEX TO CHAPTER 4

Hypothetical composition of future governing bodies

1. The following table illustrates how the proportional division of places on the governing body described in chapter 4 might be applied across a range of primary and secondary schools serving a variety of communities:

	School Staff (1)	Parents (2)	Local Education Authority (3)	Local Community (4)	Total
Primary (100 pupils, 6 teachers, 1 full-time and 4 part-time ancillaries) ...	2	2	2	2	8
Primary (200 pupils, 9 teachers, 3 full-time and 15 part-time ancillaries) ...	3	3	3	3	12
Junior (7-11) (350 pupils, 18 teachers, 2 full-time and 25 part-time ancillaries)	3	3	3	3	12
Middle (9-13) (600 pupils, 30 teachers, 1 full-time and 40 part-time ancillaries)	4	4	4	4	16
Secondary (600 pupils, 40 teachers, 2 full-time and 35 part-time ancillaries)	4	4	4	4	16
Secondary (1100 pupils, 65 teachers, 5 full-time and 50 part-time ancillaries)	5	5	5	5	20
High (11-16) with Adult Education Centre (1300 pupils, 70 teachers, 5 full-time and 50 part-time ancillaries. 2300 student enrolments, 125 part-time tutors, 20 part-time ancillaries)	6	6	6	6	24
Secondary 1,500 pupils, 90 teachers, 8 full-time and 75 part-time ancillaries)	6	6	6	6	24
Secondary (1,900 pupils, 110 teachers, 15 full-time and 95 part-time ancillaries)	6	6	6	6	24

(1) These figures include the place to be reserved for the headteacher and any places allocated by the local education authority for supporting staff.

(2) Any allocation of places for eligible pupils, within these totals, would be determined by the local education authority.

(3) The individuals filling these places could, at the LEA discretion, include members of other local authorities in the area served by the school.

(4) These places would be filled on the recommendation of the governors appointed to represent the 3 other categories of membership. They could include members of local authorities mentioned in (3) above who did not find representation in the LEA group.

CHAPTER 5—COMMUNICATION AND CO-OPERATION

5.1. To achieve their full potential the newly constituted governing bodies should maintain good communications and work in close co-operation with the groups from which their members are drawn. In this chapter we consider ways and means of establishing effective communication and co-operation, first arrangements within the school and then the school's relations with the parents and the community as a whole.

Underlying problems

5.2. In their evidence the Association of County Councils argued that if governing bodies did not exist they would have to be created in order to provide channels of communication between school, parents, local community and local education authority. This was the argument most commonly advanced by witnesses in favour of governing bodies*. Although we believe that governing bodies should play a more positive part than serving as channels of communication, and should include nominees from the interests mainly concerned, provision for efficient lines of communication remains essential. However they are composed, governing bodies will, in our view, remain susceptible to two structural failings. First, because their members comprise only a small number of the many people concerned with the schools, they run the risk of becoming detached from the very people they are intended to serve. Second, in looking after the interests of their schools, there is a danger of their becoming inward-looking and single minded, little concerned with the wider implications of their policies. We believe that both risks can be significantly reduced.

5.3. We believe that the new governing bodies, with their broadened composition, will interest more people in their work and that of the schools. But in our view the involvement of the staff, parents and the local community in general should not cease once they have chosen their nominees to sit on the governing body. On the contrary they should all be given the opportunity to keep abreast of developments within and about the school and to offer their views and suggestions upon these and other matters to the governing body.

5.4. A governing body with responsibility for one school will, quite naturally and properly, tend to concentrate on the interests of that school. We believe that this partisanship must be modified to ensure that every school plays its proper part in the education system of which it is part. Clearly the local education authority has the major responsibility in this respect, but there is also scope for

---

*It was concisely stated in the evidence of the Society of Education Officers:—

"Since our objective must be to provide the best possible education in our schools, it is essential that there should be some machinery to facilitate co-operation between the various interests who contribute to this end – the local education authority, the head and staff, parents and the local community. This should provide a framework for fostering relationships between them, for developing an appreciation of the issues involved, and for formulating policies through a creative interchange of ideas".

action by the governing bodies themselves. We develop this point later in this chapter.

5.5. At this point, however, we must strike a note of caution. An excess of consultation and participation could prove more harmful than the problems they are designed to solve. We have no intention of creating an elaborate system in which formal consultation must take place at every turn. The schools must not be deflected from their basic task of educating their pupils and the simple and informal measures which we propose below have been worked out with this overriding objective in mind.

Relations and communications within the school

5.6 Under this heading we consider the organisation and relations of the three groups who work and study in the school: the head and other teachers, the supporting staff, and the pupils.

The headteacher and his teaching staff

5.7 In his letter of 5 May, 1975 to the Chairman the then Secretary of State for Education and Science took the opportunity

"to pick out for special mention one issue among the many which will fall to be examined under the Committee's terms of reference. This is whether the arrangements for the management and government of schools should impose an obligation on the head to consult his staff on matters relating to the internal organisation, management and discipline of the school. I know that strong views are held on this by various interests concerned in the running of the schools. John Morris and I have no doubt that the Committee will accept, as we do, that such consultation is always desirable; we trust that the Committee, in the course of reviewing the present arrangements, will consider whether or not it should be made a mandatory requirement. If the Committee conclude that it should, we would expect them to want to offer advice on the scope and form of the provision which would be needed to ensure its smooth and effective working, to identify the various elements having a part to play in the procedure and to express their views on the respective functions which each of the parties would need to be given".

5.8. We accept the desirability of consultation between the headteacher and his colleagues. Indeed in our view it would be wrong for schools to attempt to operate without adequate and suitable arrangements for such consultation.

5.9. The 1945 model articles provide for the headteacher to "control the internal organisation, management and discipline of the school". Of course he can exercise this control in different ways. As one headteacher noted in his submission of evidence,

"some headteachers in the past have been excessively authoritarian and have been reluctant ... to discuss matters of importance concerning the school with their own staff ... such heads have tended to be used as a model ..."

Despite the hold of this authoritarian model upon the popular imagination, our evidence suggests that headteachers are increasingly preferring a consultative style of leadership. According to the National Association of Head Teachers "the vast majority of headteachers consult with their teaching staff frequently and effectively"; the National Union of Teachers noted that "well-developed consultative procedures exist in many schools". The value of consultation between the headteacher and his colleagues is not at issue. The question is whether such consultation should be made mandatory.

5.10. We have recommended that, subject to the overriding functions of the local education authority, governing bodies should be in a position to determine the lines on which their particular schools are organised and run. Against this background the need is for consultative arrangements which will give teachers the opportunity to submit their views or proposals to the governing body on matters for which it is responsible and to the headteacher on day-to-day decisions within the policies approved by the governing body. We do not envisage any major difficulty in arranging for a full interchange of views and information between the headteacher, the teaching staff and the governing body. The first point of contact would be the teacher governors, to and through whom the other teachers could express their views; though, as we made clear in the previous chapter, the teacher governors would not be delegates of their colleagues. It should be open to the teaching staff generally to present papers on particular issues through the headteacher for consideration by the governing body. The governing body and the teaching staff will, we hope, invite each other to present contributions on specific topics at their own meetings.

5.11. *We RECOMMEND that, subject to our recommendation* concerning confidentiality, the minutes of the governors' proceedings, together with the notices and agenda for their meetings, should be made available in the teachers' common room.*

5.12. It is more difficult to ensure that the headteacher consults his colleagues on day-to-day decisions. The proponents of mandatory consultation see it as a means of compelling those heads who are unwilling to engage voluntarily in genuine consultation with their colleagues to do so. Its opponents argue that mandatory consultation would not only fail to change the attitude of those few headteachers who have no use for consultation, but would also provide the opportunity for a minority of teachers bent on obstruction to insist upon consultation about the most trivial matters. We believe that the newly constituted governing bodies which we propose—whose members will include the head and at least one other teacher—will be able to deal with either of these rare eventualities. *We RECOMMEND that the governing body should invite the headteacher to submit his general proposals for consultation with his staff on day-to-day matters, should satisfy itself upon the adequacy and suitability of these proposals in general*

---

* See paragraph 11.9

*and in particular satisfy itself that they afford facilities for discussion between members of the teaching staff and the expression of collective views.** Whenever necessary, the governing body should examine the operation of the consultative arrangements.

5.13. We recognise that the arrangements adopted for this purpose will differ, just as the size, character and circumstances of schools differ. The consultative machinery used in a small village primary school will bear scant resemblance to that adopted in a large secondary school. We believe that the detailed arrangements should be left to the judgement of those on the spot.

The supporting staff

5.14. Depending upon their size, schools employ a wide range of non-teaching personnel such as caretakers, cleaners, cooks, groundsmen, school meals staff, secretaries and technicians. These supporting staff play an important part in the effective running of a school and their work and working conditions can be directly affected by many decisions reached by the governing body and the headteachers. We believe that such decisions should take account of the views of the supporting staff.

5.15. Given their widely assorted occupations, the supporting staff may not always find it necessary or appropriate to formulate views as a whole. In such cases the occupational group concerned could make their views known to the governing body or the headteacher independently. Where a member of the supporting staff is appointed as a governor, he would provide a first point of contact with the governing body for his colleagues. In schools where this does not prove possible other means should be found.

5.16. *We RECOMMEND that:*

a. *supporting staff be kept informed of the governing body's work by means to be determined by the governors after consultation with the staff concerned;*

b. *supporting staff be given the opportunity to submit their views or proposals to the governing body and the headteacher on any matter which is of special concern to them;*

c. *arrangements for consultation between the supporting staff and the head-teacher should be made by the governing body on the same basis as that proposed for teaching staff in paragraph 5.12.*

Secondary school pupils

5.17. School councils or similar pupil organisations are fairly common in secondary schools today. They are generally composed of elected representa-

---

* In smaller schools all members of staff might take part. In larger schools this might not be practicable; in such cases consultation could take place between the headteacher and representatives elected by the staff.

tives—usually of classes or tutor groups—who are given facilities to raise and discuss matters which affect the pupils of the school and to make representations to the head or other responsible teacher. The initiative for the creation of these organisations has come mainly from teachers, who regard them as a means of increasing the pupils' awareness of the issues involved in running their school and of introducing them to some of the basic procedures and realities of representative democracy.

5.18. Although not all school councils have succeeded in achieving these two purposes, we believe that their efforts deserve encouragement and support. The governing body is well-placed to provide such backing. Contact between the governing body and the pupils would be enhanced by inviting pupils to sit in on a regular basis at governors' meetings. In any event *we RECOMMEND that:*

a. *the governing body should be empowered to authorise the establishment of a school council or similar organisation by the pupils, and should be responsible for ensuring that arrangements within the school are adequate and suitable for its effective operation;*

b. *as a general rule the pupils themselves should decide upon the agenda for their organisation's meetings;*

c. *the pupils should be given access to the governing body should they wish to express a view on a particular matter or to question the adequacy or suitability of the arrangements made for them to do so.*

Relations and communications with parents

5.19. Both individually and collectively the parents constitute a major source of support for the school. It is not a source which has been tapped fully in the past. We believe that governing bodies should encourage the widest and deepest possible parental commitment to their schools. We go on to consider how the parents as a whole might most effectively contribute to the work of the governing body, and also how the relation between the school and the individual parent, with his special interest in his own children's work and welfare, might be given open recognition on a basis that will benefit both.

The parent body

5.20. We look first at the parents as a group. We have already recommended that they should have at least one quarter of the places on the governing body of every school. The special role of the parent governors is to foster relationships between the school and its governing body and the general body of parents. We do not underestimate the difficulties. In the past parent governors have often found themselves isolated and without a base from which to draw upon the full potential support of their fellow parents. Many of the latter have either been unaware of the parent governors' existence or have had no part in the process by which they were chosen. We believe that these problems can be solved. We have already recommended that every governing body should include representatives of the parents and that these should be elected by the general body of parents. In addition *we RECOMMEND that parents' organisations should be encouraged and facilities for their work should be made available within the school.*

5.21. The election of parent governors should be one of many activities bringing together parents and involving them in the life of the school and so a valuable way of developing their sense of collective identity and purpose. Although they have a common interest in the school which their children attend, parents have no readily available means for the regular expression of that interest. Special arrangements must therefore be made for parents to be able to meet and exchange views.

5.22. In recent years a popular means of pursuing these ends has been the parent-teacher association (PTA). Many of these associations have increased parents' commitment to their schools and have established closer and better relations between parents and teachers. Some PTAs however, have succeeded in attracting the more articulate and committed proponents of parental participation but have failed to win the support of the generality of parents as well. With a view to involving a wider group of parents many school associations have adopted a more informal approach, giving automatic membership to all parents, dispensing with subscriptions and inviting all those interested in the welfare of the school and its children to take part in their functions. Whilst we welcome the spread of this looser form of association, we believe that the parents themselves should be free to choose what type of organisation, if any, is best suited to their needs. We therefore confine ourselves to the *RECOMMEN-DATION that the parents should have the opportunity to set up an organisation based upon the school, developing its aims and methods of working in consultation with the headteacher and the governing body.*

5.23. Whether or not the parents take up this opportunity we *RECOMMEND that as a basic minimum the governing body should ensure that parents have access to the school for a weekday evening meeting once a term and the means of publicising their activities.*

5.24. We are confident that in most schools the teachers would welcome and assist a more active parental contribution, but we have stipulated these minimum requirements because there is evidence that in a small minority of schools parents are discouraged from meeting. It is worth noting the benefits which would accrue from just a termly meeting and opportunities for publicity. Parents would be given opportunities for getting to know other parents with similar interests, choosing their candidates for the governing body and referring queries and proposals through them to the governing body. In their turn parent governors would be better able to keep their fellow parents informed of the issues facing the school and their fellow governors informed of the parents' views.

5.25. Thus even the most rudimentary parent organisation would perform an important service to both the parents and the governing body. Of course we would not expect such an organisation to achieve the active involvement of all parents. While most parents are interested in the progress and prospects of their own children, fewer show a desire to participate in school affairs generally or take an interest in broader questions of educational theory and practice. Yet decisions on such matters affect, directly or otherwise, the education of the individual children. The best approach, we think, is to seek to build on the natural interest of parents in their own children to the point where they can be drawn into collective discussion of wider educational issues. By helping the parents to speak and act collectively the governing body could more effectively draw upon the views of the parents in exercising its responsibility for the school. Moreover, we would expect the parents to join with the teachers in arranging regular contact and discussion on both an individual and a group basis.

The individual parent

5.26. It is the individual parent who is in law responsible for securing his child's education* and whose support in this task is vital. There should therefore be at the individual level also a partnership between home and school. The individual parent will want the school to be an open and welcoming place. He will expect it to provide a framework within which he can communicate with his own child's teachers, in a spirit of partnership, about the child's welfare and progress.

5.27. We believe that such aspirations are wholly reasonable and that every parent has a right to expect a school's teachers to recognise his status in the education of his child by the practical arrangements they make to communicate with him and the spirit in which they accept his interest. If there is no such recognition, the measures we have advocated for parents collectively will be of limited value, and may be seen by many parents and teachers as no more than a means of increasing the influence of those who are already enthusiastic participators. We wish to produce a structure within which every parent will have a role in supporting the school and increasing its effectiveness. We believe that the governing body should continually seek to improve the arrangements for individual parents to inform themselves of their children's education, behaviour and development in the school. We sympathise with the many teachers who feel that their increasing problems in educating poorly-motivated children with a low level of home support are not enough appreciated. They often say, rightly, that the priority given to education in many homes of all classes is too low, that talk of parents' "rights" often ignores their corresponding responsibilities, that parents indeed often expect teachers, especially in disciplinary matters, to assume responsibilities which they are no longer able or

---

*Section 36, Education Act 1944. (See Appendix D).

willing to assume themselves. A minority of parents feel only a slight commitment to their child's school, but most conscientious parents would welcome positive encouragement and help from teachers in doing their duty to see that their children are educated.

5.28. We have therefore considered what the headteacher and his colleagues can do to build on parents' sense of responsibility and enlist their support in the education of their children. The staff of a good school already tries to make parents feel at ease there, welcomes their help and continuously seeks better ways of communicating which are appropriate to local needs. The headteacher will encourage parents to join the school association and make arrangements for parents to see their child's teachers regularly, by individual appointment if necessary. Where problems arise with a child the headteacher will at once contact parents, encouraging them to contact him about any problems they have encountered. He will give clear information about school rules and the reasons for them, seek parents' support in upholding them and try to make sure that parents understand the school's teaching aims and how they can help. He will make it clear that parents can have access to a teacher by reasonable arrangement especially if they are worried, puzzled or dissatisfied, and that they have a right to information and explanation on school policies, and to regular reports on the progress of the individual child.* We repeat that we endorse the right of every parent to expect these things, and *RECOMMEND that the governing body should satisfy itself that adequate arrangements are made to inform parents, to involve them in their children's progress and welfare, to enlist their support, and to ensure their access to the school and a teacher by reasonable arrangement.*

5.29. We believe that better forms of communication will, in time, increase parents' sense of commitment. We think there is one measure which could make an immediate contribution to a recognition of linked rights and responsibilities. *We RECOMMEND that the nature of the relation between the school and the individual parent should be set down in a letter sent by the governors to every parent at the time of their formal acceptance of a place at the school.* The letter would set out, in the terms indicated in paragraph 5.28, what those concerned at the school are doing to involve parents and what parents can in turn do to support their child at school, reminding them of their legal responsibility for ensuring regular attendance but also indicating the many other ways they can help the staff of the school in their task. An idea of the kind of letter a governing body might send is given in Appendix F. We would, however, emphasise that we do not wish this to be taken as a model for all schools in England and Wales: the form and content is very much a matter for decision by individual governing bodies in the light of their knowledge and experience of the local situation.

---

*After giving careful consideration to the question of parental access to educational records kept in the school on their own children, we decided that it would be premature to express a view since we understand that this matter is at present being considered by the DES and that the local authority and teacher associations and other interested bodies are being consulted.

5.30. There is of course no suggestion that what the school has to offer the child is in any way conditional on home support but to issue such a letter at the same time as inviting the parents formally to confirm their acceptance of a place at the school would give more solemnity both to the act of enrolment and to the contents of the letter. It would have the incidental benefit of acquainting new parents with the governors and their role in promoting good relationships. Its main object would be to increase parents' sense of commitment to the school, to remind teachers of their responsibility to parents, to encourage both to value their partnership in the education process, and to increase the sum of the joint effort made on the child's behalf.

The school in its wider setting

5.31. Under this heading we consider ways and means of improving communications and encouraging co-operation between governing bodies and the community or communities which their schools serve. We also look at communication and consultation between local education authorities and the governing bodies of their schools.

5.32. Some schools serve a compact and readily identifiable community. Others draw their children from a wide or diverse area and cannot easily be identified with a single community. For a school in this position, a first task of the governing body is to survey the range and nature of the community interest. This task could usefully begin when the local education authority, staff and parent governors meet to co-opt their "community" colleagues, as the latter will be seen and will act as intermediaries between the school and the different elements of its community.

5.33. Whether or not it provides a community governor, any organisation or group operating in or connected with the community should be able to put questions, views or proposals to the governing body. Governing bodies should make known their readiness to consider representations from members of the community, perhaps looking to the local press and radio to publicise their intention to work in co-operation with the community. Another means of demonstrating this intention would be to encourage local people to attend school functions and to make the school premises available, when practicable, for use by the local community. (We discuss this aspect of school-community co-operation in chapter 9.)

5.34. The practical details of such co-operation are obviously best left to those on the spot. Nevertheless we urge all governing bodies to pay particular attention to liaison with other governing bodies, with prospective employers, and with agencies concerned for children's welfare.

5.35. When children move up from one stage of primary education to the next, and especially when they move from the contained world of the primary school to the larger world of secondary school life, there is a danger that they may lose direction and momentum in the crossing of the transfer gap. We are told that the danger often becomes fact. Too often this is because of inadequate communication between schools. The need for children to gain the maximum advantage from their obligatory time at school is clear, and their education should be a continuous progression. Now that this country is moving rapidly to the point at which all maintained schools, both primary and secondary, are comprehensive in character and in which the vertical relationships between receiving and contributory schools are more clearly established, there is every good reason for unnecessary discontinuity to be avoided. Governing bodies should take it as an important task to develop these relationships and to look for the co-ordination that will enhance the overall effectiveness of the school system.

5.36. Another matter of considerable concern, which has given rise to substantial public discussion is the recognition of a gap between schools and the wealth-producing sector of the economy. *We RECOMMEND that governing bodies should do what they can to narrow this gap.*

5.37 There has also been a good deal of disquiet recently about the inadequate liaison between the various professions and agencies which have responsibility for the well-being of children. This has been highlighted by several well-publicised tragedies. We believe that governing bodies should encourage the further extension of co-operation between teachers and other people concerned for the welfare of children, such as school doctors, dentists, nurses and social workers. Each governing body will wish to keep itself informed of the child health service arrangements in its own school and in particular of any changes in the service which may be made in the light of the Court Report*

5.38. It will not be possible for all the governors nominated by local education authorities under our proposals to be members of local authorities, because there will not be enough of them. As well as ensuring that all governors whom they nominate are briefed on authority policy, local education authorities should consider further measures to ensure efficient communication and informed consultation with the governing bodies of their schools. We believe that such measures are best worked out locally. We therefore confine ourselves to the *RECOMMENDATION that on those occasions when the local education authority wishes to obtain local opinion on educational issues it should ensure that the consultation process draws on the knowledge and experience of the members of the newly constituted governing bodies.*

5.39. We believe that co-operation between groups of governing bodies can be very useful. Reference has already been made in paragraph 5.35 to co-operative arrangements between schools catering for the same pupils at different stages; *we RECOMMEND that in the same way governing bodies with other shared interests or concerns should be encouraged to make arrangements for consulting each other about them.*

---

*Department of Health and Social Security. Fit for the Future. The Report of the Committee on Child Health Services; Chairman Emeritus Professor S. D. M. Court, C.B.E., M.D., F.R.C.P., F.C.S.T. (Cmnd. 6684-1) HMSO 1976.

CHAPTER 6—CURRICULUM

6.1. In this chapter we set out the basic issues involved in assigning responsibility for the school curriculum, outline our general approach to those issues and describe its application in concrete terms.

The 1944 arrangements

6.2. Section 23 of the 1944 Act provides that the secular instruction to be given to pupils shall, subject to the school's rules of management or articles of government, be under the control of the local education authority. The model articles provide for the local education authority to "determine the general educational character of the school and its place in the local education system"; subject to this, for the governors to "have the general direction of the conduct and curriculum of the school" and, subject to this and other provisions in the articles, for the head to "control the internal organisation, management and discipline of the school" (the full text of the provision is given in Appendix E). When the relevant legislation was before the House of Commons in 1944 the then President of the Board of Education, Mr R A Butler, explained the division of responsibility as he saw it: " . . . the local education authority will have the responsibility for the broad type of education given in the . . . school . . . and its place in the local system. . . The broad picture will be governed . . . by the needs of the district and the needs of the children . . . The governing body would, in our view, have the general direction of the curriculum as actually given from day to day, within the school. The head teacher would have, again in our view, responsibility for the internal organisation of the school, including the discipline that is necessary to keep the pupils applied to their study, and to carry out the curriculum in the sense desired by the governing body "*

Evidence

6.3. Responsibility for the school curriculum was described by many witnesses as the most difficult, sensitive and controversial of the issues we had to consider. Even so, despite the wide range of views on this topic and the variety of definitions of the term curriculum, the evidence revealed a good deal of unchallenged common ground.

6.4. Many witnesses considered the wording used in the model articles to be "vague", "woolly," and even "meaningless". In their view the manner in which the responsibilities are set out in the model articles is too blurred to be of any practical value in the event of a dispute between the three parties involved: to avoid confusion and harmful demarcation disputes, the responsibilities of those concerned should be clearly differentiated and defined. † On the other hand a number of witnesses claimed that the 1945 wording, by virtue of its vagueness,

---

*Hansard. House of Commons. Vol. 397 10 March 1944. Column 2363.

†We have noted that the difficulties of the William Tyndale Junior School were exacerbated by the confusion about the respective roles of the LEA, the managers, the headteacher and the local inspectorate; William Tyndale Junior and Infant Schools Public Inquiry– see especially Chapter X. (See 1.10 footnote).

had important advantages: the absence of strict boundaries encouraged people to co-operate and made it possible for new initiatives on the curriculum for an individual school to come from any of the interested parties.

6.5. There was no suggestion that the local education authority should not retain its present statutory responsibility for the secular instruction given in the schools in its area. Similarly, witnesses were generally agreed that the head and the other teachers should play a leading part in formulating and implementing the curriculum of their particular school. There was, however, no such consensus on the role of the governors. At one extreme it was held that governors should be completely excluded from involvement in curriculum matters. At the other it was argued that governing bodies should not only oversee the implementation of the school's curriculum but also help in its formulation and development.

6.6. It should be noted that when referring to governors in this context, most witnesses, even those who favoured the appointment of teachers as governors of their own schools, seem to have in mind people not employed as teachers in the school concerned. The fundamental question at issue therefore was whether subject to the overall guidance of the local education authority, responsibility in this field—requiring professional skills but also with broad social and personal implications—should be borne by the school's teachers alone or be subject to some degree of external guidance and participation.

6.7. In the following brief review of witnesses' answers to this question we shall take in turn the views of organisations and individuals belonging to the four major interest groups. Most of the teachers' associations, including the National Union of Teachers and the National Association of Schoolmasters/ Union of Women Teachers, took the view that the curriculum should remain, as in their opinion it had become in practice, essentially the preserve of the school's own teachers. Some individual teachers who submitted evidence were less certain that such an approach was justified.

6.8. The bodies representing local education authorities, as well as the authorities which submitted evidence individually, tended to favour the retention of the existing arrangements.

6.9. Most organisations representing parents considered that governing bodies—reconstituted to include a greater number of parent governors—should have a say in drawing up the general educational aims of the school, and should have greater access to information on the school and education in general and more opportunities for questioning the teachers on specific matters. Though some of the individual parents and governors who submitted evidence urged a greater degree of parental involvement, on our visits we met a large number of parents and governors who did not question the convention that they should defer to the headteacher on all educational matters.

6.10. Those witnesses who can be regarded as representative of the communities and wider society served by the schools were a widely assorted group and we have found it difficult to generalise about their views. Nonetheless, there was a general tendency amongst them to advance the claims of members of the community not engaged in teaching to take some part in decisions about the school curriculum.

6.11. To conclude this brief summary of the evidence received on this topic, it should be mentioned that, although we heard arguments in favour of an exclusively teachers' control of the curriculum, we received no evidence suggesting that teachers should be formally excluded from decisions on the curriculum at the level of the individual school, as they are in some other educational systems.

Teachers' control or shared control?

6.12. We first consider the claim that the curriculum should be regarded as a preserve of the school's teachers. This does not imply, as is sometimes suggested, that the teachers would have complete freedom to decide the curriculum to be offered and how it should be taught. Although England and Wales do not have the centralised control of the curriculum that characterises some other educational systems, there are important constraints upon the freedom of headteachers and their staffs to decide what teaching and other educational activities should be carried on in their schools and how the schools should be organised. Every teacher must take account of the physical and intellectual characteristics of the pupils and the resources available to him. At the secondary level the teaching will be influenced by the public examination system controlled by the GCE and CSE examining boards and by the qualifications required for entry to various occupations. Both primary and secondary schools may be helped or hindered by the successes and problems of other schools in their area. Their curricular decisions may also have implications for the curricula of the other schools. Furthermore, each local education authority will have an overall policy that includes a view on the curriculum and it will also influence the decisions of individual schools through, for example, the work of its advisory service. Nevertheless, notwithstanding the above constraints and influences, a very real power of decision over curricular matters remains at the level of the individual school.

6.13. In their written submissions to us, most of the teachers' associations claimed that teachers alone should exercise this power of decision on the ground that, to quote the evidence of the Assistant Masters' Association, the curriculum "best falls within the competence of professionally trained, experienced and practising teachers". On our visits we took the opportunity to ask head and other teachers if they could justify such claims. The answers we received stressed the professional training and experience of the teachers and their objective understanding of the abilities, aptitudes and needs of the children they teach. It was claimed that these qualities offered the best basis for curricular decisions and it was suggested that people not engaged in education tended to over-simplify complex educational problems.

6.14. We do not believe that these arguments justify regarding the curriculum at school level as the responsibility solely of the teachers nor are we convinced that it is right for teachers to carry this responsibility alone. In a recent communication to the Schools Council the Secretaries of State have pointed out that curricula must meet, and be responsive to, the needs of society. In our view a school is not an end in itself: it is an institution set up and financed by society to achieve certain objectives which society regards as desirable and it is subject to all the stresses to which society itself is subject. It is vital therefore that teachers have the support of people outside the school in the increasingly difficult task of attaining those objectives and dealing with those stresses.* If ordinary people do not, as some teachers suggest, understand what schools are trying to do, it is in part because they have traditionally not taken an active part in determining the educational policy of the schools. Certainly there are substantial difficulties involved in fostering such participation, especially in the early stages, but we think that it will eventually promote fuller understanding, better relations and a wider knowledge and appreciation of the education provided by schools and of the skills which teachers bring to a difficult task.

6.15. A basic difficulty in evaluating the evidence on this subject was that different witnesses meant different things by "the curriculum". One of the main reasons for this diversity of interpretation, in our view, is that over the past thirty years most people not directly involved in education have for various reasons not kept abreast of new ideas and developments in the classroom. Although a great deal has been done in many parts of England and Wales to improve links between home and school and community and school, when adults come to examine (whether as parents, prospective employers, or rate/tax payers) the performance of schools today, their starting point may well be a comparison with memories of their own schooling when, in many cases, the approach to teaching was of a basically "instructional" kind and the curriculum was viewed somewhat narrowly as a range of separate subjects for study. It is also important to bear in mind that anyone who is today aged 45 or over attended school when compulsory education ended at fourteen. Not surprisingly some of these people find it difficult to understand the new problems which face schools in providing an education for all young people up to the age of sixteen.

6.16. The breadth of the aims towards which today's schools must strive is illustrated by the following statement which appeared in a paper"† prepared by the Department of Education and Science in 1976:

"i. to enable children to acquire the basic skills of literacy, oracy and numeracy and to stimulate their curiosity and imagination.

ii. to enable them to acquire the basic knowledge, practice in skills and in reasoning to equip them to enter a world of work which is becoming increasingly sophisticated in its processes and techniques, which is competitive, and which is likely to demand the ability to adapt oneself to learn new processes from time to time.

---

*A Schools Council Working Party has accepted the "controversial and negotiable nature of the curriculum", believing that pupils, parents, teachers and society should acknowledge each other's legitimate expectations and responsibilities and seek to effect a reconciliation of view. Schools Council, The Whole Curriculum, 13–16 (Working Paper 53) Evans/Methuen Educational 1975.

†Department of Education & Science. Getting Ready for Work (Report of Conference 23/24 March 1976) D.E.S. 1976. This statement can be applied, with different emphasis, to the curricula of both primary and secondary schools.

iii. to leave children at the end of their period of compulsory schooling with an appetite for acquiring further knowledge, experience and skills at different periods in later life; and able to benefit from additional education to a variety of levels.

iv. to prepare them to live and work with others in adult life; and to develop attitudes enabling them to be responsible members of the community . . .

v. to help them develop aesthetic sensitivity and appreciation, and skills and interests for leisure time.

vi. to mitigate the educational disadvantages that many children suffer through poor home conditions, limited ability or serious physical or mental handicap".

6.17. We do not think it is necessary to go into the historical developments underlying the widespread adoption and acceptance of aims of this kind for the school. We should simply like to draw attention to three points. First, insofar as teachers have adopted such aims their object has not been primarily to extend their own functions. Rather they have seen themselves as responding to changes in educational ideas and to changes in society and social values. Second, the pursuit of such aims has led to changes in teaching methods and school organisation which have attracted a good deal of public interest and comment. Third, curricula based upon aims of this kind interact with a child's behaviour, experience and development outside school and may affect his relations with and attitudes towards his family and community.

6.18. Modern developments in curriculum theory and practice have puzzled and worried many people not involved in school education. They have, in our view, strengthened the case for bringing such people together with teachers to determine the school's educational programme. We think this must be entirely a joint enterprise because, as we shall explain, it does not seem to us feasible or desirable to make any clear-cut division between different functions and activities of the school, for the purpose of allocating responsibility for decision-making.

6.19. Many teachers and governors to whom we have spoken seem to have attempted explicitly or implicitly, to distinguish an element of essentially instructional responsibility to be assigned to the school's head and his colleagues, and other elements of a more administrative, social or political kind in which other people—be they governors or the local education authorities—might play an important part. In our view this approach implies an artificial distinction between the more obvious and less obvious* aspects of the education offered by the school and would hinder people other than the school's teachers in making a contribution to the development of the school as a whole. Nor can we see any logical way of dividing responsibility by defining different sets of functions at different levels of generality, for which final decision-making might be assigned

---

*The less obvious aspects of the curriculum are often referred to as the 'hidden curriculum'. The essence of this notion is that the preparation and management of lessons, planning syllabuses and timetables, organising resources and assessing pupils are the surface aspects of the curriculum; the total curriculum is however much wider. It includes also the hidden elements— the incidental acquisition of values as well as academic learning arising for example from the interaction with other pupils and staff, from the variety of situations which arise at school, and from the written and unwritten rules and procedures by which these are governed.

to the local education authority, the governing body and the head teacher respectively. We have concluded that there is no aspect of the school's activities from which the governing body should be excluded nor any aspect for which the headteacher and his colleagues should be accountable only to themselves or to the local education authority. It follows that the responsibility for deciding the school's curriculum, in every sense of that word, must be shared between all levels and between all those concerned at every level.

6.20. To sum up, teachers need informed support. The society of which schools are a part can and does question their performance, but schools in turn need the understanding and help of society in their difficult task. Only a working partnership can meet these needs. We believe that governing bodies can provide a most appropriate setting for the conduct of this partnership.

Nature of the partnership

6.21. We have no intention of suggesting that governing bodies be asked to perform tasks which can be carried out properly only by the school's own teachers in the course of their work. Members of the governing body should not in their capacity as governors assume the mantle of teachers, still less that of inspectors. We think of the governing body as a partnership bringing together all the parties concerned for the school's success so that they can discuss, debate and justify the matters which any one of them may seek to implement. This task will demand of its members, no matter what their personal background and experience may be, no more than can be reasonably expected of informed, interested and responsible lay people. Having said this we can go on to consider the way in which the governing body can be expected to deal with the educational matters before it.

Curriculum responsibility in action

6.22. As we have seen, our preferred concept of the school curriculum effectively comprehends the sum of experiences to which a child is exposed at school. Strictly speaking therefore in exercising, as we propose, responsibility for the education provided in the school the governors will always have the whole curriculum before them since no single aspect of the life and work of the school can be properly understood if considered in isolation. In practice, however, the planning and development of a school curriculum can be broken down into four basic, and to a large extent overlapping, stages;

i. establishing the school's aims;

ii. translating those aims into more specific goals and organising the school and developing teaching methods and other practical steps to achieve them;

iii. keeping the education provided under continuous review and making periodic appraisals of the school's progress towards its goals and aims;

iv. deciding upon and taking action to facilitate such progress.

6.23. We take it as given that policies decided nationally and at the local education authority level will provide the framework within which individual schools and their governing bodies will operate. As we made clear in chapter 3, the governing body must be subject to any general policies, regulations or directions made by the local education authority. Within this general framework we *RECOMMEND that the governing body should be given by the local education authority the responsibility for setting the aims of the school, for considering the means by which they are pursued, for keeping under review the school's progress towards them, and for deciding upon action to facilitate such progress.* In the remainder of this chapter we consider these four aspects of the governors' task in turn.

Setting the aims of the school

6.24. We propose that when looking to the governing bodies to set the aims of the schools for which they are responsible, the local education authority should alert them to the difficulties experienced, first, by schools whose aims are too frequently questioned and changed and, second, by schools whose aims become unalterably fixed. We believe that both extremes could be avoided if the governing bodies were to reconsider the particular aims of the school periodically. We return to this point in paragraph 6.45.

6.25. It is not for us to draw up model aims since this might limit the initiative of governors. It might be useful, however, if local education authorities were to draw the attention of governing bodies to some general statement such as the one quoted in paragraph 6.16. This would at least provide a starting point for discussion on the particular aims of the school concerned. The head and his colleagues might then be invited to submit a first draft of the school's aims for the governing body's consideration. The procedures adopted and the time spent upon them will probably vary from area to area and school to school and the only specific *RECOMMENDATION we would make is that in setting the school's aims the governing bodies should give consideration to constructive suggestions made by any individuals or organisation with a concern for the school's welfare.*

Translating the school's aims into practice

6.26. When the governing body has reached conclusions on any of the aims which it wishes its school to follow, it should consider whether the organisation, teaching methods, disciplinary practices and other measures used in the school are appropriate for the pursuit of their aims. Obviously there can be no question of a simple, staged progression from an agreement on the aims of the school, in their totality, to the preparation and adoption of a "master plan" for pursuing them. We have in mind a fluid procedure in which action on any aim could be initiated as and when it was agreed by the governors.

6.27. *We RECOMMEND that the governing body invite the headteacher in consultation with his staff to prepare papers setting out the means by which they propose to pursue the aims adopted.* In the case of well-established aims, the school's existing practice might need no revision but where some new aim was being considered it would be necessary to examine whether its pursuit required the introduction of new activities into the school. After discussion and consideration of any alternative suggestions it would be for the governing body to decide whether to adopt (or confirm) these proposals.

6.28. In considering the arrangements for pursuing the school's aims, the governing body's attention would focus upon the setting of specific goals or objectives and upon the school's organisation and teaching methods, examining both the educational experience and pastoral care available for the children and the educational and social effects of particular ways of arranging the provision of teaching.

6.29. These operations would, in our view, be of considerable educational value. Teachers would have an opportunity to discuss, explain and justify their decisions in terms which could be understood by people not belonging to the teaching profession; their skill as professionals can only grow from such an experience. Lack of confidence may often have lain behind the reluctance of many teachers in the past to discuss their work with people from outside the school. The latter also would come to recognise the importance and difficulty of reconciling the different objectives of the school and of producing unified plans for achieving them. We do not wish to lay down detailed procedures for governors to follow. As a practical aid we have set out in Appendix G a number of examples which illustrate how governing bodies might approach the sort of issues which they can expect to have put before them. We also wish to draw particular attention to the governors' role in respect of teaching methods, school timetables, and school discipline.

6.30. As regards teaching methods we must draw a distinction between the methods adopted by the individual classroom teacher and broader questions of method which affect the education provided by the school as a whole (or at least large departments within it). Obviously the individual teacher should continue, subject to the constraints noted in paragraph 6.12, to be responsible for deciding how to teach the members of his class, in the light of his own capacities and any general teaching policies adopted generally in the school. Nonetheless we believe there are at least two other considerations which should influence and could limit the making of decisions by individual teachers or even by the school's teachers in general. First, all decisions involving questions of consistency of approach and continuity of method are likely to be of sufficient importance to concern the governing body.* Second, we believe that people not engaged in education have an important contribution to make in expressing public opinion and concern generally on how children are taught and we hope that the governing body will become the forum for considering the suitability of new educational ideas and methods for the school. Proposed innovations might originate within or without the school. The governing body should encourage a two-way flow of ideas, examining developments initiated by its own teachers and discussing with them the implications of developments elsewhere. We believe that the governing body should concern itself with the professional development of the teachers in its school and should be active in promoting this, for example

---

*Such a decision is considered in Example a of Appendix G.

by encouraging them to take full advantage of opportunities for in-service training.

6.31. The construction of a timetable for a secondary school is a complicated task which is properly carried out by senior teachers; the purpose is clearly to provide the organisation within which teachers can teach and children can learn. It might be thought that this is a technical process which concerns only the teachers and pupils. But in fact there are often much wider issues involved, including the ordering of curricular balance and priorities to secure the fair distribution of opportunities for children of all abilities. The effectiveness of the timetabling from both the educational and the social points of view is, we believe, a matter of concern for the governing body.

6.32. We stress throughout this report the indivisibility of a school's activities. To be effective the learning experience must be supported first by an organisation which directs resources in accordance with the needs of each child, second by sensitive pastoral care, and third by the encouragement, through precept and example, of the consideration for others which alone in the long run can ensure pleasant and orderly behaviour. Put conversely, the best guarantee that high standards of conduct will be observed by the majority is a curriculum devised to give every child experience of success, and a structure of care which not only seeks to deal with any personal problems which jeopardise that success, but also makes him feel valued as an individual. We therefore regret that so often "discipline" should be equated with the treatment of indiscipline, and urge that part of the governors' responsibility is to ensure that theirs is the kind of school in which the more positive concept outlined above is consciously promoted. We also emphasise—and have set out elsewhere—the need to involve parents and the community in supporting schools in their task. In such conditions we believe that pupils will increasingly be encouraged to become identified with the work of the school, to participate fully, and to feel responsible for their own conduct. The growth of such involvement we consider to be vital to their development as individuals and to the success of their school.

6.33. Accordingly *we RECOMMEND that within the framework of any general policy made by the local education authority the governing body should have the responsibility for formulating guidelines which promote high standards of behaviour and for making such minimum rules and sanctions as are necessary to maintain such standards in the school.* It must also be their responsibility to ensure that staff, parents and pupils are made fully aware of these policies and rules and the reasons for them and have an opportunity to express their views. In this way we should hope to bring about not a weakening of the head's authority, but rather an increase in the support he received in a task which is not becoming any easier.

Keeping under review the life and activities of the school

6.34. As a first step in keeping under review the degree to which the school is achieving its goals and making progress towards its aims, the governing body will want to decide what information and advice it will need in respect of those activities of the school which it considers of particular importance as indicators of the school's progress.

6.35. The primary source for this information and advice will be the head-teacher and especially his staff, and the success of the operation will depend upon their contribution. Like all other organisations, schools produce in the course of their everyday business a great deal of information about many aspects of their work. Often this serves a single, specific purpose and is then discarded. Even when preserved it is not always in a form which facilitates its further use. We think that this represents a lost opportunity. The information flowing into and within the school, on those matters which can indicate progress in important respects, should be assembled and processed in such a way that it can be readily used by the governing body. Whilst the information required by the governors will vary from school to school it might be helpful to mention a few obvious items which we would expect to be collected. In all schools information about applications for places at the school, records of attendance and suspensions would be helpful, together with records of out of school activities including details of school societies and educational visits. In the case of primary schools information about relevant secondary provision and, in the case of secondary schools, information about examination results and employment opportunities in the area, might be added. In addition to basic information of this kind, the governors would no doubt also wish to have periodic reports of a more qualitative nature on the major departments of the school and its pastoral system as well as the headteacher's assessment of the school's general progress.

6.36. The governing body would also be concerned to obtain information on how the school is seen by the community which it serves. It would be for the governing body to decide upon the type of information required and the means of obtaining it but again, for purely illustrative purposes, we note some possibilities: the views of the school's parents, pupils and supporting staff: the pre-school provision available locally; the views of the governing bodies of other schools, to which pupils, in the case of primary or middle schools, normally transfer; the views of local people (based on observation and experience) and, in the case of secondary schools, the views of employers and institutions of higher and further education.

6.37. We believe that it will help individual governors to gain insight into the nature of the educational opportunities being provided and into the complexities of the teacher's task if they visit classes in progress. We therefore *RECOMMEND that where the governing body considers it appropriate and desirable and has worked out with the teachers procedures for the purpose, individual governors should have the opportunity of seeing classes at work.* It should be emphasised that governors should not see themselves in the role of inspectors. Where the attention of a governor is drawn to difficulties affecting a particular class or teacher, he should inform the chairman in order that the matter can if necessary be taken up in the first place with the headteacher and perhaps with the local education authority adviser concerned.

6.38. The total number in the local education authority Advisory/Inspection service has grown substantially in recent years to the present level of about 1,800 advisers in England and Wales. The purpose of the advisory service is to promote high standards of performance by teachers and of attainment by pupils both in basic skills and studies and in education in its wider sense. This purpose is principally achieved through the provision of advice, based on wide experience and knowledge, to head and other teachers and by reference to example to show where and how high standards are achieved and maintained. Whilst the relationship of advisers with teaching staff will normally be one of mutual support, the advisory team exercises a leadership role in the area of curriculum innovation, in-service training and staff development programmes. In those circumstances where the efficiency of a particular school or teacher is giving cause for concern, the advisory team may assume an inspectorial role and report as required to the governing body and to the local education authority.

6.39. Viewed overall, the local education authority advisory service has developed in a haphazard way. In the past a local interest in, or current concern about, a particular area of the curriculum, for instance mathematics, modern languages, English, physical education or religious education, often resulted in the appointment of a specialist adviser to work in this field. This has led to the local education authority advisory service having at present in some areas a certain imbalance. Although the opportunity presented by local government reorganisation was taken to achieve a better balance and improved structure, there nevertheless remains a preponderance of advisers who are primarily subject specialists rather than general advisers who, in addition to having a specialist role, are able to take an overview, to assess and to give advice upon the school as a whole, its organisation, overall development and progress, following the tradition and practice of H.M Inspectorate. The Inspectorate has become smaller (there are now only about 300 HM Inspectors available for work in approximately 28,000 schools in England and Wales) and there are heavy demands upon it to assist in preparing policy advice on national issues for the Secretaries of State, as well as for HM Inspectors to concern themselves with the work and standards of individual schools. We therefore regard it as a matter of urgency that more general advisers should be made available through the local education authority advisory service. This will be essential if the role we have envisaged for the new governing bodies is to be filled.

6.40. We have considered the important question of the level of local education authority advisory service which ought to be provided. Because of the variations between local education authorities in the organisation and function of their advisory teams and the differing demands made on them at present and likely to continue in the future, we have concluded that the level of provision must ultimately be a matter for each local education authority to judge in the light of its own circumstances and requirements. We have noted the view of the National Association of Inspectors and Educational Advisers that a reasonable establishment is one adviser for each 20,000 population, so that, for example, an authority of 500,000 would have an advisory team of 25. We consider that this level of provision should be an immediate objective for the local education authorities. Money used in providing a balanced and effective advisory team is in our view money well spent and should be high in the priorities of any local education authority.

6.41. We recognise that any increase in the number of general advisers will also mean a substantial extension of the in-service training programme for advisers at present in post. At the same time, it is clear to us that if any general adviser is to work effectively, this adviser must be able to call on support from, and work within, a well-balanced advisory team.

6.42. We therefore *RECOMMEND that:*

a. *Every local education authority should take steps to ensure that the services of a general adviser are regularly available to each of its schools and that the general adviser will be available for consultation with, and report to, the governing body on request.*

b. *All local education authorities should review the adequacy of their advisory/ inspection service in the light of the requirements which we propose for the new governing bodies and should take early steps to strengthen these services as necessary, aiming at a minimum of one adviser to every 20,000 of its total population at the earliest possible date.*

c. *Local education authorities, grouped on an area basis and in collaboration with HM Inspectorate, should establish panels consisting of local education authority advisers, HM Inspectors, and other appropriate agencies to arrange in-service training to assist local education authority advisers to identify and to develop the necessary skills to work more effectively as general advisers.*

6.43. We recognise that in some areas these proposals will involve substantial additional expenditure but we regard them as of the highest priority. We also recognise that the establishment of a local education authority network of general advisers throughout the country may take some time to achieve and that until this position is reached, some governing bodies may find themselves exceptionally in urgent need of the assistance of a general adviser before one has been assigned to their school. In these circumstances, we hope that chief education officers and education committees will deal sympathetically with requests for assistance from governing bodies.

6.44. In paragraphs 6.35 to 6.43 we have indicated the major sources from which the governing body will derive its information and advice on the life and activities of the school. *We RECOMMEND that this material should be brought together in each school with the purpose of creating an effective but unobtrusive information system for the governing body.* Individual governing bodies will have their own views on what is best in their local situation and we do not suggest that there should be any standard pattern. *We RECOMMEND that the head-teacher be made responsible for developing the governing body's information system, working with general guidance provided by the governing body about the aspects of the school's activities on which information is required and the form in which it is required.*

6.45. The governing body would be able to put the information collected to short- medium- and long-term use. We would not wish to lay down any firm guidelines on how governing bodies should use their information systems in the short and medium terms. By quickly reflecting any substantial changes over a wide range of the school's activities it would be an important aid in keeping the school under continuous review. When any particular question arose, the governing body could look to the school's information system to provide up-to-date material with a helpful bearing upon the matter. In the course of each school year we think the governing body should ask the headteacher to arrange for the relevant information to be brought together in reports on particular sectors of the school (e.g. the school's pastoral system or a teaching department). Finally, the system would be the basis on which at longer intervals the governing body would ask for the production of a complete and coherent picture of the school so as to appraise the school's progress as a whole and consider the extent to which its development matched their intentions. This would also be an appropriate occasion for a periodic general reconsideration of the school's aims and objectives (see paragraph 6.24).

6.46. In considering how often governing bodies should appraise the progress of their schools in this way, we must distinguish between the first and subsequent occasions. In general we think it unlikely that the information for a first complete appraisal would be available for several years after the introduction of this approach. Some governing bodies will find it relatively easy to conduct such an appraisal sooner than this but we would not wish others to feel obliged to do likewise. We think that each governing body should be encouraged to work at a pace which it finds appropriate to its particular situation. Nonetheless we think it important to set a limit to the time spent by any governing body in producing its first appraisal of its school's progress. We therefore *RECOMMEND that every governing body produce a first general appraisal, however incomplete, within four years of its formation.* We are reluctant to specify a term for subsequent appraisals as the experience of the first few years will provide the only basis for a well-informed decision. We hope that governing bodies would be able to appraise their school's progress in total every two or three years, and certainly not less often than every four years. *We RECOMMEND that the exact term should be decided by the local education authority after consultation with the governing bodies of the schools in its area.*

6.47. The procedures outlined in paragraphs 6.34 to 6.46 have two advantages to which we wish to draw particular attention. First, neither the continuous reviewing nor the periodic appraisals of the school's progress should interrupt the normal running of the school. Second, the direct involvement of the teachers and others working in the school would, we believe, not only improve the quality of the review and appraisal processes but also facilitate the staff's acceptance of proposals for any action needed in consequence.

Deciding upon action to facilitate the school's progress

6.48. Throughout all the stages of planning and developing the curriculum, the headteacher and his colleagues must of course continue to exercise their responsibilities for the day-to-day running of the school. As we made clear in chapter 3, we believe that if the headteacher and his colleagues are to be able to do their work efficiently they must take "day-to-day" decisions. We accept that this discretion could, if consistently abused, vitiate policies determined by the local education authority or the governing bodies. Nonetheless we think it is unnecessary, and in any event impractical and undesirable, to attempt to define the exact limits of the teachers' discretion: unnecessary because we believe that the vast majority of teachers will wish to co-operate constructively in the implementation of the policies adopted in whose determination they will have had an effective voice; impractical because it would be impossible to prescribe procedures sufficiently comprehensive to guide the teachers in dealing with every question which might arise in a school; and undesirable because such procedures would deny trained and experienced teachers the right to exercise their proper professional judgement.

6.49. In exercising their discretion, the teachers would have regard to local education authorities' policies and the general policy framework provided by the governing body in setting the school's particular aims. They would also be able to draw guidance from previous decisions reached by the local education authority and their governing body. When confronted with an important curriculum issue for which this external guidance proved insufficient, the headteacher would refer to his governing body. We do not wish to propose specific procedures since much will depend upon the importance and urgency of the question at issue. However, it might be generally accepted that the headteacher should consult the chairman of governors on such questions, and, if the latter agreed and if time allowed, a special meeting of the governing body should be convened. In the absence of such a meeting the governors could be informed of developments at their next scheduled meeting. Where the resolution of the problem was not of great urgency, the point at issue could be referred to an ordinary governors' meeting.

6.50. Whatever the exact procedures adopted, the headteacher and his colleagues should look to the governing body for general guidance on the exercise of their responsibility for the day-to-day running of the school. We are confident that most headteachers would welcome guidance of this kind. Today's headteachers are increasingly called upon to explain and justify their own and their colleagues' decisions. A headteacher today can base his decisions upon his authority as the person appointed by the local education authority to run the school; or as the agent of the school governing body; or as the leader of the school's teaching staff; or as the adult responsible for his pupils *in loco parentis*. In our view, it is desirable that in each of these capacities the headteacher should have the guidance and support of his governing body.

Consequences for the local education authority

6.51. For the local education authority the sum of the consequences of a firmer relationship with governing bodies is considerable. Education departments will need to take full account of the new approach to school government.

We envisage (see paragraphs 6.38—6.43) that the chief education officer and his staff will be mobilised to support schools and their governing bodies in a systematic way as developments at school level proceed. This does not entail more work or more administrative staff for education departments; it may well mean a readjustment of effort and emphasis. Education departments may expect to have to treat the aims of the school curriculum, and the means to help schools to achieve them, as a priority.

6.52. The education committee in turn will need to develop its responses and linked processes. Reports from governing bodies concerned with the educational needs and qualities of their schools will call for matching judgement and evaluation from the committee, so that it can form a view about the total character of the education effort for which the local education authority is providing resources. Movements to realise schools' aims and objectives, as expressed through the reports of individual governing bodies will come together to be assessed as a collective movement towards the achievement of the general education policies of the education committee and the local education authority.

6.53. It is not for us to discuss in detail how these processes should be translated into structure by education committees. But we do suggest that they will need to consider seriously what analysis or research function, and what definition of local education authority aim and objective, should be established. We also suggest that, just as we expect governing bodies to communicate continuously with their supporting local communities, so on a larger scale should education committees aim to communicate effectively with the population and interests in their areas.

6.54. We expect too that education committees will be looking for the means to relate performance in their own areas to standards revealed elsewhere. Cross referenced in this way education committees' analyses would be a major contribution to that body of knowledge about the state of the nation's schools which we think must be available to central government for the purposes of the supervisory function given to the Secretary of State by statute.

6.55. *We RECOMMEND that the governing body of every school should send the local education authority a short report upon the completion of its periodic general appraisal.* This would provide the local education authority with a regularly up-dated record of the progress of its schools. It is not for us to prescribe how the local education authorities should handle these periodic reports but we would hope that selected aspects could be distilled into papers to be presented to the education committee. In this way committee members would be given progress reports from the field on the implementation of particular local education authority policies. In this connection, we would advise caution as to the publication of the reports of individual schools. Whilst we recognise the benefits of publicity in certain cases, we believe that a general commitment to publish the reports in full might not be in the interests of the schools. In submitting their reports to the local education authority the governing body should specify any items which they would wish to be withheld in the event of publication.

CHAPTER 7—FINANCE

7.1. In this chapter we deal with the financial responsibilities of school governing bodies, first in general and then, more specifically, in relation to the use of the resources allocated to a particular school and also to building work. We begin by reviewing practice as it has developed since 1944 and summarising the evidence we have received.

The 1944 arrangements

7.2. In 1944 it was expected that governing bodies would have a significant financial role. The White Paper said:

"The practice will no doubt generally obtain by which governors prepare estimates covering a suitable period and submit them to the local education authority. Within the broad headings of the approved estimate the governors should have latitude to exercise reasonable discretion. It may be desirable that a small margin for contingencies should be allowed, particularly under the heading of "Books, apparatus and stationery"; in any case the allowance under this heading, which is commonly calculated on a capitation basis, should not be too rigidly defined and a school should be entitled to present a case for a higher rate to meet special difficulties and developments. There is general agreement that the school library, the special needs of which have often been overlooked in the past, should be given a separate allowance".

7.3. The relevant articles in the 1945 model provided that:

"a. The Governors shall in the month of   in each year submit for the consideration of the Local Education Authority an estimate of the income and expenditure required for the purpose of the school for the 12 months ending   in the following year, in such form as the Local Education Authority may require.

b. The Local Education Authority shall consider the estimate and make such variation in it as they think fit.

c. Where the Governors are empowered by the Local Education Authority to incur expenditure they shall not exceed the amount approved by the Local Education Authority under each head of the estimate in any year without the previous consent of the Local Education Authority."

Study by Baron and Howell

7.4. At the time Baron and Howell conducted their study they found that of the then 159 local education authorities slightly more than half (41 county councils and 43 county borough councils) had followed the model, in some cases with additions. There were eight authorities which limited governing bodies to making proposals for special expenditure and gave them no say in the preparation of estimates. One authority omitted the financial clauses altogether. In addition, there was the substantial number of (mainly county borough) authorities which had adopted grouping arrangements, which afforded little, if any, scope for decision at the level of the individual school.

7.5. In those areas where the articles gave the governing body some financial responsibility, practice did not always conform with the theory. Even where governing bodies were encouraged to scrutinize the estimates and to put forward their own suggestions, they were liable to find that the estimates they had put forward, whether in their original draft or in a revised form, were liable to be revised further by the education committee with little, if indeed any, opportunity for reference back to the governing body. In other areas, the governors' role in preparing and submitting estimates sometimes amounted to no more than "rubber-stamping" draft estimates which had been drawn up by officers of the authority, either on their own or in consultation with the head teacher. Some authorities dispensed altogether with the submission of estimates for individual schools.

7.6. The position in primary schools was very similar.

7.7. The reasons for this state of affairs are not far to seek—the facts that by far the greatest part of any school's expenditure is on salaries and wages, that rates of pay are determined on a national basis and standards of staffing on an area basis; a succession of shortages of one sort or another and the consequential need for the determination of priorities necessitating at least some degree of central control; the development of centralised budgeting and accounting processes and techniques; and also, owing to the timing of the determination of the amount of rate support grant, the exigencies of authorities' financial time-tables.

Evidence

7.8. It was generally accepted throughout our enquiries that overall responsibility for the financing of schools must remain with the local education authority. At the same time, there was a widely expressed opinion that more discretion in deciding the use of the resources made available to schools by the local education authority should be allowed at the school level. There were differing ideas as to the extent to which, in practice, such discretion might be exercised and by whom, but the majority view was that control of the allotted resources, insofar as there was scope for variation in their use, should be exercised by the governing body, in consultation with the head and staff.

7.9. Various arguments were put forward in support of this approach. Some witnesses suggested that such financial responsibility would help to give governing bodies a feeling that they were serving a useful purpose. Others argued more strongly that it would not be possible for the governing body to make a reality of their plans for the school unless they had a real measure of responsibility for the disbursement of at least some of the resources made available by the local education authority. Those who thought it desirable for governing bodies to have this responsibility had differing views about the way in which it should be exercised. Many felt that the governing body should be responsible not only for the preparation of draft annual estimates for submission to the local education authority for approval but also should be able to exercise virement between the various heads of the approved estimates, provided the total sum authorised by the local education authority for spending by the school was not exceeded.

7.10. Our attention was also drawn to certain recently introduced schemes which are designed to give schools the opportunity not only to consider how they should spend their capitation allowances on minor equipment and materials but also to look at such matters in direct relation to expenditure on, for example, extra teaching hours for small groups, new curriculum projects, additional clerical support etc. Such schemes generally distinguish two kinds of expenditure. First, that which must in the local education authority's view be handled centrally and therefore remains the responsibility of the authority; second, that which is capable of being deployed in different ways to suit the particular requirements of individual schools. In deciding on the resources to be made available in the latter category, the authority remains free to discriminate between schools according to their special needs. Within the overall sums made available and subject to certain restrictions, the individual school can vary the use of the resources in this category and can make plans in advance to ensure their most effective use.

7.11. Representatives of some local authorities with whom we discussed schemes of this kind during our visits said that, although they accepted in principle the advantages to be gained from increasing opportunities for school-based initiative, they would have reservations about introducing such arrangements at present since the difficult economic situation made it necessary, in their view, to have a greater rather than a lesser measure of centralised financial control. Head teachers with whom we discussed these schemes also had differing views. Those who had experience of their operation were generally in favour of them. Others, who had no such direct experience, were doubtful whether the benefits to be obtained from a limited power to re-allocate resources would compensate for the additional responsibilities and problems involved in administering the arrangements at the school level.

7.12. Nor did all those who believed that some measure of financial responsibility should rest with the individual school agree that this responsibility should lie with the governing body. A minority argument, which was presented with some force, particularly by some head teachers, was that there were practical difficulties which militated against the direct involvement of governors in this field. Their meetings were regarded as too infrequent and there were doubts about their being in a position fully to appreciate the educational implications of expenditure decisions. It was therefore suggested that the governors should act in a supervisory capacity, and that the head teacher, in consultation with the staff, should be responsible for the detailed administration of capitation and other funds made available by the local education authority.

The Committee's views

7.13. We regard it as axiomatic that power to control expenditure overall must, in the last resort, remain with whoever is responsible for financing the expenditure and this means the local education authority. We therefore take it as given that the local education authority must, even if only in the last resort, be in a position to exercise effective control over the levels of expenditure by governors. We recognise that each year the local authority must balance the needs of the education service in its area against those of other services for which it is responsible, and must divide the global sum available for the education service between the various branches and stages of education. But having said that, we regard it as important that at the right time each year governors should spend time in carefully considering an estimate of the financial needs of their school for the coming financial year. The governors will add to, subtract from, or otherwise amend, the estimate as they think necessary and then submit it for approval by the local education authority, supplying such additional information on the special needs of the school as they may wish to bring to the attention of the authority. In the light of the total resources available to the local education authority and in accordance with their judgement on priorities in the allocation of resources between schools because of differing needs, the authority should amend this estimate, approve it, and return it to the governors with authority to incur expenditure accordingly. This procedure, which was envisaged in the 1945 model articles, is at present not widely followed. We think it should be, in order that governors become more fully informed of the economics of education and exercise a more effective control over the management of the school for which they have responsibility. In wishing to see the extension of the practice envisaged in 1945, we recognise that a phased operation may be necessary in view of the additional work which will be involved initially in introducing this procedure. We therefore *RECOMMEND that provisions corresponding to those in the 1945 model articles on the submission of estimates should be applied to all schools as soon as this is practicable.*

Capitation and other school allowances

7.14. In our view, it is in determining the use to be made of the resources available for individual schools, capable of being used for different purposes that there is the greatest scope for governing bodies to play an effective and worthwhile part. In theory, they might be allowed entire discretion limited only by the local education authority's ultimate power to dismiss them if the discretion were flagrantly abused. In reality few local education authorities, probably, would consider that this power was reliably available to them in practice or sufficiently effective to ensure proper control of expenditure in ordinary circumstances. These arguments have additional force in the light of our proposals for the constitution of governing bodies under which the appointment of the majority of the members is effectively outside the control of the local education authority.

7.15. We have assumed therefore that most local education authorities would wish to exercise some control over the structure of the school's budget and place some standing restrictions on the uses to which resources allocated to the school might be put, so as to ensure that basic standards of provision are maintained. They would necessarily have to ensure that the school complied with any relevant national or local agreements regarding the terms and conditions of service of staff; they would presumably wish to stipulate that the school's general financial policies should, especially in time of great financial stringency, conform with those of the local education authorities' education committee, and they would presumably also take steps to ensure that no decision entailing the use of resources was taken without regard to its future implications, particularly in the case of those involving continuing expenditure. The school's basic establishment, which accounts for much the largest part of its expenditure, must clearly continue to be a matter for the local education authority to decide.

7.16. We consider, however, that every local education authority should keep to the minimum necessary the restrictions which, for financial reasons, they impose on freedom of action at the school level. Indeed, we believe that authorities should encourage initiative and independent action to the utmost extent that is compatible with their own education responsibilities. *We RECOMMEND that they study the possibilities of making financial arrangements to facilitate this.* At the very least, those responsible at school level ought, in our judgement, to be given, wherever possible, a choice between alternative ways of achieving a given object. We hope, however, that authorities will find it possible to go further in many respects, that their general approach will be positive rather than negative and that their guiding principle will be to encourage independence of thought and action wherever there is no need for restriction. We are convinced that such a policy would have advantages which would more than outweigh the additional administrative costs that this might involve. We also believe it would lead to a continuing pursuit of economy and ways in which savings could be beneficially redeployed. We consider too that a more effective use of resources would be secured by locating decisions with the users in the schools and that this in turn would foster a sense of responsibility in heads and senior staff and help to ensure that all the various interests involved in the running of the school were engaged in a constant examination of the school's needs and ways of meeting them effectively and economically.

7.17. A detailed examination of the various procedures at present used by authorities would be necessary before firm conclusions could be reached about the advantages and disadvantages of particular allocation systems and related discretionary procedures and precise recommendations made. We have not been able to undertake such a study. Nevertheless we are satisfied that there continues to be a very wide variety of practice in the arrangements made by authorities for the allocation of capitation allowances to schools. Some authorities have highly centralised systems of control and very little discretion is allowed to the schools. Other authorities, as we have noted in paragraph 7.10, have introduced schemes (admittedly in certain instances on an experimental basis) which are specifically designed to give schools greater opportunity to determine for themselves how best to deploy, and get the best return from, the resources placed at their disposal by the authority.

7.18. This state of affairs was first investigated by the two Central Advisory Councils—see the Plowden* report of 1966 and the Gittins† report of 1967. The most recent review was by the Bullock Committee‡ which reported in 1974 on the development of language and the teaching of reading. They concluded that the whole question of determining the allowances for schools and the ways of distributing them needed detailed examination. We believe this is a matter of

---

*See footnote to 3.25.

†See footnote to 3.25.

‡Department of Education and Science. A Language for Life. Chairman Sir Alan Bullock, F.B.A. HMSO 1975.

continuing general concern and with the present economic difficulties has become very urgent. *We therefore RECOMMEND that early action should be taken by the Secretaries of State on the Bullock Committee's proposal that a joint working party of representatives of the Department of Education and Science and local education authorities should be established to investigate the whole question of determining the allowances for schools and the ways of distributing them.*

7.19. Though for these reasons we have not felt able to recommend any particular system for the allocation of resources to schools, we consider that the principles we have recommended in paragraph 7.16 should be applied by local education authorities so as to give governors the power of virement between the various heads of the approved school estimate. To exercise such a power effectively, the governing body will need to draw up its draft estimate and after consideration and approval by the local education authority, the approved estimate will become the working budget for the school. At the same time the governing body will also need to ensure that there are arrangements for the collection of the various facts (rate of consumption of materials, equipment needs etc) which will assist in the preparation of the draft estimate and which can also be drawn on readily when decisions with resource implications have to be made. This information will also be useful to the governing body whenever the need arises for that body to review the financial situation or prepare a general report to the local education authority on the school's progress towards its overall aims and objectives.

7.20. When the draft estimate has been submitted, the governing body will be able to make tentative plans for the use of the resources requested from the local education authority for the coming financial year. It is, however, in the nature of things that authorities will rarely be able to meet all the hopes and wishes of those responsible at the school level. The school's provisional budget will therefore need to be reviewed as soon as the local education authority's decisions on central resource allocation have been announced. In making these decisions, the local education authority will, we assume, have taken into account so far as possible the needs of individual schools as submitted to them by individual governing bodies during the early stages of the estimates procedures. We regard it as essential, therefore, that as soon as possible after the allocation for the school has been announced, the governors should meet to consider any changes that may have to be made in their plans for the use of the resources which will be available in the year ahead.

7.21. Once the budget has been finally agreed by the governing body on the basis of the resources that can be made available by the local education authority, we would expect the day-to-day decisions on school-controlled expenditure, within the limits approved under each main heading, to be made by the head-teacher (subject to consultation, as appropriate, with the staff).

School building projects

7.22. A proposal submitted to us was that local education authorities should make funds available to governing bodies to meet the cost of small improvements to the school buildings. It was also suggested that individual governing bodies should be fully involved in discussions about proposed major building projects affecting their school.

7.23. These suggestions have to be considered against the background of the arrangements by which capital expenditure* is controlled by the Education Departments. The lump sum authorisations given by the Department for capital expenditure on school building include an element for minor works, which for this purpose are defined as building projects costing less than £75,000. Minor works (unlike major works) do not have to be submitted to the Departments for approval†. This provides a measure of flexibility which we understand is highly valued by local education authorities.

7.24. It is evident that a local education authority will need to retain the power to determine centrally the proportion of the available resources to be devoted to minor works in its area. It has also been strongly represented to us, and we accept, that the allocation of the monies to be spent on minor works must also be determined centrally, with due regard, of course, for the needs of individual schools.

7.25. Responsibility at the school level for expenditure to be met from the authority's revenue account on minor repairs and other small building jobs could well be considered on the same basis as school allowances and capitation grants. We return to the question of minor repairs in chapter 9.

7.26. In any event, *we RECOMMEND that local education authorities should see that there is the maximum possible consultation with individual governing bodies before decisions are taken about building work, major or minor, at their schools, and also that the governing bodies are consulted about developments during the subsequent planning and building stages.*

Conclusion

7.27. The financial responsibilities we have proposed for governing bodies should be considered not in isolation but in relation to their other functions since most, if not indeed all, of the decisions taken in the exercise of these other functions, will have resource implications. The financial responsibilities of governors are, therefore, both necessary and important and, although they may add to the volume of their work, they are in our view the minimum compatible with the role of governing bodies as we conceive it. The administrative work of the headteacher and other members of the staff may also be increased as more decisions are taken at the school level. We are confident, however, that these effects will be outweighed by the benefits foreshadowed in paragraph 7.16.

---

*i.e. expenditure on major and minor school building projects which is not met from the authority's revenue account as are the sums allocated through the capitation allowances.

†It should be noted, however, that the Departments' approval is required for minor projects at aided and special agreement schools for which the managers or governors are responsible.

CHAPTER 8—APPOINTMENTS

8.1. In county schools staff are the employees of the authority even though, as is frequently the case, they are appointed to serve in a particular school. The model articles lay down fairly detailed procedures for the appointment and dismissal of the headteacher, assistant teachers and non-teaching staff. These procedures are reproduced in Appendix E.

8.2. At present the extent to which rules of management or articles of government provide for managers or governors to be involved in the appointment of staff varies fairly widely with the nature of the school and the attitude of the local education authority. The latter determines the size of the staffing establishment in all maintained schools but managers and governors are often empowered to make proposals concerning the designation of posts carrying additional remuneration for special responsibility, within an overall structure determined by the authority.

8.3. In drawing up rules of management and articles of government many authorities have followed the model closely. Others have sought to minimise the role played by governors in the exercise of these functions. For example, in the case of headteacher appointments governing bodies are sometimes given no part in the short-listing of candidates or are involved only to a limited extent at this stage through consultation by the chief education officer with the chairman of the governors. In addition, some authorities have weakened the part played by the governing body in the final decision by reducing or eliminating its representation on the joint committee appointed to select a candidate to fill the vacancy, or dispensing with such a committee.

8.4. There are similar variations in procedures for the appointment of deputy heads. In the case of the appointment of teachers below this level there are even wider differences of practice. In some areas, for example, the arrangements for the filling of vacancies are entirely in the hands of the authority's education committee and the governors are able to make recommendations only about promotions of staff already employed in the school. During the years when teachers were in short supply some authorities argued that it was not always practicable to involve the governors in first teaching appointments, or other appointments to lower scale posts, because of the need to act quickly when applications from suitable candidates were received. They pointed out that where a large number of interview meetings had to be held to fill such vacancies the involvement of governors had sometimes caused delays, good candidates had been lost and much professional and administrative time had been wasted. These arguments are recognised to have less force now that the balance of teacher supply and demand has changed but they are still felt to be relevant for certain subjects, such as mathematics, where there continues to be a limited supply of well qualified teachers.

Evidence

8.5. A few witnesses argued that the appointment of teaching staff should be left entirely to the local education authority. Others expressed the view that

71

only members of the teaching profession were equipped to take on this responsibility. Most, however, of those who submitted evidence suggested that the governing body should play a part in the procedure, so as to help ensure the selection of candidates best suited to meet the needs of their school. There was, however, a range of views on the extent to which the participation of the governing body was desirable, with most support for their direct involvement in the appointment of the head, the deputy head and the senior staff. The appointment of the head was frequently mentioned as being of special importance in the life of the school and it was widely held, particularly by some of the local authority organisations, teachers' associations and voluntary bodies, that responsibility for this should be shared between the local education authority and the governing body.

8.6. In general less emphasis was placed by witnesses on the need for the local education authority to be directly involved, through the participation of elected members, in the appointment of teachers other than the head, although we received some suggestions that the authority should be given the ultimate right to veto a selected candidate on educational grounds. Our evidence points to a fairly wide recognition of the concern of governors in all teaching appointments, but many people thought the inclusion of the head, and, where appropriate, heads of departments in the selection process was important. There were suggestions that decisions on appointments to junior posts might be left entirely to the head or that the interests of the governing body might be safeguarded by a right to veto the appointment of the candidate selected by the head, or by arranging for the head and the chairman of the governors to act together.

Appointment of the headteacher

8.7. We shall discuss separately the appointment of the headteacher, because he has a key position in the school and, under our proposals, will have a vital part to play in the activities of the governing body itself. It is obviously essential that the headteacher should be generally acceptable to all the interested parties. We conclude that this appointment should not be made without regard to the views either of the local education authority or of the governing body.

8.8. The interest of the local education authority in the appointment of a headteacher derives in a large measure from their statutory responsibility for ensuring educational standards. The need to appoint a new head arises infrequently in any particular school but the local education authority's concern with all the schools in their area gives them considerable experience in such appointments; they can call on expert advice and see candidates against a broad background.

8.9. The governing body also has a distinctive interest in this matter. The needs of particular schools vary considerably and are affected by, for example, their size, locality and the social nature of the areas they serve. The general character of the school can also have a bearing on its particular needs. These needs, as seen by the governors, ought to be a very important consideration in the appointment of the headteacher.

8.10. *We RECOMMEND that the procedure for the appointment of heads should provide for a small selection committee consisting equally of members of the governing body and representatives of the local education authority.* The governors should elect their own representatives to serve on the selection committee but we consider that the retiring headteacher should not be among them; he should take no part in the appointment of his successor because he cannot have any responsibility for the latter's future actions.

8.11. We assume that local education authorities will wish to ensure that their representatives on the selection committee include members of the education committee. *We RECOMMEND that one of the latter should be elected by the selection committee to serve as its chairman and should, if necessary, have a casting vote.* The selection committee should itself determine the extent to which it wished to be involved in the arrangements for advertisement and in the short listing of candidates. In making its selection the committee should make the greatest possible use of professional guidance and advice from the chief education officer and his staff. In particular, we believe that it would be helpful if the selection committee could count on having available to it the experience and knowledge of the school acquired by the authority's advisers. There might also be circumstances when it could benefit from advice from professionals outside the authority's service.

Appointment of other teachers

8.12. These arguments for involving the governing body in the appointment of the headteacher apply also in our view to appointments of deputy heads and higher scale posts. Since the post of deputy head can be regarded as in part a training post for further advancement there is a case for involving the authority in this appointment in a similar way. However, on balance *we RECOMMEND that the selection of deputy heads and other teachers should rest with the governing body, who should give due weight to the professional advice made available through the local education authority and in particular to the responsibility of the local education authority to find suitable posts for teachers whose schools are closed or reorganised.*

8.13. So far as appointments at the other levels are concerned, we recognise that candidates often have to be interviewed at short notice and that difficulties might arise in arranging for members of the governing body, other than the staff members, to be present on all occasions. Nevertheless we believe that the responsibility for choosing—the formal appointment is, of course, for the local education authority—should be vested in the governing body and that the latter should itself settle the procedures by which it would discharge this responsibility. It will probably arrange for the chairman or his nominee(s) normally to undertake the interviewing with the headteacher and appropriate members of the teaching staff and the authority's professional advisers. It is important, however, that the governing body should retain the power to change these arrangements for delegation and play a more active role if at any time they had reason for disquiet about how the procedure was working.

8.14. For the reason set out in paragraph 8.10 above, we consider that it would be inappropriate for any member of staff to be involved in the appointment of his or her successor. If a teacher governor finds himself in this situation we would expect him to withdraw from the proceedings.

Dismissal of teachers

8.15. Teachers' conditions of service are generally similar throughout the country and model agreements generally adopted by local education authorities include provision for termination of appointment (usually on two or three months notice) and for suspension, on lines similar to those laid down in articles of government and rules of management. A teacher is normally given the right to be present, accompanied by a "friend" if desired, at any meeting of governors, managers or local education authority at which his dismissal is to be considered (although the teacher involved need not be present when the question of suspension is initially raised), and must be given seven days notice of the meeting and a written statement of any complaint or charge. The Employment Protection Act 1975 requires that if dismissed he must be given a written statement of the reasons, and under the Trade Unions and Industrial Relations Act 1974 he could complain to an industrial tribunal if he thought his dismissal unfair.

8.16. In general the existing procedures relating to the dismissal of teachers seem to be working satisfactorily. Nonetheless difficulties exist. First, information on the procedures is not always readily available*. *We RECOMMEND that every governing body should have access to a copy of the Local Education Authority's conditions of service relating to teachers.* Second, there remains the problem of the professionally incompetent teacher. Such teachers have never numbered more than a small proportion of the total of the profession but where they exist they are an embarrassment to their colleagues, cause anxiety to parents and are an impediment to the progress of their pupils.

8.17. All teachers have a period of probation after completing their initial training when their performance is assessed by their local education authority. Some local education authorities in addition have a period of probation for all teachers appointed to a new post—not necessarily their initial teaching post— and this is supervised by the local education authority inspectors (or advisers). Unfortunately a minority of teachers either fall into a borderline category and do not live up to initial expectations or actually regress after a period of satisfactory service and find it difficult to meet their professional obligations. We think that one means of overcoming this problem in the longer term would be the closer involvement (which we suggested in chapter 6†) of the governing body in the promotion of in-service training and career development of their school's teachers. We have not felt that the conditions of service of teachers fall within

---

*As Mr. Auld's report makes clear, this can have serious consequences for the efficient conduct of a school.
†See paragraph 6.30.

our remit. Nonetheless, we believe that some governing bodies may find the problem an obstacle to fulfilling the duties we have proposed for them. Accordingly *we RECOMMEND that the Secretaries of State should initiate discussions on the subject with the local education authority and teachers' associations as soon as possible.*

Appointment and dismissal of supporting staff

8.18. The model articles include the following provision:—
"The non-teaching staff shall, subject to any general directions of the Local Education Authority, be appointed by the Governors, after consultation with the Head Master, to the service of the Authority and shall be dismissed by the Local Education Authority upon the recommendation of the Governors".

Our evidence did not reveal that there are any major problems in this field and it is our impression that the present arrangements have in general worked satisfactorily. *We accordingly RECOMMEND that they should continue.*

CHAPTER 9—OTHER FUNCTIONS

9.1. We have dealt in the previous chapters with some of the most important responsibilities of the governing body. In this chapter we turn to other functions in relation to which the model articles provided for some involvement on the part of the governing body and which merit separate consideration here if the future role of these bodies is to be properly defined.

Admissions

9.2. Article 10 of the model dealt with the admission of children to a county school as follows:

"The admission of pupils to the school shall be in accordance with arrangements made by the local education authority, which will take into account the wishes of the parents, any school records and other information which may be available, the general type of education most suitable for the particular child and the views of the governors and headmaster as to the admission of the child to the school".

9.3. Baron and Howell found that the model wording had been generally adopted at the time of their study. More recently, following the reorganisation of secondary education on comprehensive lines, authorities have tended to omit references to the factors to be taken into account by them when drawing up admission arrangements but continue to include provision for consultation with the governors. The following version is now fairly common:

"The admission of pupils to the school shall be in accordance with arrangements made by the local education authority, in consultation with the governors".

9.4. It has been suggested by some local education authorities that there is no place for consultation with governors over admissions and that if differing policies were pursued by the various governing bodies there would inevitably be intolerable friction. We see no necessary connection between these two statements. Consultation need not imply the pursuit of different policies but may be helpful in establishing a general policy as well as identifying any possible need for exceptions to it. In general it seems to us desirable that the local education authority should continue to settle policy on admissions, in consultation with the governing bodies of the schools concerned. We believe that the latter ought to have the chance both to advise on the formulation of local education authority policy and, if they thought it desirable in the interests of their own schools, to propose exceptions to it. In some cases, for example, when catchment area boundaries are being drawn up or revised, conflicting views might be put forward by governing bodies of the schools affected. The ultimate decisions on such questions will have to be taken by the local education authority after taking into account all the relevant factors. It should, however, always be open to a governing body, once decisions have been taken on the general arrangements for the area, to ask the local education authority to make an exception in their case.

9.5. It appears to us that the present arrangements for determining the responsibility for admissions to school have worked well. *We accordingly RECOMMEND that they should continue. We also RECOMMEND that when the local education authority has settled its admissions policy, it should make public the principles and criteria upon which school places are to be allocated in order to avoid any uncertainty about the local position among parents and governing bodies.*

Suspension and expulsion

9.6. We begin this section by acknowledging that many schools in England and Wales are run without the need for frequent recourse to suspension and expulsion. However, we think it important to devote careful attention to this subject since cases of suspension and expulsion have often caused genuine difficulties for those concerned.

9.7. A registered pupil of compulsory school age is required to attend school regularly and his parents are under a statutory duty to see that he does so. In certain circumstances he may be debarred from attendance, temporarily or permanently. A number of serious problems have arisen through uncertainty about the meaning of the terms that are used and about the objectives being pursued and the procedures to be employed.

Use of terms

9.8. "Exclusion" is a term that is commonly used in this connection. Those who use it do not always agree on its meaning. It is used, without definition, in regulation 4 of the Pupils' Registration Regulations 1956 and in regulation 7(1) of the Schools Regulations 1959, in contexts where it appears to cover a variety of situations in which pupils might be barred from school. It is possible to distinguish three main situations in which the term "exclusion" is used:

a. permanent debarment, commonly known as expulsion. We discuss this in paragraph 17.

b. temporary debarment on medical grounds under section 54(7) of the Education Act 1944 (which expressly uses the term "exclusion") or under section 150(1) of the Public Health Act 1936.

c. temporary debarment for other reasons, commonly thought of as "suspension" but in practice not always based on the use of the power of suspension conferred by articles of government.*

9.9. The lack of authoritative definition of the terms exclusion, expulsion and suspension has given rise to considerable confusion in the minds of governors, teachers and parents. It appears also to have given rise in some quarters to an impression that governors and headteachers need not comply with the procedures

---

*The courts have distinguished between the exercise by a headteacher of the power of suspension conferred on him by articles of government and the action of a headteacher in refusing to allow a child to attend school until certain conditions have been met. Cf. Spiers v Warrington Corporation [1953] 2 All ER 1052; [1954] 1 QB 61.

specified for suspension (see paragraph 9.13) if the action taken is denoted by a different term. In our view, the term "exclusion" should be limited to debarment on medical grounds as specified in paragraph 9.8b. We see no need to concern ourselves with cases of this kind. We think the term "suspension" ought to be defined in such a way as to cover all temporary debarments from school on any other ground. We shall use the term "suspension" only in this sense.

Other problems

9.10. The practice of suspension is widespread. Articles of government commonly confer on the headteacher power to suspend a pupil from attendance for any cause that he considers adequate. We have heard of instances in which this power appears to have been used in connection with minor infringements of school discipline or of school rules. We have recommended in paragraph 33 of chapter 6 that responsibility for deciding on the measures to be taken generally to promote good discipline in the school, and making the rules necessary to maintain it, should be placed on the governing body, which will include the head. This will, we think, help to ensure adequate protection and guidance both for the head and for the pupil and his parents; it should permit disciplinary action to be taken, when necessary, within a clearly defined framework sanctioned by the governing body.

9.11. There has been public concern about suspended pupils remaining out of school, often with no provision for the continuation of their education or indeed for any supervision outside their homes, in some cases for as long as a year or more. The implications for juvenile delinquency have been a matter of special anxiety. It is not for us to express any view as to the responsibility for this state of affairs in any particular case. We recognise that the educational interests of a suspended pupil have to be weighed carefully against other factors. However, it seems to us that the present arrangements in general lack any provision to ensure that everybody concerned will feel a proper sense of urgency and will press forward vigorously to put an end to a suspension, in one way or another, as quickly as possible. In our view there should be a strict limit on the time for which a pupil may remain debarred from attendance at school without a systematic review of his case by the local education authority in consultation with all those concerned, including representatives of the governors and social agencies, with a view to finding an acceptable solution.

The objectives of suspension

9.12. These problems seem to be accompanied by—and perhaps to stem from—a general uncertainty about the objectives of suspension. Since 1944 the Education Departments have consistently taken the view that debarment from attendance, in whatever circumstances and for whatever period, should not be used as a punishment. We agree. Suspension should be seen as providing a breathing-space to allow rational consideration, discussion and accommodation between the parties concerned or, depending on the seriousness of the problem, a search for more fundamental solutions, including, in an extreme case, the possibility of education elsewhere. The objectives of the procedure should be:

a. to allow the school to function satisfactorily while problems are solved;

b. to allow the headteacher reasonable discretion to take very short term action in an emergency without excessive formality but with suitable safeguards;

c. to avoid unnecessary interruption to the child's education and to keep the period of non-attendance as short as possible;

d. to bring all relevant considerations and all interested parties quickly together to this end.

Procedures for suspension

9.13. It also seems to us that these problems are aggravated by the lack of reasonably uniform, comprehensive and well understood procedures relating to suspension. Articles of government commonly require the head to report any suspension forthwith to the governors. The articles often have nothing to say about what the governors can or should do when the headteacher reports to them, except to require them to consult the authority. They say nothing whatsoever about what the authority can or should do when consulted. As a result, procedures differ widely in different areas. In some a suspension is reported to the governors immediately, in others only at the next formal meeting of the governors. The articles of some county schools provide for an appeal, but seldom specify a time within which governors have to be informed or have to hear appeals.

9.14. Parents are often given little information either about the procedures which are being followed or about the grounds on which the procedures have been set in motion. There is no assurance, except in a very few areas where the local education authority regulations specify it, that they will have been consulted even if their child's behaviour has been giving cause for concern over a period. In some cases their first notification that it has had serious consequences may be a notification of suspension conveyed by the child himself (which is clearly undesirable), expressed in terms which they may not understand and without any indication of the action which may be open to them to remedy the situation.

The need for properly prescribed procedures

9.15. We think it unsatisfactory that there are wide differences from area to area in the procedures for suspension. There are stringent and carefully defined suspension procedures for students at further education institutions, although they are outside the age limits of compulsory education. We consider that the corresponding procedures for school pupils should be prescribed more carefully. We do not think it necessary to lay down detailed procedures for local education authorities to follow. At the very least, local education authorities should be required to establish clear rules of procedure and to ensure that heads, teachers, governors, parents and pupils are familiar with them. Given the objectives in paragraph 9.12, one local education authority might, for example, lay down a flexible procedure which allowed a headteacher, on his own responsibility, to send a pupil home* for up to three days while those concerned "cool off",

---

*Especial care should be taken to avoid the possibility of a young child being suspended and arriving home unexpectedly at a time when he cannot gain admission.

subject only to informing parents of the reasons for the suspensions and making a written record in the school in a register kept specifically for the purpose and available to the governing body. This will enable the latter to review constructively the problems which have given rise to such action. The local education authority might prescribe a different procedure for longer suspensions (up to five days, for instance), and in exceptional cases for suspensions up to a maximum of, say, four weeks with provision, in the latter cases, for appeal by the parents against the suspension. The local education authority might require that any suspension longer than the prescribed "cooling-off time" should be the subject of immediate consultation with all those concerned, on lines laid down by the authority. Another local education authority might of course consider these time limits excessive. We have given them simply for illustrative purposes.

9.16. The school needs to be protected against threats to its orderly running and the pupils against excessive resort to suspension. The guiding principle in making these procedural arrangements should be, in our view, to strike a balance between the provision of elaborate safeguards intended to protect the individual from any possibility of injustice and the desirability, in his own interest and that of the school, of solving the problem promptly.

9.17. Clearly the governing body, with its concern for the welfare of the school and the pupils, will be the obvious agency to undertake this task and it should be their responsibility to bring together the interested parties, in an effort to find an acceptable solution; in particular the education welfare officer has a key role to play in these cases. If agreement cannot be reached and recourse to appeal procedure is necessary, we think the governing body should continue to work towards a solution. Because of its wide responsibilities for the general interests of the school, however, the parent concerned might not feel confident of its impartiality in his particular case. In our view therefore the governing body should not itself determine the appeal. It should be the function of the local education authority to decide, finally, whether the pupil should be allowed to resume attendance or should be debarred for a further period, or permanently, from the school at which he has been a pupil. The local education authority is responsible for the control of admissions to the school, has a continuing duty to provide for the education of the child and will need, taking account of the parent's statutory duty to secure the education of his child and his moral duty to help in the maintenance of discipline, to make arrangements for the resumption of his education either at another school or in some other way. For these reasons we think it is undesirable that the power to expel a pupil should rest with the governing body, as by implication it has been assumed to do at present in the absence of any provision to other effect in articles of government. In our view no final decision on expulsion, in any circumstances, ought to be taken except by the local education authority after taking into account the views expressed by the governing body.

Recommendations

9.18. Accordingly *we RECOMMEND that:*

1. the terms exclusion, suspension and expulsion, wherever they are used in statutory regulations or in local education authorities' regulations or instruc-

tions, should be authoritatively defined and differentiated in the way we have suggested;

2. *every local education authority should be required to make and publish arrangements for the procedures to be followed in its area with regard to the suspension of pupils from attendance at school which satisfy the following general requirements;*

    i. *when a pupil's behaviour over a period gives rise to a real possibility that he will have to be suspended from attendance if it continues, opportunity for consultation and discussion should be accorded to his parents;*

    ii. *it should be clearly known by all concerned who has the power to decide that a pupil should be suspended from attendance, or should remain suspended after a specified period;*

    iii. *a time limit of not more than three days should be fixed for the duration of any suspension by the headteacher;*

    iv. *provision should be made to avoid danger to the pupil concerned, or to others, as a result of his suspension;*

    v. *when a decision is made to suspend a particular pupil the parents should be informed by a quick and reliable means, should be told how long the suspension is to last and should be given full particulars of the reason for it. A record should be made in a register kept specifically for the purpose within the school and available to the governing body;*

    vi. *the governing body should be empowered to extend the suspension for a strictly limited period, specified by the local education authority for all cases, during which the interested parties should be brought together to seek an acceptable solution;*

    vii. *if no satisfactory solution is found within this period the case should be referred to the local education authority;*

    viii. *there should be provision for appeal by the parents to the local education authority, to be heard within a specified period, against the continuation of a suspension beyond a specified period or against any other action proposed as an alternative to the child's resumption of attendance at the school. Parents should be told how, and to whom they should appeal, when the appeal will be heard and what procedure will be followed;*

3. *legislative steps be taken to ensure that:*

    i. *no registered pupil is debarred from attendance at his school, except on medical grounds, otherwise than in compliance with the suspension procedures arranged by the local education authority;*

    ii. *no registered pupil is expelled from a school except by the decision of the local education authority responsible for maintaining the school, who should inform the governing body.*

School premises

9.19. The model articles dealt with the responsibilities of the governing body in relation to the condition and state of repair of the premises and also with regard to their use out of school hours.

Care and maintenance

9.20. As regards the condition and state of repair of the premises, the model provides that:

"The Governors shall from time to time inspect, and keep the Local Education Authority informed as to, the condition and state of repair of the school premises, and, where the Local Education Authority so permit, the Governors shall have power to carry out urgent repairs up to such an amount as may be approved by the Local Education Authority."

9.21. We have little to say about the first half of this provision. We think it sensible that the local education authority, being legally responsible for the safety of county school premises, should look to those on the spot to keep it informed about the condition of such premises. *We therefore RECOMMEND that the governing body should continue to be responsible for inspecting the school premises and for keeping the local education authority informed of their condition and state of repair.*

9.22. In considering who should be responsible for undertaking minor repairs of a kind which can be dealt with from the authority's revenue account, we have been concerned to balance the need for local education authority control of expenditure on school buildings (which we have already discussed in chapter 7) against the need for urgency in keeping school premises in sound condition. Prompt repairs are desirable not only for the convenience and safety of those who use the school but also, in certain cases, as a means of containing the spread of damage through vandalism.* We believe that prompt action often provides considerable savings in the long term. We therefore *RECOMMEND that the local education authority should authorise the governing body to have urgent minor repairs carried out up to a limit set by the authority.* In view of the importance of speedy action we would expect the headteacher to be given discretion to put in hand any necessary work and to report his action at the next meeting of the governing body.

---

*Home Office Standing Committee on Crime Prevention; Protection Against Vandalism. Home Office 1975.

9.23. The model also provides that:

"The Governors shall, subject to any direction of the Local Education Authority, determine the use to which school premises, or any part thereof, may be put out of school hours."

9.24. In considering this function it is necessary to draw a distinction between the use for extraneous community purposes of ordinary schools and the use of those schools which have been designed from the outset for dual use or have been enlarged to provide youth, adult or adult community services. We deal initially with the community use of schools in the first category.

9.25. The study of current practice carried out by Baron and Howell indicated that most authorities made provision on the lines of the model. The exceptions were a few county boroughs who either omitted it altogether or made themselves responsible for determining lettings.

9.26. School premises are a public resource and we think that it is generally accepted that they should continue to be used as widely as possible by the whole community, provided that such use does not reduce the facilities available to the children whose education must remain the school's primary purpose. Not surprisingly, this view was confirmed in our evidence by those associations which are concerned with the encouragement of sports and physical activities. A point they made was that in relatively sparsely populated areas, school premises often provide the only means by which adult participation in sport is possible. In such an area the school may be the main focal point for local community activities, whereas in a large urban district the community interest might well come from a wider area than that served by the school.

9.27. A survey of the use of school premises outside school hours conducted in 1976 by the Advisory Centre for Education (ACE)* revealed that not all local education authorities conformed with the model; a substantial number gave responsibility for lettings wholly to the local education authority. It appears that with very few exceptions local education authorities set the scale of charges for the use of county school premises. The uses identified by most local education authorities included activities which were school-linked, recreational, or organised for youth, adult or further education purposes; Sunday schools; meetings of community, political and industrial groups; and hirings to private individuals. The actual sums charged and the ways in which they were compiled varied very widely.

9.28. The task of dealing with applications can be a considerable administrative burden and in many cases governors simply do not have the resources

---

*Stone Judith and Taylor Felicity, Who Can Use Your School. Where, No. 118 July 1976, pages 190–194.

to cope with it. In areas where there is a large community demand for the use of school premises the task is either delegated to the headteacher or sometimes handled by a team in the education office. Centralised arrangements are less likely to be found in rural areas where small village schools are used informally by wide sections of the community.

9.29. On the whole our evidence revealed a wish for governing bodies to decide on the use of premises out of school hours. Witnesses tended, however, to take little account of the problems caused by community use. As well as giving rise to additional costs—for example, for lighting, heating, cleaning and other maintenance—community use can put caretakers under pressure to work excessive overtime and cause administrative and managerial difficulties by blurring lines of control and responsibility. The National Union of Teachers drew attention to some of these problems and suggested that the headteacher and his staff should have the power to veto certain types of use.

9.30. In any assessment of the cost of the community use of school premises it is appropriate to take into account the fact that savings can be achieved through a reduction in damage by vandalism. The Home Office Working Party which looked into this question in 1975* took the view that "playgrounds should be open as often as possible out of school hours, at weekends and on public holidays". They urged "the greater use of school premises for such purposes in order that young children can identify more readily with the schools as their property and not as places which, when not used for school work proper, are bolted and barred by 'them' and as such present a challenge for assault and destruction."

The Committee's views

9.31. It seems to us essential that a public body should have control of the use to which school premises are put out of school hours. The local education authority is in a position to assess the merits of competing demands throughout its area and to determine any legal questions which might arise. We therefore *RECOMMEND that it should, after consultation with the governing bodies of all county schools in its area, formulate an overall policy on the letting of those schools.* This overall policy would be implemented in the schools by the governing bodies. In practice we would not expect them to concern themselves with every application to use the school. In our view this task is best left to the headteacher as the person most accessible to applicants. It is important that the headteacher should operate from a firm basis in exercising this responsibility. *We RECOMMEND, therefore, that the governing body should provide the headteacher with a set of guidelines for the consideration of applications to use the school premises.* It would then be for the head to refer to the governing body in any case where a decision could not be reached within the guidelines.

---

*See paragraph 9.22 (footnote).

9.32. *We RECOMMEND that in any dispute between the governing body and an outside organisation about the use of the premises, the final decision should rest with the local education authority.*

9.33. The role of the governing body in relation to the problems of school use can be illustrated by reference to those occasions when the premises are required for electoral purposes. Their use for these purposes is within the control not of the governing body but of the Returning Officer. He can direct that schools which are used as polling stations should be closed on the day of the election and that no part of the premises should be used for any other purpose. If the Returning Officer were not to make such an all-embracing direction it would, in our view, be important for the governing body to consider, in consultation with the staff, the possibility of avoiding the complete closure of the school for education, by making use of any part of the premises not required for the electoral purposes. The governing body could also suggest for the consideration of the Returning Officer the possibility of other premises being used as the polling station as an alternative to the complete or partial closure of the school.

9.34. We have given some thought to the difficult question of charges for school lettings. There seems little doubt that these charges, which have risen considerably in recent years, place financial barriers in the way of many potential users. We are aware of the financial difficulties that confront local education authorities at the present time and we do not therefore make any specific recommendations in relation to the level of hire charges. Nevertheless we remain convinced of the need for local education authorities to ensure that school premises, including playing fields and sports facilities, are as widely available for community use as is practically possible. In our view it is of primary importance that school premises should be accessible to parents for purposes related to the welfare of the school. (We discussed the parents' needs in this respect and made a recommendation in chapter 5). In the longer term, as and when the economic climate improves, we hope that local education authorities will consider ways in which the community use of schools can be expanded.

Community schools

9.35. Under this heading we are concerned with those schools, possibly purpose-built, which cater not only for pupils of primary or secondary school age but provide in addition a variety of educational and other facilities (eg libraries, social service provision etc). In the remainder of this section we refer to them as "community schools".

9.36. The concept of community schools goes back more than fifty years to the ideas pioneered by Cambridgeshire's Henry Morris but interest in this kind of development has increased noticeably over the past decade. This is due to the increased interest in the development of links between the school and the community as well as to economic pressures (since pooled resources allow more economical and extensive provision).

9.37. Community schools exist in a wide variety of forms and cannot be described in precise terms. Several community schools were visited by members of the Committee and we were interested to learn that the Department of Education and Science are sponsoring a five-year research project, under the direction of Professor M D S Stephens of Nottingham University, which is designed to investigate, in co-operation with the local authority, the impact of a community centre at Sutton on the life of the town.

9.38. It has not been possible to include a detailed examination of all the management implications of community schools within the scope of our review. Further experience of the operation of these institutions is likely to throw up a variety of management problems. Some of these may be identified in the report of a Working Party set up by HM Inspectorate which carried out a detailed survey of community school provisions in 1975-76. We understand that, in addition to this general survey, the Department of Education and Science has recently carried out a study of the Abraham Moss Centre in Manchester and that this is likely to include reference to aspects of the management structure. We were also interested to learn that the Department is sponsoring an evaluation of the development of Coventry's Community Colleges. This project, which was begun in October 1975 under the direction of Dr A H Halsey of the Department of Social and Administrative Studies at the University of Oxford, and is expected to last three years, includes studies of the organisation and management of the colleges, and of the extent to which they promote involvement and participation of local people and groups.

9.39. Further consideration may well need to be given to the functions of community school governing bodies in the light of the further information which will become available when the reports on these projects have been published. We see no reason, however, why the various proposals we have put forward with regard to the functions of school governing bodies in general should not apply in principle to the governing bodies of community schools, at least in relation to the activities of their "school" sides.

Holidays

9.40. The model articles include the following provision:
"Holidays for the school shall be fixed by the local education authority, but the governors shall have power to grant mid-term or other occasional holidays not exceeding 10 days in any year".

9.41. This power given to governors to grant occasional school holidays was clearly intended to reflect the individuality of schools and to give them some opportunity to recognise particular occasions (eg outstanding achievements of former pupils). Some variations of practice were noted in the study conducted by Baron and Howell. In come cases provision was made for the local education authority to determine the number of days to be taken as occasional holidays; in others the number of days were limited to 6 or to a quota of half days.

9.42. Decisions on school holidays can have far reaching effects. When they are being considered, the following factors, obviously, need to be taken into account:

i. the problems caused for working parents and parents with children at other schools where the occasional holidays do not coincide;

ii. the consequential difficulties for any local industry employing mothers of school children if a substantial proportion of the labour force has to absent itself; and the possible serious economic effect of reduced production;

iii. the effects on school bus services, school meals and arrangements for linked school facilities;

iv. the dates of industrial holidays.

9.43. Although, as we have indicated, the occasional holiday has in the past been used mainly as a means of commemorating an event in which a school has a separate interest from those of other schools, it has, in our view, become an increasingly inappropriate manner in which to achieve this end since it inevitably conveys the out of date impression that school is an irksome place from which it is desirable to escape as frequently as possible.

9.44. Occasional days are now commonly used to provide a full week's holiday at mid-term on dates fixed by the local education authority for all the maintained schools in its area. In our view this should be the universal practice. Since there can be no question of any reduction in the statutory school year it follows that the scope for granting other occasional holidays is limited. Even so, the power to grant a limited number of holidays for special reasons still seems to us to be of some value. We accordingly *RECOMMEND that governing bodies should continue to have the power to grant occasional school holidays other than the mid-term holidays, subject to the agreement of the local education authority in each case.* This should ensure that a uniform policy is applied throughout an area. We would expect local education authorities to adopt a fairly flexible approach when formulating their general policy, so as not to rule out reasons that might genuinely be regarded by schools as "special", and to bear in mind local factors of the kind mentioned above when specific applications are being considered.

CHAPTER 10—TRAINING THE NEW GOVERNORS

10.1. If the tasks described in the previous four chapters are to be performed effectively, governors must be trained for the job. This is particularly necessary in view of the more active part which we wish governing bodies to play in formulating and developing the school's curricular policy. In our view all governors should be given the opportunity to inform themselves on matters of educational theory and practice which will play a more central part in their deliberations. In addition to this basic need, we believe that there are a number of difficulties faced by governors today which a basic training programme could help to overcome:

i. many are uncertain of the nature and extent of their powers and unfamiliar with committee procedures;

ii. they are sometimes confused by the complexities of laws and regulations and puzzled by educational terminology;

iii. they do not always understand how the administrative machine works or the process by which educational policy decisions are reached;

iv. some feel isolated because there are few opportunities for exchanges of views with other governors.

10.2. Only a few of those submitting written evidence mentioned the need for training, but among those who did there was a strongly expressed view that local education authorities should accept responsibility for ensuring that governors are adequately trained. Several practical proposals were put forward. It was suggested that, in view of the common content of course material and the widespread potential demand, there might be scope for courses to be provided at national level through the further education facilities of the BBC and for Open University courses. Also emphasised were the advantages of courses organised jointly by local education authorities and universities, colleges of further education or voluntary educational associations. Another possibility suggested to us was the use of teachers' centres.

10.3. In some areas little or no action seems to be taken by the local education authority to keep governors informed of their duties and responsibilities, not even to the extent of supplying a copy of the instrument and articles of government. Fortunately a growing number of authorities are recognising the need for training and taking positive steps to establish training courses and issue written guidance in the form of handbooks and manuals. The standard of these booklets varies considerably. Some consist of little more than a copy of the relevant instrument and articles, other are more detailed and include such things as a glossary of educational terms, an explanation in lay terms of the practical effect of each article and information about educational finance.

10.4. Courses of the kind suggested by witnesses have in fact been organised in some areas. They have included lectures and discussions, group work, tutorial guidance and simulation exercises in which the participants play the part of governors at "mock" meetings. In addition to "core subjects" they have emphasised different aspects of school government ranging from broad topics such as "Community Politics in Contemporary Britain" to "The Disturbed and Disturbing Child".

10.5. The introduction of participatory school government need not and should not be deferred until all the prospective participants have been trained. Nevertheless it will create a need for training in effective participation, not only for the parent and community governors but also for the local authority and teacher members who will in future have a broader and more specific obligation to explain their aims and techniques to those who are not familiar with them. The job of ensuring that the partnership foreshadowed in this report is successful should be conceived positively, the more so since education tends to be the subject of much unhelpful publicity. Clearly local education authorities are the right people to assume responsibility for this task, and the suggestions and recommendations which follow are intended to take account of their varying circumstances and resources.

10.6. As regards the content of programmes, we accept that, as at present, there will be differing views on local needs. We would not wish to lay down a rigid training format or advocate any particular pattern as being more effective than another. Clearly one basic requirement is to see that new governors know the powers and duties of governing bodies and the rules of procedure within which they operate. This, however, is only a beginning. They must also be familiar with the structure of the education service and have some knowledge of the working of a school. Further, high priority should be given to providing governors with an opportunity to become familiar with the more important current topics in education generally, so that they know something of the framework within which educational decisions are taken. It is important that they should be encouraged to think independently within this framework, not simply to obey the rules (written and unwritten). There is therefore positive advantage, from the point of view of effectiveness as well as economic sense, in the local education authority's sharing the task with other agencies.

10.7. We see merit in the suggestion that courses should, if possible, be provided at national and local level through radio and television and by the Open University. As we have already mentioned, some local education authorities have found it helpful to organise courses jointly with other bodies and indeed small authorities may not be able to provide the full range of training opportunities suggested above without such co-operation. Where there is no local university the local education authority might run a course in conjunction with an adult college or with the Workers' Educational Association, the National Association of Governors and Managers or the Confederation for the Advancement of State Education. As a minimum, governors need contact with members of other governing bodies; opportunities for this can be combined with lectures and question sessions. The suggested use of teachers' centres to provide a continuing back-up information service for school governors is also in our opinion worthy of consideration. We also think that there is scope for the governing body to build up its own collection of relevant books and documents*.

---

*For example the LEA's conditions of service relating to teachers referred to in paragraph 8.16.

These might be housed in the school library where governors could be given reference facilities.

10.8. People holding other forms of public office are trained. In our view, it is important that school governors too should be trained. We therefore *RECOM-MEND that all local education authorities should be required to ensure that initial and in-service training courses are available for governors. We also RECOM-MEND that:*

    i. all governors should have a short period of initial training as soon as this is practicable;

    ii. all governors should attend in-service training courses regularly;

    iii. a person to be designated by the local education authority should be responsible for co-ordinating the training of school governors.

CHAPTER 11—PROCEDURAL ARRANGEMENTS FOR THE NEW GOVERNING BODIES

11.1. The effectiveness of a governing body, like that of any other organisation, will be increased if the procedural arrangements for its work are efficient. We do not wish to burden governing bodies with a detailed set of standing orders. Within the general guidelines provided in this chapter, we believe that governing bodies should be free to work out their own rules and procedures.

Meetings and proceedings

11.2. The Fourth Schedule to the Education Act 1944 (Appendix C) provides that "the quorum of the managers or governors shall not be less than three, or one third of the whole number of managers or governors, whichever is the greater". In our view this requirement will continue to be appropriate for the new pattern of school government which we propose.

11.3. The fifth paragraph of the Fourth Schedule provides that a meeting of the governors may be convened by any two of their number. It seems to us desirable that this provision should be brought more into line with the quorum requirement. This would help to ensure that a meeting of the governing body is not convened unless there is likely to be a quorum of members present. We accordingly *RECOMMEND that the provision should be amended to make it necessary for the agreement of at least one third of the members of the whole governing body to be obtained to the convening of any meeting other than one arranged by the chairman and clerk in the ordinary way.*

Frequency and time of meetings

11.4. The Fourth Schedule specifies that the managers or governors shall hold a meeting once in every term.

11.5. It will be clear from what we have already said about the functions of the new governing bodies that the scale of their responsibilities and duties will be considerably greater than they are at present. We are aware of the possible manpower and financial implications of frequent meetings but it seems to us unavoidable that governing bodies will need to meet more than once a term if they are to achieve any measure of success in their new role.

11.6. *We therefore RECOMMEND that the Fourth Schedule should be amended to provide for meetings to be held at least twice in each school term.**

---

*The following members disagree with this recommendation: Professor Baron, Mr. Browning, Mr. Currie-Jones, Councillor Hett, Miss Lynn, Miss Millett, Canon Reilly, Mr. Turner. In the view of these members the frequency of meetings of governing bodies should be determined by local circumstances and needs. An increase in activity is to be expected from the new governing bodies but this could well be expressed through the work of sub-committees, specialist panels or working parties. In these circumstances, the formal requirement for the whole governing body to meet as a minimum twice a term could prove an unnnecessary encumbrance. The minimum requirement for meetings of the governing body as a whole should remain once a term.

11.7. The time of day at which meetings of governing bodies are held is not in our view a matter on which there can be any central prescription. Attendance at meetings of school governing bodies is specifically recognised in the Employment Protection Act 1975 as a service for which employers are required to allow time off from work. Nevertheless, the personal circumstances of individual governors may make it more convenient for them to attend meetings at one time of the day rather than another. There are also other factors, such as the prior commitments of LEA advisers and senior officers, local transport problems and the availability of accommodation for meetings, which will need to be taken into account.

11.8. We accordingly *RECOMMEND that the time at which meetings are held should be left for decision by the individual governing body so that they can be arranged at a time convenient for most of the members.* To minimise any interference with work and to ensure maximum attendance it will be desirable to avoid, as far as possible, holding meetings of the governing body during the normal working hours of its members.

Confidentiality and the dissemination of information

11.9. *We RECOMMEND that proceedings should not be confidential unless a governing body specifically so decides in regard to a particular item of its business, in which case any confidential items in the minutes should be recorded separately.* We think it should be for the individual governing body to decide whether non-members, including journalists, should be admitted to its meetings.

11.10. We attach importance to the need for all those concerned in school government to be kept fully informed. *We RECOMMEND that copies of all agenda, reports and minutes of proceedings of governing bodies should be sent to the local education authority and to all members of the governing body.* It will not, of course, be sufficient for the governing body to use this routine procedure for the purpose of drawing the LEA's attention to any of its resolutions or recommendations which require specific consideration by the authority. Such items should be the subject of separate communications to the local education authority.

11.11. It became apparent to us during our visits that there is very little public awareness of the part assigned to governing bodies in the running of schools. It is a very important element of our new approach that the existence and accessibility of school governors should be generally recognised. We therefore *RECOMMEND that information about the membership of governing bodies should be made widely available to parents and others.* It would be helpful, for example, if such detail could be included in any school handbook issued to parents or in other appropriate communications sent to the home. Local education authorities will no doubt wish to consider additional ways in which suitable publicity might be given.

Chairman of the governing body

11.12. The chairman of the governing body has a particularly important part to play. The responsibilities of this post require not only that he (or she) ensures the smooth and efficient conduct of meetings but that he should be available to represent the governing body and fulfil the additional duties required. He may also, on occasions, have to take action on his own on behalf of the governing body.

11.13. The election of the chairman will normally take place at the first meeting of the governing body. *We RECOMMEND that it should be open to the governing body to elect as chairman any one of its members, except those who are paid members of the staff of the school.*

Clerking

11.14. The 1944 White Paper suggested that "it would be usual for the Education Officer or his representative to be the clerk to the governing body". The model instrument provided that "the Clerk of the Governors shall be the Chief Education Officer or such other person as may be appointed by the local education authority". Although it is a fairly widespread practice for the clerk to be appointed by the local education authority from its own staff ("central clerking") there are some areas where the governors have appointed as their clerk a person from the staff of the school or its locality ("local clerking"), either for practical or economic reasons or as a positive attempt to give managing and governing bodies greater independence.

11.15. Clerking arrangements were not regarded as a major issue by our witnesses. The only question of any substance concerned the relative advantages of central and local clerking. Of those who made specific reference to the subject well over half favoured the latter. They pointed to the greater independence of the governing body that has the right to appoint its own clerk; the advantage of having a clerk with local knowledge and personal interest in the school; the saving in economic terms and the relief afforded to the authority who would otherwise carry a very substantial administrative burden. It was also suggested that the presence of a representative from the local education authority office inhibits members of the governing body from speaking freely and that problems can arise because of the conflicting claims on the loyalties of an officer from the education department serving as clerk.

11.16. On our visits we found support for central clerking arrangements. It was argued that when meetings were serviced by officers of appropriate standing, a reasonable standard of proficiency and the certainty of regular meetings could be assured, authoritative answers could be given on the spot and the local education authority office be kept in better touch with the local situation. The latter point was regarded as particularly important by some local education authorities faced with the problems of maintaining communications in widely spread rural areas. Significantly, however, the Association of County Councils, basing themselves on the experience of those local education authorities that have dispensed wholly or largely with central clerking, expressed the view it was not essential to have clerking done by the staff of the local education authority.

11.17. We do not deny the force of the arguments for central clerking but on balance we consider that they are outweighed by the advantages of a local appointment. Of these, we regard the greater independence of the governing body and the personal interest of the local clerk in the activities of his "own" school as of particular importance. In our opinion the work that is involved could, in most cases, be undertaken by the school secretary where there is one in a large school, and in a smaller school by one of the governors or by someone else living locally. Such an appointment could provide interesting part-time work without being excessively demanding.

11.18. However, the varied views that have been expressed on this subject lead us to the conclusion that the differences between urban and rural areas and between London and the provinces are so considerable that the choice of system must remain with the local education authority. We therefore *RECOM-MEND that the local education authority should decide in the light of the local situation the most effective, practical and economic system of clerking for its governing bodies.*

Payments to members of school governing bodies

11.19. Local authorities have power, under the Local Government Act 1972, to pay allowances to their members in respect of a wide range of "approved duties". These duties may include, for those council or committee members asked to serve as managers and governors of schools, attendance at meetings of the managing and governing bodies. Where the authority has decided to recognise such service as an "approved duty" (no details were available to us of the number who have done so) the individual members concerned are able to claim attendance allowance, at present up to £10 a day. Co-opted members of local authority committees (who are treated as local authority members for allowance purposes) are not entitled to receive attendance allowance but may claim financial loss allowance payable only where loss of earnings, or specific extra expenditure, can be proved for "approved duty". Where their service on the governing body has been recognised in this way by the local education authority, both councillors and co-opted committee members may also claim travelling and subsistence allowances.

11.20. Under the 1972 Act, arrangements may also be made for all the members of a school managing or governing body to be paid travelling, subsistence and financial loss allowance in respect of attendance at meetings of the bodies concerned. Such arrangements have however been confined to a handful of boarding schools. We understand that the Government's view has been that the arrangements should be limited to those schools whose special characteristics have made it essential to have a governing body composed of other than local persons, with the result that all or nearly all the governors are involved in long journeys to meetings. The argument against any more general application has been that, by their very nature, schools are usually local institutions, and their governors usually local people whose attendance at meetings does not normally involve much in the way of expenses.

11.21. The consequence is that, whilst the majority of governors do not receive allowances of any kind, different conditions can in practice apply to individual members of the same governing body. We regard it as particularly invidious that there should be this financial discrimination in some cases between one governor and another. We recognise that there is a long established and valuable tradition of voluntary service in school government. We trust it will long continue. Nevertheless, in our view the most important consideration is that no one should be debarred from serving as a school governor because of financial considerations. So, in addition to recommending that meetings be arranged outside the normal working hours of members (paragraph 11.8), *we RECOMMEND that:*

i. attendance allowance should not be payable to any school governor;

ii. financial loss allowance should be payable to all governors in respect of proved loss of earnings;

iii. local education authorities should be empowered to pay travelling and incidental expenses to members of governing bodies in accordance with arrangements made by authorities with the object of securing that no individual would be debarred from membership of a governing body by reason of the cost of attending meetings of the body.

CHAPTER 12—THE GOVERNMENT OF VOLUNTARY SCHOOLS

12.1. About one-third of all maintained schools,* whose running costs, including teachers' salaries, are met by local education authorities, have been provided by voluntary foundations (mainly associated with the Anglican and Roman Catholic Churches). The contribution made by these bodies is recognised in certain statutory features which distinguish the arrangements for the management and government of such schools from those for county schools, which are wholly provided as well as maintained by local education authorities. In his letter of 5 May 1975 to our Chairman the then Secretary of State for Education and Science said, among other things:

"We think the Committee will find it helpful if we say at the outset that we do not expect the Committee to concern itself with those aspects of the present arrangements for voluntary schools which arise essentially from their voluntary character and which reflect the respective interests of the providing body and of the local education authority in the provision and administration of a voluntary school. These aspects include particularly the relative responsibilities of the authority and the providing body for the provision of premises and finance; their relative shares in appointing the persons who are to be responsible for the conduct of the school and, directly or indirectly, in the appointment of its staff; the arrangements for determining the character of the school, for the admission of pupils, for denominational religious worship and teaching, and for the use of the school premises outside school hours.

It is not the Government's intention to review at present the structure of the 'dual system' of county and voluntary schools, which was established after the most careful consideration and clearly remains generally acceptable to educational and public opinion. In considering the conclusions and recommendations of the Committee in due course, however, we shall have regard to any implications they may have for the matters mentioned above."

We have followed this guidance.

12.2. Voluntary schools are of three kinds, each of which has in some respects different arrangements for management and government. Some of the more important features of each are the following:

a. An aided school, in respect of which the providing foundation has certain continuing financial responsibilities†, has a governing body of whose members two-thirds (the "foundation" governors) are appointed by the providing body and one-third (the "representative" governors) by the local education authority.

---

*In January 1976, there were approximately 9,000 voluntary schools with 2 million pupils, and 19,000 county schools with 7 million pupils.

†The managing or governing body of an aided school is responsible for providing the site and school buildings, including any significant enlargements that may be needed, and for keeping the exterior of the building in good repair. Eighty-five per cent. of their approved expenditure in carrying out these responsibilities is met by the Secretary of State. All other costs are borne by the local education authority.

The governing body of such a school has statutory responsibility for appointing the head and teachers (subject to some safeguards as regards dismissals), for controlling the religious—and also, in the case of a secondary school, the secular—instruction given to the pupils, and (subject to some limited powers conferred on the local education authority) for the occupation and use of the school premises.

b. A controlled school, in respect of which the foundation has no continuing financial responsibility, has a governing body of whose members two-thirds are appointed by the local education authority and one-third by the foundation. The governing body of such a school has a statutory duty to provide a limited amount of denominational religious instruction at parents' request, certain functions in relation to the appointment of religious education teachers, and limited powers to determine the use of school premises.

c. A special agreement school, in respect of which the financial responsibilities of the foundation are similar to those relating to an aided school, has a governing body similarly constituted. Its governing body has powers similar to those of an aided school's in respect of religious education and the use of the school premises.

12.3. In addition to the particular features to be found in connection with each type of voluntary school, the governing body of every voluntary school occupies a special position in two major respects: it alone may take the formal steps necessary to initiate a significant change in the character of the school and it decides the arrangements for the admission of pupils, normally, under the articles of government, after consultation with the local education authority.

12.4. Our evidence included proposals for changes in the management and government of voluntary schools. Both the Catholic Education Council and the Board of Education of the General Synod of the Church of England (the latter presenting evidence jointly with the National Society for Promoting Religious Education) recognised the need for widening the basis of representation on the managing and governing bodies of voluntary schools. Teacher and other organisations connected with voluntary schools also favoured reform to facilitate wider participation. The churches have been active in promoting discussion of ways to do this without damaging the essential features which characterise the voluntary school and make it an important component of the public education service. We are conscious that they look to us to offer a lead, by pointing out the directions in which the management and government of county schools ought to develop, so that they can move consistently and avoid the risk of unnecessarily widening the differences between the two elements of the "dual system".

12.5. Some of the recommendations we have made in earlier chapters, and very many of the observations which lead up to and amplify our recommendations, will be applicable to voluntary schools without difficulty. For example, the abolition of grouping, the training of governors, acceptance of the LEA's decisions on the dates of school holidays, and the payment of necessary expenses, are matters which can be put in hand without distinction between one kind of school and another.

12.6. Our main recommendations, however, have implications which would make their implementation in voluntary schools difficult, if not impossible, without some changes in the essential distinguishing characteristics of a voluntary school in the "dual system" as at present structured. Even our basic assumption about the proper relationship between the governing body and the local education authority (paragraph 3.17) does not hold good in the case of a voluntary school. The powers and duties of voluntary school governors derive not only from those of the local education authority but also from those of the providing body, and the individual governor is not only the holder of a public office but also the guardian of a trust.* The broadening of membership would be hard to accomplish without either an increase in size or a diminution in the representation of the providing body, because the latter's representatives have statutory functions in relation to the character of the school and therefore could not be selected by other interests. The composition of a voluntary school governing body on the "four equal shares" principle that we have recommended for county schools (paragraph 4.6) would clearly be incompatible, in the present framework of the "dual system", with its exercise of some of the responsibilities and powers which we think appropriate for a governing body. Even a matter which might at first sight seem to be of minor importance, such as the availability of the school buildings for community purposes (paragraphs 9.23—9.34) could have major implications for the conduct of an aided school and the financial responsibilities of its governors.

12.7. Some of our witnesses have suggested means by which attempts might be made to solve these problems. For example, the Board of Education of the General Synod of the Church of England discussed in their evidence to us "several possible ways of reconciling size with a reasonable spread of representation" and the Catholic Education Council were willing to contemplate some reduction in the representation of providing bodies. It would not be hard to think of other possiblities which would merit consideration. It is not for us, however, to enter into a detailed discussion of the problems or their possible solutions. Even if the Secretary of State had not guided our main efforts in other directions, we should have been very conscious that our own recommendations have in certain respects made the issues relating to voluntary school government rather different from those to which our witnesses were addressing themselves and that in the course of any full consideration of those issues there may well emerge new questions and new initiatives which could be properly followed up only by those with a continuing responsibility for the relevant aspects of the education service.

12.8. If the recommendations we have proposed for county schools were, in the main, to be implemented within a five-year period and during that time nothing were done by way of consultation and subsequent recommendation about the arrangements for voluntary schools, it is obvious that there would develop increasing differences between the arrangements for the government of county and voluntary schools. This, we believe, could cause difficulties.

12.9. *We RECOMMEND therefore that:*

a. to the extent that our other recommendations can be implemented without

---

*Section 114 Education Act, 1944. (See Appendix D).

giving rise to any issue of principle in relation to the structure of the "dual system", their application in respect of voluntary schools should be given by those concerned equal consideration with their application in respect of county schools; and

b. the Secretaries of State should put in hand as soon as possible consultation with representatives of the providing bodies, the local education authorities and all other parties concerned with a view to the adoption for voluntary schools of arrangements for management and government following as closely as practicable the lines of those we have recommended for county schools.

CHAPTER 13—OUR RECOMMENDATIONS AND THEIR IMPLEMENTATION

13.1. In the preceding chapters, in addition to many observations which we hope will be heeded by all those concerned with school government in the future, we have made a number of recommendations about the establishment and composition of governing bodies, the functions of local education authorities, governing bodies and headteachers, and various procedural and other incidental matters. Taken together, our recommendations constitute a new approach to school government which in our view will solve the main problems of the present arrangements, will encourage and carry forward the progress already being made and will set school government on a firm footing for many years to come. The essential features of this approach are the full and equal involvement of the four interests mainly concerned in school government; the definition of a direct line of responsibility running from the local education authority to the governing body and through the latter to the headteacher and staff; and, as we propose in this chapter, the replacement of individual schools' instruments, rules and articles of management and government by a general framework of national legislation and local ordinance.

13.2. The implementation of our recommendations will be a matter for everyone concerned in school government. It will be for the Secretaries of State, after the usual consultations, to decide the general lines of national policy, to frame and put before Parliament the legislation needed to ensure that national policy is followed in its broad and essential aspects and to keep the working of the system under review. As the Secretaries of State will no doubt wish these consultations to be as wide as possible, we suggest that consideration might be given to the production of an abridged version of this report for use in this connection as appropriate. We discuss later in this chapter the basis on which legislation and monitoring should be put in hand.

13.3. It will be for local education authorities to decide how the broad outlines of the new approach should be filled in so as to provide the best arrangements for their own areas. Those who have already made substantial progress in the recommended directions will be able to offer the benefit of their experience to those who have further to go. All authorities will wish to discuss the position with local organisations of teachers and parents before formulating firm proposals. They will, we hope, as a matter of high priority set about making arrangements for training all those who will in due course be concerned. The teachers' organisations at national and local level, and the staff of each school in their particular context, will need to consider the implications of the new approach for themselves and especially its implications for the form and character of staff representation in the new governing bodies. Parents' organisations, where they already exist, will find many questions to which they will need to address themselves and which they will wish to discuss with heads and staffs of schools. Where such organisations do not exist, we hope that individual parents and others with an active concern in promoting wider participation in school government will come forward to stimulate local interest and action. Throughout the community, voluntary organisations—both those specially concerned with education and those with more general interests—will have an opportunity of taking an active part in the development, in practical local form, of the general ideas we have put forward. We foresee a lively period of activity by all concerned, at every level.

13.4. The cornerstone of the new structure, in legal and administrative terms, will be the provision made in new legislation. We think the time has come to dispense with the complex and involved requirements of instruments and articles or rules for each school, at least as far as county schools are concerned. Many, if not most, local education authorities have always made these in standard form for all their schools. In our view there would be advantage in replacing them by a general order made, and given wide publicity, by the local education authority specifying the arrangements for the government of all its county schools, or at least for each broad group of schools such as all the primary, and all the secondary, schools in its area. This would at the same time ensure both that those features of school government which the local education authority regarded as essential were carried into effect in every school, and that all those concerned were aware of the local education authority's general requirements.

13.5. We do not think it would be appropriate, however, to leave the making and the content of these general arrangements solely to the discretion of the local education authority. There are certain requirements which we consider so essential to the successful implementation of the new approach to school government that they should, we consider, be laid down by statute or statutory regulations made by the Secretaries of State.

13.6. *We RECOMMEND that a statutory duty should be imposed on every local education authority to make, by order, arrangements conforming to the following requirements for the government of county schools in its area, to publicise them and to make them known to all concerned:*

1. Establishment and functions of governing bodies
A separate governing body should be set up for each primary and secondary school, to which the authority should delegate the exercise of such of its own functions as may be prescribed in regulations made by the Secretaries of State and, in addition, such other functions as the local education authority considers appropriate, having regard to its own responsibility for the running of the schools in the area.

2. Composition
*i. The governing body should consist, in equal numbers, of local education authority representatives, school staff (including the head teacher ex **officio**, and with first priority given to teachers), elected parents (and eligible pupils) and representatives of the local community.*
ii. Rules and procedures for the election of parent governors should be drawn up, and their implementation supervised, by the local education authority.

iii. The present "*minor authority*" requirements having been removed, elected members of statutory local authorities in the area served by the school should be eligible for appointment as local education authority or community representatives.

iv. There should be a prohibition on the appointment of any person to the governing body of a school catering for children in an age group served by any other school of which he is already a governor.

3. Consultation with staff

Provision should be made, to the satisfaction of the governing body, for the headteacher to consult his teaching staff on day-to-day matters with opportunities for discussion among staff and the expression of collective views; for supporting staff to be consulted likewise and to be kept informed of the governing body's work; and for supporting staff to have opportunities to submit their views and proposals to the governing body and the headteacher on any matter of special concern to them.

4. Parents' organisations

Parents should be permitted at any time to set up an organisation based on the school and be given facilities for their activities within the school.

5. Relations and communications with individual parents

Adequate arrangements should be made in the school, to the satisfaction of the governing body, to inform parents, to involve them in their children's progress and welfare, to enlist their support, and to ensure their access to the school and a teacher by reasonable arrangement.

6. General activities (including curriculum)

i. The governing body should be given the responsibility for determining the particular aims of its school, for considering the means by which they are pursued, for keeping under review the school's progress towards them, and for deciding upon action to facilitate such progress, and for making and reporting briefly to the local education authority a first general appraisal of the school's progress within four years of its formation.

ii. The governing body should have the responsibility for formulating guidelines on behaviour and for making the necessary school rules and sanctions regarding pupil's behaviour.

7. Finance

Provisions should be made corresponding to those in the 1945 model articles regarding the preparation and submission of estimates for all secondary schools; these provisions should be extended to primary schools as soon as the local education authority considered it practicable.

8. Staff appointments

i. The procedure for the appointment of heads should provide for a small selection committee consisting equally of members of the governing body and

representatives of the local education authority and for a member of the latter's education committee to serve as chairman with a casting vote if necessary.
ii. The selection of deputy heads and other staff should rest with the governing body.

9. *Training*
   i. Provision should be made for initial and in-service training courses for governors.
   ii. All governors should be required to undertake a short period of initial training as soon as this is practicable and to attend in-service training courses regularly.

10. *Procedure, etc.*
   i. There should be provision for each governing body to elect as its chairman any member who is not one of the paid staff of the school, for ordinary meetings to be held at least twice in the school term, for the agreement of one-third of the members to be required for the convening of a special meeting, for copies of minutes of all meetings to be sent to all members and to the local education authority.
   ii. The local education authority should make the membership of each governing body known to parents and others concerned.
   *iii. The payment of attendance allowance in respect of school governors' duties should be prohibited.**

13.7. The intended effect of these measures, the timing of which we discuss later in this chapter, would be that every local education authority would be required by law to make, by a formal order, arrangements which in respect of certain basic features conformed with a nationally prescribed pattern but in other respects differed from area to area. We hope that each authority, in turn, will leave scope within its own general arrangements for differences in the workings of school government between one school and another.

13.8. Provision on these lines would lend itself to both local and national review and amendment from time to time without the need for further main legislation. At the national level we RECOMMEND *that the Secretaries of State should, within five years after the legislation comes into effect call for reports from local education authorities on the working of the new system and in the light of these reports issue such further guidance as may be thought desirable and also, if need be, amend the regulations.* We assume that if at any time the situation in a particular area appeared to call for the intervention of the Secretary of State appropriate action would be taken. In order to provide a

---

*We have recommended in paragraph 11.19 that the local education authorities should be empowered to pay financial loss allowance to governors in respect of proved loss of earnings and should be provided for, to pay governors' travelling and incidental expenses in accordance with arrangements made by the local education authority with the object of securing that no individual should be debarred from membership of a school governing body by reason of the cost of attending meetings.

comparative and synoptic view for consideration together with the local education authority's reports, we *RECOMMEND that the Secretaries of State should arrange for the progress and problems to be monitored and reported, and to be studied from an early stage by an independent agency such as a university research group, working in close association with local education authorities and the Department of Education and Science.*

13.9.　We have given very careful consideration to the extent to which the implementation of our recommendations by local education authorities might require administrative control by central government departments in addition to the general requirements set out in the legislation which we have recommended. There are, of course, major problems in exercising effective control over the actions of authorities in such matters. It is difficult for a central government department to ascertain and assess the local circumstances which must be an important, if not the decisive, consideration in relation to a proposed departure from some general pattern. Indeed the desirability of trying to preserve such a pattern, extending beyond the essential features we have set out above, is open to question. We have also been informed that the detailed scrutiny and discussion of individual authorities' arrangements would impose a severe burden on the limited manpower available in the Departments concerned and would divert substantial effort from other important educational purposes. We recognise, too, that central control can never do more than prevent developments which might be undesirable. It cannot ensure that desirable developments will take place.

13.10.　We believe that the impetus towards the full implementation of our recommendations must come from local sources, acting within a broad framework laid down by the Secretaries of State. There may be occasions, hard to foresee and to guard against in general terms, when a particular authority may make changes in its school government arrangements which give rise to controversy or even dismay. The Secretaries of State already have power to call for information and to intervene where a local education authority are in default of a duty or are acting (or propose to act) unreasonably. Even granting that the circumstances in which the latter powers can be used are, rightly, very limited, there seems no need to subject the school government arrangements of all authorities to a detailed control which might be needed, if at all, only for a few and on rare occasions. In such cases, as indeed in all others, the most potent instrument is the pressure of public opinion.

13.11.　In some areas there has already been significant movement in the direction we advocate. These advances could be carried further without greatly increased resources. Where the need for change is greatest, the opportunities are available to take now those steps which the more progressive authorities have already been able to take without special encouragement. Immediately there is only one statutory barrier in the way of the full implementation of the substance of our recommendations in any area. This is the requirement (in section 18 of the 1944 Act) for minor authority representation on the managing bodies of certain primary schools, which could prevent the implementation in those schools of the "four equal shares" principle. Otherwise the present statutory requirements regarding instruments, rules and articles do not prevent the implementation of our recommendations. Their administration could be made less onerous by the Secretaries of State giving general approval to the making or changing by any local education authority of articles of government for any county secondary school during a transitional period, so that authorities would be free to move on the lines of our main recommendations in advance of the introduction of general requirements to do so. Local education authorities should ensure that appropriate changes in the composition of governing bodies accompany or precede any changes in their functions. We hope that the period of transition will be short. In our view, even in an area where very little progress has been made in the directions we recommend, not more than five years should be needed to undertake the local consultations and make the practical arrangements necessary for having in effective operation a system of school government of the kind we propose.

13.12. A start can be made by progressively replacing the "grouping" arrangements which still exist in some areas by establishing separate managing/ governing bodies for each school with members drawn from the school's parents and staff and the local community. Such an approach would permit the provision of training on whatever scale was practicable in the locality, and could be accompanied by general encouragement of the school's staff and parents bodies to equip themselves for participation in school government as we propose. All governing bodies could, in close co-operation with the heads and staffs of their schools, begin the process of defining the aims and objectives of their schools and bringing into being the information systems which will be needed as a basis for some of their main functions. Many of our other recommendations—for example, those relating to the use of premises—could be put into effect on a similar basis.

13.13. Thus it would not be unrealistic to expect that within five years there would have been sufficient progress to permit easy compliance with the statutory requirements we have recommended. To provide a clear objective and to ensure proper momentum towards it, the eventual position and the date for its achievement should in our view be laid down in legislation from the outset.

13.14. *We RECOMMEND accordingly that legislation should be initiated as soon as possible to give effect within five years to Recommendation 86 (paragraph 13.6) and, immediately, to Recommendations 3 (paragraph 3.24); 7 (paragraph 4.10) and 60, 61, 62, (paragraph 9.18).*

13.15. We are aware that the implementation of our recommendations will involve significant resources of money, manpower and time. Much, though by no means all, will be additional to the resources already employed in this field. For example, on the basis of one local education authority's present costs it could be estimated that twice-termly meetings of separate governing bodies for every primary and secondary school will involve annual administrative expenditure by local education authorities of £4.3m. On the assumption that 10 per cent of members will be eligible to claim financial loss allowance of—for illustrative purposes—£4 for each meeting, additional expenditure of £0.55m will be required for this purpose. Some basic training for all members of the new governing bodies can be provided, on one local education authority's estimate, for £1 a head, a total of £0.23m. Judging from one local education authority's recent experience, elections for parent governors throughout England and Wales would cost at least £0.1m, with an additional £0.5m for any postal delivery required. None of the estimates we have mentioned, however, can be more than a very rough indication of the order of cost that might be involved. It will vary widely according to the accounting procedure adopted (whether, for example, account is taken of facilities already available which could be used without additional provision) and according to the speed with which these developments are pressed forward. We believe, however, that the increased effectiveness of school government, and the increase in the educational efficiency of our schools which we would look for as a consequence, will justify a significant diversion of resources whenever and wherever the opportunity can be seized.

13.16. More significant, perhaps, than the financial implications of our recommendations are their implications for the involvement in school government, on a new basis and on a scale different from anything experienced in the past, of people whose interests in school education derive not from their engagement in it as a professional or political pursuit but from their personal concern with it in relation to their children and their social concern in relation to the community in which they live. We have no illusions about the difficulties there will be in making this wider involvement an effective and constructive reality. It will require many thousands of people to take on new responsibilities and to give up substantial amounts of their time. It will also require a major effort of accommodation on the part of those who have hitherto borne these responsibilities. Nevertheless we believe that the approach which we have recommended is a direct and logical development of a tradition in which this country has led the civilised world—and has now a further contribution to make in respect of school government—a tradition of local democracy, community co-operation and individual freedom, a positive view of the relation between the school and the society which it serves and, above all, a care for the wellbeing of every individual child. We are confident that the problems of the new approach will be met and overcome and that it will help to carry forward the best features of our school system for at least a generation to come.

SUMMARY OF RECOMMENDATIONS

Chapter 3:   A new approach to school government

1. All the powers relevant to school government should be formally vested in the local education authority. (3.15)

2. There should be as much delegation of these powers by the local education authority to the governing body as is compatible with the local education authority's ultimate responsibility for the running of the schools in its area, and as much discretion in turn granted to the headteacher by the governing body as is compatible with the latter's responsibility for the success of the school in all its activities. (3.17)

3. Section 20 of the Education Act 1944 should be repealed as soon as possible and from a date to be fixed by the Secretaries of State, every school should have its own separate governing body. (3.24)

4. The term governing body should be retained and applied by law to all bodies whether they serve primary or secondary schools. (3.26)

Chapter 4:   Membership of the new governing bodies

5. The membership of governing bodies should consist of equal numbers of local education authority representatives, school staff, parents (with, where appropriate, pupils) and representatives of the local community. (4.6)

6. There shall never be less than two members in any one category and 24 members shall normally be regarded as the maximum for efficient operation. (4.7)

7. The provisions of Section 18 of the Education Act 1944 relating to the representation of minor authorities on the managing bodies of primary schools should be repealed. (4.10)

8. Any elected member of a local authority in the area served by the school should be eligible for appointment to the school governing body in either the "local education authority" or the "community" category. (4.11)

9. The headteacher of a school should always be a member of its governing body and be included *ex officio* in the group of members representing the school staff. (4.16)

10. Priority in the allocation of places within the school staff group on the governing body should be given to teachers, the opportunity being taken to add representatives of the supporting staff where size permits. (4.17)

11. Those to be appointed as the school's parent governors should be elected by the parents of the children attending that school. (4.22)

12. The local education authority should be made responsible for drawing up the rules and procedures for the election of parent governors in its area, and for ensuring that they are put into effect. (4.23)

13. All elections of parent governors should be school-based, and combine meetings and other procedures to ensure maximum participation; and the procedures should satisfy the following broad criteria: (4.23)

i. communications with parents should be in plain words;

ii. every parent with a child at the school should be eligible to nominate candidates, to stand for election, and to cast one vote;

iii. nomination and voting papers should be sent to every eligible parent;

iv. the results of the election should be communicated to all eligible parents.

14. The Secretaries of State should take definitive advice on whether it is possible to change the law to enable pupils to serve as governors at 16 without opening the whole question of the age of majority and the holding of public office. (4.26)

15. Senior secondary school pupils should participate in school government to the fullest extent allowed by law until they are eligible for membership. (4.26)

16. The procedures for the appointment of community representatives should be based on the principle that the individuals concerned should be co-opted by the governors representing the three other interest groups. The task of drawing up lists of people willing to serve in this capacity should be the responsibility of the local education authority. In compiling such lists for secondary school governing bodies, local education authorities should always invite both local employers' (or business) organisations and trade unions to submit nominations. (4.30)

17. A person should be disqualified if he is an undischarged bankrupt, has been convicted of a serious offence or if, having been appointed, he has not attended an ordinary governors' meeting for a year or is incapacitated from acting as a governor. (4.37 i)

18. Any person who, holding office as a governor, ceases to be qualified for appointment as a governor, either in one of the respects mentioned in recommendation 17 (paragraph 4.37 i) or in respect of the capacity in which he was appointed should forthwith cease to be a governor. (4.37 ii)

19. The term of office for governors should in general be within a four year framework. (4.39)

20. No person should be eligible to serve on the governing body of a primary or secondary school catering for children in an age group served by any other school of which he is already a governor. (4.42)

Chapter 5: Communication and co-operation

21. Subject to recommendation 76 (paragraph 11.9) the minutes of governors' proceedings, together with the notices and agenda for their meetings, should be made available in the teachers' common room.   (5.11)

22. The governing body should invite the headteacher to submit general proposals for consultation with his staff on day-to-day matters, should satisfy itself upon the adequacy and suitability of these proposals in general and in particular should satisfy itself that they afford facilities for discussion between members of the teaching staff and the expression of collective views.
(5.12–5.13)

23. Supporting staff should be kept informed of the governing body's work by means to be determined by the governors after consultation with the staff concerned.   (5.16a)

24. Supporting staff should be given the opportunity to submit their views or proposals to the governing body and the headteacher on any matter which is of special concern to them.   (5.16b)

25. Arrangements for consultation between the supporting staff and the head-teacher should be made by the governing body on the same basis as that proposed for teaching staff in recommendation 22.   (5.16c)

26. The governing body should be empowered to authorise the establishment of a school council or similar organisation by the pupils and should be responsible for ensuring that arrangements within the school are adequate and suitable for its effective operation.   (5.18a)

27. As a general rule the pupils themselves should decide upon the agenda for their organisation's meetings.   (5.18b)

28. Pupils should be given access to the governing body should they wish to express a view on a particular matter or to question the adequacy or suitability of the arrangements made for them to do so.   (5.18c)

29. Parents' organisations should be encouraged and facilities for their work should be made available within the school.   (5.20)

30. Parents should have the opportunity to set up an organisation based upon the school, developing its aims and methods of working in consultation with the headteacher and the governing body.   (5.22)

31. As a basic minimum the governing body should ensure that parents have access to the school for a weekday evening meeting once a term and the means of publicising their activities.   (5.23)

32. The governing body should satisfy itself that adequate arrangements are made to inform parents, to involve them in their children's progress and welfare,

to enlist their support, and to ensure their access to the school and a teacher by reasonable arrangement. (5.28)

33. The nature of the relation between the school and the individual parent should be set down in a letter sent by the governors to every parent at the time of their formal acceptance of a place at the school. (5.29)

34. Governing bodies should do what they can to narrow the gap between schools and the wealth-producing sector of the economy. (5.36)

35. On those occasions when the local education authority wishes to obtain local opinion on educational issues it should ensure that the consultation process draws on the knowledge and experience of the members of the newly constituted governing bodies. (5.38)

36. Governing bodies with shared interests or concerns should be encouraged to make arrangements for consulting each other about them. (5.39)

Chapter 6: Curriculum

37. The governing body should be given by the local education authority the responsibility for setting the aims of the school, for considering the means by which they are pursued, for keeping under review the school's progress towards them, and for deciding upon action to facilitate such progress. (6.23)

38. In setting the school's aims the governing body should give consideration to constructive suggestions made by any individuals or organisations with a concern for the school's welfare. (6.25)

39. The governing body should invite the headteacher in consultation with his staff to prepare papers setting out the means by which they propose to pursue the aims adopted. (6.27)

40. Within the framework of any general policy made by the local education authority the governing body should have the responsibility for formulating guidelines which promote high standards of behaviour and for making such minimum rules and sanctions as are necessary to maintain such standards in the school. (6.33)

41. Where the governing body considers it appropriate and desirable and has worked out with the teachers procedures for the purpose, individual governors should have the opportunity of seeing classes at work. (6.37)

42. Every local education authority should take steps to ensure that the services of a general adviser are regularly available to each of its schools and that the general adviser will be available for consultation with, and report to, the governing body on request. (6.42a)

43. All local education authorities should review the adequacy of their advisory/inspection service in the light of the requirements proposed for the new governing bodies and should take early steps to strengthen these services as necessary, aiming at a minimum of one adviser to every 20,000 of its total population at the earliest possible date. (6.42b)

44. Local education authorities, grouped on an area basis and in collaboration with HM Inspectorate, should establish panels consisting of LEA advisers, HM Inspectors, and other appropriate agencies to arrange in-service training to assist LEA advisers to identify and to develop the necessary skills to work effectively as general advisers. (6.42c)

45. Information and advice on the life and activities of the school should be brought together in each school with the purpose of creating an effective but unobtrusive information system for the governing body. The headteacher should be made responsible for the development of the system, working with general guidance provided by the governing body about the aspects of the school's activities on which information is required and the form in which it is required. (6.44)

46. Every governing body should produce a first general appraisal of the school's progress, however incomplete, within four years of its formation. The exact term for subsequent appraisals should be decided by the local education authority after consultation with the governing bodies of the schools in its area. (6.46)

47. The governing body of every school should send the local education authority a short report upon the completion of its periodic general appraisal. (6.55)

Chapter 7: Finance

48. Provisions corresponding to those in the 1945 model articles on the submission of estimates should be applied to all schools as soon as this is practicable. (7.13)

49. Authorities should study the possibilities of making financial arrangements to facilitate initiative and independent action at the school level. (7.16)

50. Early action should be taken by the Secretaries of State on the Bullock Committee's proposal that a joint working party of representatives of the Department of Education and Science and local education authorities should be established to investigate the whole question of determining the allowances for schools and the ways of distributing them. (7.18)

51. Local education authorities should see that there is the maximum possible consultation with individual governing bodies before decisions are taken about building work, major or minor, at their schools, and also that the governing bodies are consulted about developments during the subsequent planning and building stages. (7.26)

Chapter 8: Appointments

52. The procedure for the appointment of heads should provide for a small selection committee consisting equally of members of the governing body and representatives of the local education authorities. (8.10)

53. One of the education committee members on the selection committee should be elected by the latter to serve as its chairman and should if necessary have a casting vote. (8.11)

54. The selection of deputy heads and other teachers should rest with the governing body, who should give due weight to the professional advice made available through the local education authority and in particular to the responsibility of the local education authority to find suitable posts for teachers whose schools are closed or re-organised. (8.12)

55. Every governing body should have access to a copy of the LEA's staff code relating to teachers. (8.16)

56. The Secretaries of State should initiate discussions with the local education authority and teachers' associations as soon as possible about the problem of teachers who find it difficult to meet their professional obligations. (8.17)

57. The present arrangements for the appointment and dismissal of supporting staff should continue. (8.18)

Chapter 9: Other functions

58. The present arrangements for determining the responsibility for admissions to school should continue. (9.5)

59. When the local education authority has settled its admissions policy, it should make public the principles and criteria upon which school places are to be allocated. (9.5)

60. The terms 'exclusion', 'suspension' and 'expulsion', wherever they are used in statutory regulations or in local education authorities regulations or instructions, should be authoritatively defined and differentiated in the way we have suggested. (9.18i)

61. Every local education authority should be required to make and publish arrangements for the procedures to be followed in its area with regard to the suspension of pupils from attendance at school which satisfy the following general requirements:

i When a pupil's behaviour over a period gives rise to a real possibility that he will have to be suspended from attendance if it continues, opportunity for consultation and discussion should be accorded to his parents;

ii it should be clearly known by all concerned who has the power to decide that a pupil should be suspended from attendance, or should remain suspended after a specified period;

iii a time limit of not more than three days should be fixed for the duration of any suspension by the headteacher;

iv provision should be made to avoid danger to the pupil concerned, or to others, as a result of his suspension;

v when a decision is made to suspend a particular pupil the parents should be informed by a quick and reliable means, should be told how long the suspension is to last and should be given full particulars of the reason for it. A record should be made in a register kept specifically for the purpose within the school and available to the governing body;

vi the governing body should be empowered to extend the suspension for a strictly limited period, specified by the local education authority for all cases, during which the interested parties should be brought together to seek an acceptable solution;

vii if no satisfactory solution is found within this period the case should be referred to the local education authority;

viii. there should be provision for appeal by the parents to the local education authority, to be heard within a specified period, against the continuation of a suspension beyond a specified period or against any other action proposed as an alternative to the child's resumption of attendance at the school. Parents should be told how and to whom they should appeal, when the appeal will be heard and what procedure will be followed.   (9.18.2 i–viii)

62. Legislative steps should be taken to ensure that:

i. no registered pupil is debarred from attendance at his school, except on medical grounds, otherwise than in compliance with the suspension procedures arranged by the local education authority;

ii. no registered pupil is expelled from a school except by the decision of the local education authority responsible for maintaining the school, who should inform the governing body of its decision.   (9.18.3 i, ii)

63. The governing body should continue to be responsible for inspecting the school premises and for keeping the local education authority informed of their condition and state of repair.   (9.21)

64. The local education authority should authorise the governing body to have urgent minor repairs carried out up to a limit set by the authority.   (9.22)

65. The local education authority should, after consultation with the governing bodies of all county schools in its area, formulate an overall policy on school lettings.   (9.31)

66. The governing body should provide the headteacher with a set of guide-lines for the consideration of applications to use the school premises.   (9.31)

67. In any dispute between the governing body and an outside organisation about the use of the premises the final decision should rest with the local education authority.   (9.32)

68. Governing bodies should continue to have the power to grant occasional school holidays, other than mid-term holidays, subject to the agreement of the local education authority in each case. (9.44)

Chapter 10: Training the new governors

69. All local education authorities should be required to ensure that initial and in-service training courses are available for governors. (10.8)

70. All governors should have a short period of initial training as soon as this is practicable. (10.8 i)

71. All governors should attend in-service training courses regularly.

(10.8 ii)

72. A person to be designated by the local education authority should be responsible for co-ordinating the training of school governors. (10.8 iii)

Chapter 11: Procedural arrangements for the new governing bodies

73. The Fourth Schedule to the Education Act 1944 should be amended to make it necessary for the agreement of at least one-third of the members of the whole governing body to be obtained to the convening of any meeting other than one arranged by the chairman and clerk in the ordinary way. (11.3)

74. The Fourth Schedule should be amended to provide for meetings to be held at least twice in each school term. (11.6)

75. The time at which meetings are held should be left for decision by the individual governing body so that they can be arranged at a time convenient for most of the members. (11.8)

76. Proceedings should not be confidential unless a governing body specifically so decides in regard to a particular item of its business, in which case any confidential items in the minutes should be recorded separately. (11.9)

77. Copies of all agenda, reports and minutes of proceedings of governing bodies should be sent to the local education authority and to all members of the governing body. (11.10)

78. Information about the membership of governing bodies should be made widely available to parents and others. (11.11)

79. It should be open to the governing body to elect as chairman any one of its members, except those who are paid members of the staff of the school. (11.13)

80. The local education authority should decide in the light of the local situation the most effective, practical and economic system of clerking for its governing bodies. (11.18)

81. Attendance allowance should not be payable to any school governor.

82. Financial loss allowance should be payable to all governors in respect of proved loss of earnings.

83. Local education authorities should be empowered to pay travelling and incidental expenses to members of governing bodies in accordance with arrangements made by authorities with the object of securing that no individual would be debarred from membership of a governing body by reason of the cost of attending meetings of the body.   (11.21 i, ii, iii)

Chapter 12:   The government of voluntary schools

84. To the extent that our other recommendations can be implemented without giving rise to any issue of principle in relation to the structure of the "dual system", their application in respect of voluntary schools should be given by those concerned equal consideration with their application in respect of county schools.   (12.9a)

85. The Secretaries of State should put in hand as soon as possible consultations with representatives of the providing bodies, the local education authorities and all other parties concerned with a view to the adoption for voluntary schools of arrangements for management and government following as closely as practicable the lines of those recommended for county schools.
(12.9b)

Chapter 13:   Our recommendations and their implementation

86. A statutory duty should be imposed on all local education authorities to make arrangements for the government of the county schools in their areas conforming to the requirements which we have stipulated as essential to the implementation of the new approach to school government, to publicise the arrangements and to make them known to all concerned.   (13.6)

87. The Secretaries of State should, within five years after this legislation comes into effect, call for reports from local education authorities on the working of the new system and in the light of these reports issue such further guidance as may be thought desirable and also, if need be, amend the regulations.   (13.8)

88. The Secretaries of State should arrange for progress and problems to be monitored and reported, and to be studied from an early stage by an independent agency such as a university research group, working in close association with local education authorities and the Department of Education and Science.
(13.8)

89. Legislation should be initiated as soon as possible to give effect within five years to Recommendation 86 (paragraph 13.6) and, immediately, to Recommendations 3 (paragraph 3.24); 7 (paragraph 4.10) and 60, 61, 62 (paragraph 9.18)   (13.14)

NOTE OF EXTENSION

by Miss Barrow, Mrs Edwards, Mr Flower, Mr Hale, Mr Hett, Mrs Sallis, Mrs Stone

Parents' rights and responsibilities

We welcome the Committee's recognition of parents' aspirations, both collective and individual, to a status and a part to play in the education of their children.

The Committee has recommended that parents have rights to an equal share with other interests on school governing bodies, and a right to form associations based on the school. Their need to express their *collective* views is therefore well provided for.

The Committee has also recognised that *individual* parents have a need for information, explanation and consultation about the education of their own children, and has suggested that a good school will meet this need and that governing bodies will be responsible for ensuring that arrangements made for the purpose are satisfactory. This is all set out in chapter 5, and we think that the further step we suggest completes the logic and harmonises with the spirit of that chapter.

We suggest that it is not enough that an individual parent's access to information should be expressed as a "reasonable expectation." It should be a right. It is the individual parent who in law has the duty of seeing that his child is properly educated, and we think that the law should also give him the right to satisfy himself that he is carrying out that duty responsibly. If the governing body is a partnership, there should also be a partnership extended to the relations between individual parents and schools, and the parent must have all the means to play his part.

We therefore ask the Secretaries of State to consider giving each individual parent the right in law to the information relevant to the performance of his legal duty. This should include information and explanation about the school generally, regular consultations and reports on his child, the opportunity to see teachers at other times by reasonable arrangement, guidance about how he can best support the school, and access to information relevant to his own child's education, including records kept in a permanent form in the school. This right should be given formal expression by properly structured arrangements made in the school, the governors being responsible for ensuring that they are adequate to give effect to the parent's right, and also that they are not abused by the individual.

We should like to emphasise that this request represents no threat to the individual teacher or to the orderly running of schools. We do not intend that a parent should have access to classrooms, teachers or written material except in accordance with arrangements made by the school and approved by the governors. On the contrary, we consider that if the parent knows he has a right to information there is less danger that he will seek it in an arbitrary and unreasonable way. In the long run the well-informed parent is the best protection and support for the work of the school.

NOTE OF DISSENT

by Mr E Currie-Jones

In expressing my dissent from some of the Committee's recommendations, I wish to make it perfectly clear that I accept most of the recommendations and the new approach to school government as set out in chapter 3 of this report. My disagreement is confined to the Committee's recommendations in respect of the functions to be allotted to the new governing bodies, in particular their financial responsibilities, and their involvement in the appointment of junior staff.

I have not dissented without a great deal of thought, and after satisfying myself that my alternative recommendations would in no way weaken the working partnership or power sharing envisaged by the Committee.

In my opinion the essential criteria for the success of the new partnership arrangements are that they should be realistic, workable, and provide a better and more satisfying job for the governing body. I believe that most of the recommendations satisfy these criteria, but I think that those contained in *Chapter 7—Finance* are unrealistic, unworkable, and would add little to the satisfaction that the governing bodies will undoubtedly have in exercising their other functions.

It may be true that the 1945 model envisaged that governing bodies should have a large measure of financial responsibility, but it does not follow that the Committee should slavishly follow the model in every particular in 1977. There were good reasons why very few authorities followed the model, and these reasons are fully set out in para. 7, chapter 7, of this report. By today the difficult economic situation has made it necessary to have a greater rather than a lesser measure of centralised financial control.

In my view there are also many practical difficulties which militate against the involvement of governors in the field of finance to the extent suggested by the Committee, e.g. preparation of estimates. One of these difficulties would be the infrequent meetings, and the very tight budget time-table to which most local authorities have to work.

I found little evidence that there was an overwhelming body of opinion who were in the least worried about this lack of financial involvement, and most witnesses accepted that overall financial responsibility for the financing of schools must remain with the local education authority, although there were many who thought that more discretion in deciding the use of the resources made available to the schools by the local authority should be allowed at the school level. I am prepared to support such a view, and I believe that control of the allotted resources should be exercised by the governing body, in consultation with the head and staff.

It is unrealistic to suppose that the control of expenditure beyond that covered by capitation allowances can be responsibly transferred to governing bodies. Far from leading to a much more satisfied governing body, I am sure the consequences would be a perpetual state of argument between the authority and the governing body about its estimates. I am also very much afraid that the suggested procedures as to draft estimates for each school will raise false expectations, and give governing bodies a completely misleading impression of the extent to which an individual governing body can finance its own plans.

122

The evidence given by the Association of County Councils supports my view—"Much of the spending of schools must be controlled centrally by the local education authority, and the Association doubt whether any useful purpose is served by the preparation of individual school estimates. Governors should, however, be enabled to represent to the local education authority particular resource requirements of their own school. Governors should be given as much freedom as is consistent with local education authority policy to control internal spending, upon the advice of the head and local education authority staff."

Similarly the Association of Metropolitan Authorities, and the Association of Education Committees expressed the view that there are very real limits to the delegation which can be afforded to governing bodies in matters of finance.

I therefore dissent from the Committee's recommendations as set out in para. 13 of chapter 7, and would suggest the following alternative recommendations:—

1. Local education authorities should so arrange their financial procedures that if governing bodies consider it necessary to make repiesentations about any special needs of their schools they can do so at a point in time when those representations can be taken fully into account when the relevant decisions come to be taken.

2. Local education authorities should keep governing bodies suitably informed about the authority's financial position in general and also about the costs of the school for which a particular governing body is responsible, so that in discharging its functions, and in particular in considering possible changes or new developments the governing body can be informed by a sense of financial realism.

If the Secretaries of State, after concluding their consultations, formed the view that there was no objection to the Committee's recommendations in para. 13, chapter 7, I would respectfully suggest that the question of whether estimates should be prepared for each primary and secondary school should be left to the discretion of the local education authority and not made mandatory.

My second point of dissent concerns the recommendation in paras. 12 and 13 chapter 8 where it is recommended that the appointments of deputy heads, higher scale posts and other teachers should rest with the governing body. I appreciate that the precise arrangements vary from authority to authority and that the Committee's recommendations have already been adopted by some authorities. Other authorities place the responsibility for appointing deputy heads on joint selection committees as in the case of headteachers. In my view there is great merit in this arrangement, as the post of deputy head can be regarded in part as a training for further advancement.

In the case of junior teachers, the arrangements again vary from authority to authority, and some authorities and a great many teachers feel that the combined professional judgement of the Director of Education, his advisers, and the head of the particular school, results in better and more impartial appointments. This cannot always be claimed for appointments by governing bodies. I realise that there are many who would not agree with my view, but most informed persons would probably agree that there is no perfect system of appointments. I would, therefore, urge that in this particular field, the local education authorities should have the same discretion as they now have in deciding upon their appointment procedures.

We must not regard a single solution as appropriate to everybody's problems, or insist on a multiplicity of detailed prescriptions and restrictions.

Chapter 4.   Para. 24—Pupils

I agree wholeheartedly that some provision should be made for some of a school's pupils to play a part in the government of the school. This is possible for the minority of pupils of 18 and over, who can legally be full members of a governing body, and there would be no illegality in allowing pupils over 16 to sit as observers, and even take part in discussions at governing body meetings. I must, however, with others, dissent from my colleagues in their desire to have the law amended to permit pupil governors from the age of 16. In my opinion the Committee's desire to draw on pupils' knowledge and ideas for the benefit of the governing body, can be adequately realised by giving pupils over 16 observer status extending to the right to take part in discussions at the meetings of governing bodies as is suggested in the latter part of para. 26.

To allow pupil governors of 16 years of age the same right as parents, teachers and other adult members to *inter alia* appoint teachers, exercise disciplinary powers, etc., would, in my view, be most undesirable, and certainly not in the best interest of teachers or pupils.

MINORITY REPORT AND LETTER TO THE CHAIRMAN

by Mr P O Fulton

22 Chiltern Avenue,   *23rd May, 1977*
REDCAR,
Cleveland.

Dear Tom,

I am sorry that I am unable to sign the report as produced by the majority of the Committee. This is regrettable after two years hard work because there are parts of the report with which I concur but too many fundamental points with which I disagree.

In my opinion the recommendations are impracticable from the point of view of resources, (manpower, time, and finance) and they will lead eventually to the position where what goes on in schools will become the sole province of the teacher and this will not necessarily be in the best interests of the child and the community.

I fail to see how the publication of this report will suddenly produce people who are prepared to fulfil the role of governors as envisaged when in fact they have not carried out a number of the duties within their jurisdiction that they have had since 1944 (chapter 2 para. 11 Main Report shows).

I am a very firm believer in local government and would not wish to see any more authority taken away from the local education authority and the elected member who in the end is the only person held accountable. I also see the head teacher as the key figure within any school.

The majority report, if implemented, will devolve to a non-elected unrepresentative body authority without any accountability and in my opinion diminishes the role of the local education authority and the headteacher.

The crucial need for education at the present time is a restoration of confidence in our schools by parents and the community. The teachers are able to influence what goes on in schools through direct in-put, through their associations, examination boards and the Schools Council.

What is needed is that more information should be made available to parents and there should be a greater involvement of parents and the community in schools. There should be an increase in the number of advisers and inspectors to monitor, assess and review what is happening in the schools so that parents can be assured that the schools are capable of preparing children for life after school.

The concept of equal representation (one wonders how the 'proportional representation NUT' will square its conscience with this) does not help in bringing accountability any nearer a reality if experience in FE is anything to go by and I, therefore, forward with this letter the attached comments for inclusion in the report.

                                    Yours sincerely,

Committee of Enquiry into the Management and Government of Schools—Comments on Report

The Committee was established in May, 1975 at a time when the public at large were beginning to ask questions about education in general and what was happening in schools in particular. Whilst the Committee has been sitting further interest has been engendered, and to some extent the fires of controversy fuelled, by the Tyndale affair, the events in Tameside, the Prime Minister's Ruskin speech, the so-called "Yellow Paper", the Bennett Report on "Teaching Styles and Pupil Progress", and the debates and discussions relating to the proposed common examination at 16+ and the question of the core curriculum. It is clear to me that parents and the community in general, to a very considerable extent, have lost confidence in our schools. It is vital for the educational well being of the country that confidence is restored as quickly as possible.

Teachers will say that this can be achieved by devoting more resources to education, yet expenditure on education has never been greater than it is at this time, the salaries of teachers were very greatly improved following the Houghton Report, class sizes are smaller and in very many other respects conditions are so much better than they were years ago.

Industrialists and people from the commercial world will tell us that confidence will be restored when schools go back to showing a greater concern for achievement in the basic skills of numeracy and literacy; the ordinary man-in-the-street will perhaps tell us that there needs to be greater concern for discipline and good behaviour.

I believe that the restoration of confidence will only come about when the public are convinced on three points.

Firstly that there is a good return on the massive investment in education.
Secondly that the people in the education service are competent to identify and provide for the needs of children to fit them for life after school.
Thirdly that schools can be made more accountable.

The running of our schools and influence upon the curriculum hitherto has been left too much in the hands of teachers and of teacher dominated bodies like the Schools Council and examination boards. Governing bodies have had little if any, significant influence although, in theory, they have had control over the curriculum and finance (see chapter 2 paragraph 11). The education officers and advisers of the local education authorities have spent too little time in schools. For far too much of their time they have been office bound dealing with a mass of administrative matters. The burdens and pressures in this respect have increased markedly in recent years consequent upon new legislation, particularly that concerned with industrial relations and employment, with all the attendant codes of practice and procedures that relate to consultation, grievances, and the investigation of complaints. Many of the manifestations of corporate management in the post Bains era also appear to be very time consuming for professional staff in education departments as also the ever recurring budgetary exercises that the various economic crises seem to involve. I feel that in recent years far too much effort and attention has had to be devoted to staff conditions of service and questions of structure and organisation within schools and too little to the needs of children and to the assessment of the activities which are actually taking place. This I believe has much to do with the loss of confidence which a great many people feel.

The remit of this Committee was to review the arrangements for the management and government of maintained schools. I do not think this can be done effectively except in a wider context.

Three major factors will affect our schools in the immediate future.

Firstly the likely shortage of resources for education (other services will take priority).

Secondly the fall in the birthrate.

Thirdly the shortage of work for young people leaving school which will mean that employers will be more selective and demanding in terms of standards achieved.

Each of these factors suggests to me a need for a greater degree of central planning and management within local authority (or nationally) rather than devolution to thousands of non-elected, non-accountable bodies.

It is unrealistic to expect that at a time when finance is so tightly controlled through rate support grant, when growth rates are determined nationally, when the possibliity of specific grants is being canvassed and when Policy and Resources Committees are exercising such a firm control over expenditure in the local authorities that they will feel able to involve governing bodies in budgeting and finance to the degree proposed in the report.

It is unrealistic to believe, also, that with such emphasis now being placed upon the need to improve standards that local education authorities will be content to give the governing bodies the powers to organise, structure and vary the curriculum as envisaged in the report. (How can it be consistent with democracy if a local education authority determines a particular general policy and a governing body is then able to frustrate that general policy by its determination of aims for a school and by the manner in which those aims are pursued and realised?) These considerations lead me to the view that local education authorities will have to involve themselves much more directly in the management of schools in the future than they have been accustomed to do in the past. I see a need, the more so in a climate of general retrenchment, for better management of resources both human and material. I believe this is more likely to be achieved if there is more direct inter-action between the education department of the local education authority and the schools. The role as now envisaged for governors will absorb too much professional expertise and dissipate effort which could more usefully be employed.

There was very little evidence presented to us that indicated that more people want to participate actively in the government of schools where this involves the making of decisions and the shouldering of responsibility. My impression is that people are seeking rather a role that will enable them to influence rather than to control. There was evidence of difficulties and apathy in areas where parental elections are held.

I recognise, nevertheless, that all but a small number of parents want to be involved with the education of their children in school. They want information that will help them to encourage and support their children so that they can realise their full potential. They want to know how the school is organised and why. They want to know about options and the possible consequences of making particular choices. They want to know about external examinations and the currency of CSE. Above all they want to know what can be done about inadequate incompetent teachers. (It would appear that there are a great many more of these in our schools than some would have us believe.)

127

Concern about the problem posed by the incompetent teacher was expressed throughout the county and this appears to be confirmed in the reports of the "Great Debate". I feel that part of the outcome of the review of the management of schools should be the introduction of a system of annual assessment for teachers. The responsibility for dismissing a teacher should rest solely with the local education authority which could take into account any views expressed by the governors as necessary. The present procedure for suspension and dismissal which involves hearings before governors and the authority is cumbersome and protracted. Recent employment protection legislation affords safeguards which should enable the procedures currently embodied in the teacher's contract of service to be revised and simplified.

I have referred earlier to my assessment of what parents essentially are seeking in relation to schools. The vast majority are not concerned to secure representation by a very small number of them on a governing body. Their interest and concern is very much more immediate and personal and it all boils down to how the school affects their child.

If we are to have governing bodies, and I came very close to saying that we could do without them altogether, I would recommend a body that would act as a "watchdog" to ensure that the local education authority and the school fulfilled certain functions. This governing body would consist of three or five members constituted as follows:—

One parent; one member of the community in general who would desirably reflect local industry or commercial interests; and one elected member of the local education authority who would be the chairman.

Alternatively:—

Two parents; two members of the community and one elected member of the local education authority who would be the chairman.

In view of the fact that circumstances differ so widely in different areas any decision whether or not to group a number of schools under one governing body or to establish individual governing bodies for each school should be left to the discretion of the local education authority. Similarly the arrangements for the election or appointment of governors should be a matter for local discretion.

The duties and responsibilities of the governing body would be as follows:—

(i) to ensure that the aims and objectives of the school as determined by the local education authority are carried out;

(ii) to ensure that the school is structured and organised in such a way that the aims and objectives can be achieved effectively;

(iii) to receive and consider each year a detailed report from the head teacher describing the use made in the school of the resources available, including the allocation of capitation funds, and the curriculum being followed and to forward this report to the local education authority together with any observations or recommendations;

(iv) to ensure that the local education authority by means of regular visits and inspections by advisers and other professional officers maintain an up-to-date profile of the school which is available for inspection by the governors;

128

(v) to participate in the appointment of the headteacher and other staff, (the detailed arrangements for appointments procedures to be determined by the local education authority).

(vi) to satisfy themselves that effective liaison is maintained between the school and other feeder or receiver schools or establishments;

(vii) to prescribe broad guidelines for consultation and to ensure that appropriate and effective arrangements are established at the school for consultation between the head and all staff, between the staff and governors, between staff and parents and with pupils and outside agencies;

(viii) to ensure that each year arrangements are made for parents with children entering the school for the first time to meet the head and staff and to have explained to them such matters as the aims and objectives of the school, its organisation and structure, the curriculum followed, the options available, the teaching methods used, the external examinations for which pupils are entered, the nature and scope of any recording systems and the responsibilities of the parents toward the school;

(ix) to ensure that parents and interested members of the community are invited to an annual "school meeting" at which the governors and the head and staff can give an account of their stewardship;

(x) to ensure that the procedures determined by the local education authority relating to the suspension of pupils are observed.

The headteacher would have a major role in providing administrative services for the governing body and the officers and advisers of the local education authority would also be responsible for giving advice including advice about standards of achievement within the school.

The governing body would not need to meet formally more than about twice each year since day to day management and control would rest with the head teacher and the offices of the local education authority, complemented and supported by the consultative sub-structure within the school.

In conjunction with a system of school government of this type I would lay a responsibility upon each local education authority to hold a series of public meetings throughout the authority, possibly just after the budget has been determined, to inform the public about the policies that were being pursued and the resources available. Such meetings would be attended by the Chairman of the Education Committee and the Chief Education Officer or their representatives.

I would also require each local education authority to establish one or more industrial and commercial advisory committees to report annually to the Education Committee, perhaps through the medium of a Careers Advisory Committee.

In sum, it is my firm opinion that the proposals that I have outlined would ensure that local education authorities set aims and objectives for their schools; monitored performance and maintained standards that were reasonably consistent throughout the area; effected the necessary changes in response to newly ascertained needs; kept parents and the public in general fully informed and afforded them ample opportunity to be involved in school affairs if they so wished. I believe, furthermore, that such a system would help in no small way to restore the confidence in our schools which has so recently been lacking.

APPENDIX A

Evidence

I List of witnesses who gave written evidence

A. *Organisations*

Aberystwyth Labour Party
Advisory Centre for Education
Ammanford, Llandybie and District Trades Council
Anglian Regional Management Centre
Appleton Parish Council, Warrington
Assistant Masters Association
Association for Adult Education (Cumbria Branch and Northern Region)
Association of Assistant Mistresses
Association of Career Teachers
Association of Conservative Managers and Governors in Camden, London, NW3
Association of County Councils
Association of District Councils
Association of District Secretaries
Association of Education Committees
Association of Governing and Managing Bodies in Brentwood and District, Hutton, Essex
Association of Headmistresses
Association of Metropolitan Authorities
Association for Neighbourhood Councils
Association of Polytechnic Teachers
Association of Teachers in Colleges and Departments of Further Education
Association of Teaching Religious
Association of Voluntary Aided Secondary Schools
Avon County Branch of the Association of District Councils
Aylesbury Vale Community Relations Council
Bangor and District Group of the Confederation for the Advancement of State Education
Bedford Branch of the National Association of Governors and Managers
Bedford Parents' Union
Bedfordshire County Council Education Committee
Blackburn and District Community Relations Council
The Board of Education of the General Synod of the Church of England and the National Society (Church of England) for promoting Religious Education
Bollington Town Council
Bradfield Parish Council, Sheffield
Branksome School Parent/Teacher Association, Darlington
Bridgwater and District Trades Union Council, Somerset
Brighton Pavilion Labour Party
Brighton Socialist Educational Association
British Association of Social Workers
British Educational Administration Society
British Humanist Association

131

Buckinghamshire County Branch of the Association of District Councils
Campaign for Comprehensive Education
Catholic Education Council
Catholic Teachers' Federation
The Central Council of Physical Recreation
Chesterfield Division Conservative Association
Chorley Borough Council, Lancashire
Claverdon Parish Council, Warwick
Commission for Local Administration in England
Community Relations Commission
Confederation for the Advancement of State Education
Confederation of British Industry
Coombe Lodge, Academic Staff of Further Education Staff College, Blagdon,
    Bristol
Council of Citizens of Tower Hamlets
Coventry Local Education Authority
Croydon Education Association
Croydon Guild of Social Service
Crystal Palace Triangle Community Association
Cumbria Centre Members' Council
Cumbria-Cumberland Federation of Women's Institutes
Cumbria Voluntary Action
Clwyd and Gwynedd County Branch of the Association of District Councils
Dale Abbey Parish Council, Nr Ilkeston, Derby
Darlington Borough Council
Darlington Parents' Association
Derbyshire Branch of the National Association of Governors and Managers
Devon County Labour Party
Diocesan Council for Education of the Diocese of Monmouth
Dymchurch County Primary Schools' Parents/Teachers Association, Kent
Enfield Association for Education
English New Education Fellowship
Essex County Council
The Fabian Society
Federated Committee of Parent/Teacher Associations, Llandudno
Folkestone and Hythe Divisional Liberal Association, Shepway District
Forest of Dean District Council
The Free Church Federal Council
Gedling Borough Labour Group, Mapperley, Nottingham
Gosforth West Middle School Parents Association, Newcastle upon Tyne
Greater London Area Conservative Education Advisory Committee
Greenhill Home and School Association, Beauchief, Sheffield
Gwent Headmasters' Association (prepared in consultation with the one Gwent
    Member of the Headmistresses Association)
Gwent Secondary Heads Association
Gwynedd Council of Schoolmasters
Haringey Association for the Advancement of State Education
Headmasters' Association
Headmasters' Conference
Head Teachers' Association, Birmingham

Health Visitors' Association
Heron Brook Church of England Middle School, Gnosall, Stafford
Independent Schools Joint Committee
Inner London Education Authority
Inner London Education Authority Branch of the National Association of Governors and Managers
Inner London Education Authority Parents' Consultative Committee, Division 10
The Joint Four
The Joint Four, Birmingham
The Labour Party
Lambeth-Streatham Constituency Labour Party
Lancashire County Council Labour Group
Lancaster Trades Council
Leeds City Council
Leeds City Council Liberal Group
Leeds Council for Voluntary Service
Leeds Parents' Association
Leicestershire and Rutland Federation of Women's Institutes
Liberal Party Advisory Panel on Education
Lincoln Diocesan Education Committee
Lindsey Federation of Women's Institutes
Liverpool Branches of the Confederation for the Advancement of State Education and National Association of Governors
Liverpool Education Committee
Llandaff Diocesan Council for Education
London Board of Jewish Religious Education
London Borough of Bexley
London Borough of Croydon
London Borough of Ealing
London Borough of Hillingdom
London Borough of Islington
London Church Teachers' Association
Macclesfield District Labour Party
Maidstone Borough Council
Maidstone Constituency Labour Party
Mansfield District Council
Marston Parish Council, Oxford
Meopham Fabian Society, Gravesend, Kent
Merton Education Association, London SW19
The Methodist Church Division of Education and Youth
Mid Yorkshire Conservative Federation (Barnsley, Dearne Valley, Hemsworth, Normanton and Pontefract constituencies)
Nailsea Parish Council, Bristol
National Association for Multi-Racial Education
National Association of Governors and Managers
National Association of Head Teachers
National Association of Inspectors and Educational Advisers
National Association of Local Councils
National Association of Schoolmasters and Union of Women Teachers

National Association of the Teachers of Wales
National Association of Youth and Community Education Officers
National and Local Government Officers Association
National Board of Catholic Women
National Campaign for Nursery Education
National Confederation of Parent Teacher Associations
National Council of Jewish Religious Day Schools in Britain
The National Council of Social Service Community Work Division
National Council of Women of Great Britain
The National Education Association
National Joint Committee of Working Women's Organisations
National Union of Hebrew Teachers
National Union of Public Employees
National Union of School Students
National Union of Students
National Union of Teachers
Nether Stowey Parish Council, Bridgwater, Somerset
Newcastle upon Tyne Education Committee
Newham Education Concern
Newport High Schools Combined Parents' Association, Gwent
North Devon Movement
Northumberland Association of Local Councils
Northumberland County Education Committee
Ockbrook Parish Council
Oldham and District Community Council
Oldham Council for Community Relations
Parents Consultative Committee for the Hackney Area
Penlan Parent Teacher Association, Swansea, West Glamorgan
Preston and District Amalgamated Trades Council
Preston Borough Council
Primary Management Studies, London SE9
Professional Association of Teachers
Programme for Reform in Secondary Education
Provincial Council for Education of the Church in Wales
Queen Elizabeth's Grammar School for Boys Parent Teacher Association,
    Mansfield, Notts
Queens Manor Parent/Teacher Association, London SW6
Reading Borough Council
Reading Labour Party and Reading Borough Council Labour Group of
    Councillors
Richmond Association for the Advancement of State Education
The Right to Learn Group of London Teachers
Risley Parish Council, Derby
Rochdale Education Committee
Rotherham Borough Council
Salop Education Committee
St Barnabas First School Parent Teacher Association, Oxford
St Bonaventure's Parent-Teachers-Student Association, London E7
Scarborough and Filey Area Advisory Committee for Education
School Concern

Schools Council
School Without Walls (Working Group of the English New Education Fellow-
 ship)
Selsdon Group
Sheffield Association for Education
Sheffield Branch of the National Association of Governors and Managers
Slough Corporation
Socialist Educational Association
Society of Education Officers
South Bucks Association for the Advancement of State Education
The Sports Council
Sports Council for Wales
Stafford and Stone Constituency Labour Party
Stockport Council for Voluntary Service
Stocksbridge and District Ratepayers' Action Group
Stoneleigh County Middle School Parents' Association, Surrey
Suffolk County Council Education Committee
Sutton Education Association, Carshalton, Surrey
Tooting Labour Party, London SW18
Trades Union Congress
Unit for Management in the Public Services, Sheffield Polytechnic Education
 Management Teaching Team
Wanstead and Woodford Labour Party, Woodford Green, Essex
Warrington Area Committee of the Cheshire Association of Parish Councils
Welsh Joint Education Committee
Welsh Secondary Schools Association
West Glamorgan Education Committee
West Midland Labour Party Young Socialists
Westminster Campaign for the Advancement of State Education
Woking Constituency Labour Party
Young Communist League

B. *Managing and governing bodies of the following schools:*

Anthony Gell School, Winksworth, Derby
Area Primary School, Stokenham, Devon
Ballantyne Middle School, Birkenhead, Merseyside
Bebington St John's Infant and Junior Schools, Wirral
Boston Spa Grouped Primary Schools, Leeds
Brenchley and Matfield Church of England Primary School, Kent
Bromborough Pool Primary School, Wirral
Brookhurst County Primary School, Wirral
Caerleon Endowed Junior & Infants School, Newport, Gwent
Castleton Church of England Primary School, Derbyshire
The Charles Read Secondary School, Thurlby, Lincs
The Church of England School, Elvington, York
Dowdales County Secondary School, Dalton in Furness, Cumbria
Elmers Court Special School, Lymington, Hants

135

Eynsham County Primary School, Oxford
Ferndown Upper School, Wimborne, Dorset
The Grove School, St Leonards, Sussex
Higher Bebington C J School, Wirral
Hillside Middle & Primary Schools, Wirral
The Jewish Day School, Prestwich, Lancs
King Alfred's School, Oxfordshire
Manor Middle School, Birkenhead, Wirral
Mendall County Primary School, Bromborough, Wirral
Milverton County Junior and Infants' School, Leamington Spa
Parley County First School, Dorset
Park High (Co-Educational) School, Birkenhead, Merseyside
Passmores Comprehensive School, Harlow
Pensby County Infant School, Wirral
Pensby Wood Primary School, Irby, Wirral
Riverside Primary School, Wallasey, Merseyside
Saltash Comprehensive School, Cornwall
Sarah Siddons County Secondary School, London W2
St John's Church of England School, Kingsley, Cheshire
Thomas Peacocke County Primary School, Rye
Town Lane Infants' School, Bebington, Wirral
Wallace Fields County First and Middle Schools, Ewell, Surrey
Wargrave Church of England (Controlled) Grouped Schools, Reading
Wetherby High School, Leeds
Wheldrake Church of England Aided Primary School, Yorkshire
Wirral Grammar School

C. Individuals

Elizabeth Adams, Educational Consultant, London SW19
Mr M Adams, Chairman of Managers of Pottery School, Belper and Mr J
    Knutton, Chairman of Managers of Long Row School, Belper
Mr R Aitken, Director of Education, Coventry Borough Council
Mr T Aldworth, Parent, Cambridge
Mr J Allenby, Barnsley, South Yorks
Mrs D M Ansari, Parent, School Governor and Secretary of a Parent Teacher
    Association
Mr T M Artingstoll, Workington
Dr A W Bacon, Department of Extra Mural Studies, University of Sheffield
Mr & Mrs J Bailey, London N1
Mr R J S Baker, Sheffield
Mr A J Batstone, Wellington, Somerset
Mr G Baylis, Willerby, Humberside
Mrs Baxter, School Governor, Kent
Mr C J Beedell, Educational Psychologist, Bristol
Sue Bender, London SW15
Dr R C Benians, London SW17
Mr A G Blackburn, Headmaster, Cobblers Lane Junior School, Pontefract

Mr P Boulter, Director of Education, Cumbria
Fionnuala Boyd (with Mr L Evans, Mr & Mrs J Hollins, Plungar, Nottingham)
Mrs P Bradbury, Parent, Mill Hill, London NW7
Mr P Brighton, Holywell, Clwyd
Mr J Brooks, Teacher, Stevenage, Herts
Councillor P B Burke, School Manager of Drayton First and Middle Schools, Ealing
Mrs S D Chalkley, Parent Manager, Kidderminster
Mr A Chambers, Putney, London SW15
Mr W P Coldrick, Sutton Coldfield, West Midlands
Mrs A Comino-James, Denham Village, Buckinghamshire
Mr E H Conridge, Sheffield
Mr A Norman Conway, Wirral
Mr T A Coombs, Goring, Reading
Mrs J Copley, Thorugumbald, Hull
Mr P Cornall, Headmaster, Carisbrooke High School, Newport, Isle of Wight
Mr A H Crawford, Teacher, Chairman of Aldershot Constituency Labour Party
Miss A Dale, Student Governor, Swanhurst School, Birmingham
Mr P Dannhesser, with Mrs B Diamond, Mrs N Drapkin, Mr J Fecamp, Mr P Geddes, Mr R S Hill, Mr J Hunt, Mr N Toetcher, Mrs B Wegg-Prosser and Mr A P Williams, governors of Sarah Siddons Comprehensive School, London W2
Mr J C Davies, Wellington, Somerset
Mr M H Davies, Mold, Clwyd
Mr A W Davis, Harpenden, Herts
Mr F S Dawson, Oxton, Birkenhead
Mr B Divine, Parent Manager, Tithe Barn Primary School, Stockport
Mr J Dobbs, Headmaster, Skelmersdale and Holland, West Bank High School, Skelmersdale
Councillor K S Dunn, Atherstone, Warwickshire
Mr R J Ede, Headmaster, Dorking, Surrey
Mr C P England, Bromley, Kent
Mr J Evans, Castle Bromwich, Birmingham
Mr T F Evans, Ashford, Middlesex
Mr C E L Farmer, Headmaster, Alexandra High School, Tipton
Mr D Feasey, School Governor, Lancaster
Mr P H Fielden, Sheffield
Mr G E Fisher, Parent, Birmingham
Prebendary H L Franklin, Director of Religious Education, Bath and Wells Diocesan Education Committee
Mr M L Franks, Headmaster, Mytton High School, Warwick
Mr J E E Frew, Sharrington, Melton Constable
Mr R A German, Pentre Halkyn, Clwyd
Mrs O Gibbs, Leader of the Opposition, Oxfordshire County Council
Mr R Glatter, Reader in Educational Administration, University of London Institute of Education
Mr M Glazier, Mold, Clwyd
Mr R P Godber, London SW20
Mrs D S Gould, Parent, Cirencester, Gloucester
Mrs P L Govier, Parent, London W10

Mr D H Graham, Teacher, East Boldon, Tyne and Wear
Mr E Griffiths, Blaenau Ffestiniog, Gwynedd
Councillor J H Griffiths, Rhyl, Clwyd
Mr S Hatch, Chairman, Town Development Committee, Greater London Council
Mr L A Hawke, Area Principal, Harlow Adult Education, Essex
Mrs J Heath, Hampton, Middlesex
Mr D Henschel, Headmaster, The Grammar School and Sixth Form College, Henley-on-Thames
Mr J Herbert, Headmaster, Lliswerry High School, Newport, Gwent
Mr M A Hodges, Parent, Governor, Christchurch, Dorset
Mr G L Hook, Headmaster, Wisewood School, Sheffield
Mr A G Horsnail, Business Economist, Clophill, Bedford
Mr A H Hoskyns, Head of Physics Department, NUT Representative, London NW8
Mr V Ient, Wateringbury, Kent
Mr T H James and Mr J F Mitchell, Ebbw Vale School Governors, Gwent
Dr Anne M Jepson, Area Specialist in Community Medicine (Child Health), London W2 (with Miss P A Slack, Area Nurse (Child Health) London W2 and Mr J Cleary, Area Dental Officer, London W2)
Anne Johnson, Highbury, London N5
Dr W R Jondore, Parent Manager, Cambridge
Mr R T Jones, Chief Administrative Officer, Glyndŵr District Council
Col F W S Jourdain, Crawley, Sussex
Mr H S C K Kandekore, Parent, Dunstable
Mr D J Kenner, London N2
Mr J S Kent, Lecturer, Barnsley College of Technology
Beryl Kingston, Bognor Regis, West Sussex
Mr A H Klein, Community Governor, Borough of Brent
Councillor I Lauder, Lecturer, University of Newcastle-upon-Tyne
Mr H T Legg, London SE21
Mr R Leggatt, Senior Lecturer in Education, Bedford College of Education
Mr W R G Lewis, Registrar, The University of Birmingham
Mr B Livesey, Clifton, Shefford
Mr E Lloyd Williams, Headmaster, The County Secondary School, Fishguard
Mr & Mrs A R Lord, Chipping, Preston
Mr & Mrs J Maloney, Parents, London W10
Mr John Frederick Mann, Sheffield Education Department
Mr J Mann, Lecturer in Management Studies, University of Bradford
Mr K J Masters, Headmaster, St Kevin's School, Kirkby
Mr A M McMurray, Headmaster, Ernulf School, St Neots, Huntingdon
Mr F J Message, Bexleyheath, Kent
Mr D P M Michael, CBE, Headmaster, Newport High School, Newport, Gwent
Dr E Midwinter, Project Director, National Consumer Council
Mr D Miles, Cwmbran, Gwent
Miss M E Mills, Headmistress, Franche First School, Kidderminster
Mr C Mitchell, General Secretary, Stockport Council for Voluntary Service (evidence submitted on behalf of interested people brought together by the Council for Voluntary Service)

Mr D Morrish, Member of Devon County Education Committee
Mr P Nanton, Birmington 20
Mr C J Newman, Warden, Manchester Teachers' Centre
Mr C P Nicholls, Parent, School Governor, David Hughes School, Anglesey
Mr R A Nisbet, Weybridge, Surrey
Mr B H Nottage, Chairman, Leasowe Nursery School Managing Body, Wallasey
Mr D S O'Callaghan, Ripe, Sussex
Mr P O'Connell, Vice-Chairman Dunraven School Governors, London SW16
Joyce Oldham, Senior Lecturer, Sheffield Polytechnic
Mrs D M Otter, Lincolnshire
Canon G A Pare, West Kirby, Wirral
Mr D J Pharaoh, School Manager, Wirral
Sir James Pitman, KBE, London SW3
Mr W Bernard Powell, Downend, Bristol
Mr M Prescott, Secretary to Managers of William Reynolds County Infants & Junior Schools, Telford
Mrs T A Punchard, Warden, Malden Youth and Adult Centre
Mr N Ratcliffe, Buxton, Derbyshire
Mrs M Reed, Headmistress, Latton Bush Comprehensive School, Harlow, Essex
Mr A Rees Jones, Birmingham
Councillor Miss E Rhodes, Chairman of Group 4 Primary School Managers, London Borough of Bexley
Mr C R Riches, Parent, and twenty other parents of children attending Wrestlingworth Voluntary Controlled Primary School, Sandy, Bedfordshire
Mrs E M Roberts, Head of the Faculty of Communications, Friars Upper School, Bangor
Mr M F Robertson, Keston, Kent and Diana McPetrie, Slapton, Devon
Mr E E Robinson, Principal, Bradford College, Bradford
Mr I Rodger, Brill, Aylesbury
Mr V G T Rosewell, Adviser to Teachers, University of London, Institute of Education
Mr E Rudd, Department of Sociology, University of Essex
Mr D V Rugg, Ottery St Mary, Devon
Mrs W G Saurin, Northwood, Middlesex (on behalf of a group of women teachers, school governors, and parents)
Mr M Scott Archer, Headmaster, Comprehensive School, Rhdyw
Mr B Seaman, Teacher, King Edward VII School, Kings Lynn
Mr P Segal, London NW3
Mr G W Shaw, Appleton, Nr Warrington
Dr H F Shaw, School Managers, Islip, Oxford
Mr R Shaw, Meols, Wirral
Mrs S Shaw, Chairman of the Education Committee, City of Manchester
Mr A Shippey, Headmaster, Oakdale County Primary School, Southfields, Peterborough
Mrs L Simmons, Primary Headmaster, Bromsgrove
Mr A Slater, Dartford, Kent
Mr M Sloman, School Manager, London N19
Councillor L Smith, JP, Davenport, Stockport
Councillor N W Smith, Water Orton, Nr Birmingham

Councillor L Snow, Wembley, Middlesex
Mr & Mrs R E Sparry, Trowbridge, Wilts
Mr J Spooner, Headmaster, The Carr Junior School, York
Mr J Stafford, Newport, Isle of Wight
Mr B Stephens, Burton on Trent
Mr K Tanney, Headmaster, Catholic Primary School, Whitley Bay, Tyne and Wear
Mr B Taylor, Chief Education Officer, Somerset, (with Mr R Benson, Chairman of Education Committee and Mr M Waley-Cohen, Chairman of Schools Sub-Committee)
Mr D Terry, Headmaster, The Headlands School, Swindon
Mr D J R Testro, Teacher, Woodford, London E18
Mr R E Thornbury, Warden of Sherbrooke Teachers' Centre, London
Mr P J Toogood, Stratton, Dorchester
Mrs C Towers-Perkins, Cookham Dean, Berkshire
Mr R Trippier, Headmaster, Bamford County Primary School, Rochdale
Mr I Tuckett, London SE1
Mr D A Turner, Lecturer, Sheffield City College of Education
Mr B Unwin, Headmaster, Connah's Quay High School, Clwyd
Mr J E Vaughan, Tutor Librarian, University of Liverpool
Mr & Mrs R Wakely, London SE27
Mrs J Waley, Parent Manager, Oulton Primary School, Staffordshire
Mr T R Ward, School Manager and Governor, and Margaret Cole, London SE5
Dr D Warwick, Senior Lecturer in Sociology, University of Leeds
Mr B Wates, Kendal, Cumbria
Mr K M Webster, Teacher, Cuxton, Kent
Mrs J H Welch, Parent, Morecambe, Lancs
Captain A P Wells (Retd.) Hooke, Beaminster, Dorset
Mr T H Whitehouse, Horsham, Surrey
Mr E G Williams, Thingwall, Wirral
Mr A Wilson, Parent, Leatherhead, Surrey
Mr A L Wilson, Headmaster, Buckingham
Mr J T Wilson, Mayor & Chairman of Education Committee, Dudley
Mr P S Worrall, Headmaster, Sutton-upon-Derwent School, Humberside
Mr D K Wotton, Parent, London SE1
Mrs M Young and another parent manager of Broughton County First and Middle Schools, Aylesbury, Bucks

APPENDIX B

SCHOOL MANAGING AND GOVERNING BODIES

A HISTORICAL RETROSPECT 597—1945

"People will not look forward to posterity, who never look backward to their ancestors"

(Burke. "Reflections on the Revolution in France")

Introduction

1. The purpose of this note is to describe the more important developments in the development of the concept of school managing and governing bodies. Other matter is introduced only insofar as it is needed to explain how these developments came about, to give some indication of the climate of opinion at the time and to provide a modicum of relief. Secondary school governing bodies are dealt with first because their history is so much longer than that of primary (or elementary) school managing bodies.

Secondary (or Grammar) Schools

The earliest years

2. "Le doctrine et enformation des enfants est chose espiritual" stated a Chief Justice of England in deciding a case in 1410[1]. To those of his hearers who understood him, the judge's statement would have seemed a truism. The schools were adjuncts of the Church. After St Augustine had brought his mission to this country in 597 he and his successors had to establish schools as well as churches—grammar schools to teach the English priests the foreign language (Latin) in which the services of the Church were conducted and song schools for the boys who chanted the services. The concept of education that Augustine and his followers brought with them was derived from the Roman and Hellenistic schools of rhetoric. It comprised the seven liberal arts and sciences which were regarded as preparatory to the study of theology, law and medicine. Of these the trivium—grammar, rhetoric and logic—were studies in preparation for the quadrivium—arithmetic, geometry, music and astronomy. The only one systematically taught in the grammar schools was grammar, ie Latin literature and, in particular, the necessary preliminary study of Latin grammar. The aim of the schools was strictly vocational, to prepare pupils for entry to the Church, which undertook much that was subsequently to be done by other, public bodies, and later also to the legal profession. For a long time to come Latin continued to be, to a great extent, the language of theology, law, science and diplomacy.

3. The first grammar school was, in all probability, established at Canterbury in 598 and by the reign of Edward VI the Cathedrals and the major collegiate churches, such as those at Beverley and Southwell, all had their grammar schools

---

[1] Year Book, II, Henry IV, case 21, p. 17. Cited in Fleming Report on the Public Schools.

141

and their song schools. Up to the end of the 11th century the cathedrals and collegiate churches were staffed by secular, or ordinary, priests. Of the principal members of the chapter, the chancellor was usually responsible for the grammar school, as may be seen from the Institution of St Osmund, the Foundation Statutes of Salisbury Cathedral (1091)[2]. These provided that:—

"The dean presides over all canons and vicars [choral] as regards the cure of souls and correction of conduct.

The precentor ought to rule the choir as to chanting and can raise or lower the chant.

The treasurer is pre-eminent in keeping the treasures and ornaments and managing the lights. In like manner the chancellor in ruling the school and correcting the books. . . .

The school master ought to hear and determine the lessons, and carry the church seal, compose letters and deeds and mark the readers on the table. . . ."

4. At the turn of the century there was a movement towards monasticism and at a number of cathedrals and collegiate churches the secular priests were replaced by regulars. But the Archbishop or Bishop kept control of the school and it was he who appointed the master[3]. Until 1540 all school masters were clerici and so in orders, though not necessarily holy orders, and required a licence from the Bishop to conduct a school. Canon law provided that no man should teach in a public or private school unless allowed by the bishop of the diocese or the ordinary of the place. This requirement, which was often used to protect established schools from the competition of "adulterine" establishments, was not formally repealed until the Endowed Schools Act 1869[4], though for many years before that the strictness with which it was applied varied from diocese to diocese; decisions, too, of the courts in 1670 and 1700 had reduced its scope.

The foundation of Winchester

5. From about the middle of the 14th century benefactions to monasteries began to dwindle. Instead wealthy benefactors, and in some cases Guilds, established chantries, each with its own priest, to celebrate masses for the repose of the benefactors' souls, and also, in many cases, to conduct a school. Probably the earliest of these chantry schools was the grammar school founded at Wotton-under-Edge in Gloucestershire in 1384 by Katharine Lady Berkeley. But the most significant event of this period was the founding by William of Wykeham of his "Saint Marie College by Wynchester" (1382), which was to consist of a Warden and "seventy poor and needy scholars clerks, living college-wise in the same studying and becoming proficient in grammaticals or the art, faculty or science of grammar".[5]

---

2. A. F. Leach, Educational Charters pp. 72–3.
3. It is to this that A. F. Leach (loc cit pp. XXIX and 252–261) attributes the fact that at Canterbury the master had the power of excommunication. Thomas of Birchwood (a pupil) and Richard Hall and Jane Moody (citizens) have earned a place in educational history because, having assaulted an usher or a pupil (1311–23), they suffered this penalty.
4. Section 21 of that Act provided that "In every scheme the Commissioners shall provide for the abolition of all jurisdiction of the ordinary relating to the licensing of masters in any endowed school, or of any jurisdiction arising from such licensing". The earlier, and largely ineffective, Grammar Schools Act, 1840 had preserved the rights of the Visitor and the Ordinary (the Bishop).
5. Leach, Educational Charters p. 325.

6. Wykeham's immediate purpose, as with his earlier foundation of New College at Oxford (1379), was "to cure the common disease of the clerical army, which we have seen grievously wounded by lack of clerks, due to plagues, wars and other miseries".[6]

Winchester's especial significance was that, though connected with New College, it was a separate and distinct foundation for school boys, "a sovereign and independent corporation existing by and for itself, self-centred and self-governed".[7] As such it served as the model for other later foundations, notably of Eton, and as the centuries rolled by, of many others. Many former pupils became the masters of other grammar schools and "according to the use of Winchester" is a phrase often to be read in the testamentary dispositions of other benefactors. Thus was spread what A F Leach has called "the Wykehamist afflatus". As will be seen, these were not the only educational concerns which that spirit influenced.

7. Wykeham also provided for an external assessment of the work of the school and of its food. Every year between the 7th July and the 1st October the Warden of New College and two of the "discreeter" Fellows were, at the cost of that College, to go to Winchester "with no more than six horses" and there "diligently inquire and hold a scrutiny on the government of the warden of the same college and the master teacher in grammar, the ushers under him, and the scholars and other persons living in the same, and on the teaching and progress in school of the scholars of the same college, and the quality of the food provided for the same, and other articles contained in the statues of the college at Winchester; and shall correct and reform anything needing correction or reform".[8]

Government by laymen

8. In the fifteenth century, in the less inhibited atmosphere generated by the renaissance, laymen began to be more prominent both in founding and managing schools. One of the earliest schools to be managed by a mixed body of laymen and clerics was Oswestry Grammar School, for whose benefit David Holbeach, a Welsh lawyer, bequeathed land in 1404–5.[9] In 1443 John Abbott took an even more decisive step. He made the Mercers' Company Trustees of the School which he founded at Farthinghoe in Northants.[10] John Colet did the same in 1512 when he made the Mercers' Company trustees for the "new scole at Poules". His friend Erasmus recorded that his reason for doing so was that "there is no absolute certainty in human affairs, but for his part he found less corruption in such a body of citizens than in any other order or degree of mankind".[11]

9. It was a natural development to make local laymen the trustees of a school, as did Sir John Percyval, a Merchant Taylor, when he founded a "Fre Grammar Scole" at Macclesfield in 1503 "for gentilmen's sonnes and other godemennes' children of the Towne and contre thereabouts". He did so considering that "in the countie of Chester, and specially aboute the towne of Maxfield . . . God of his

---

6. The Black Death of 1349 and the plagues of 1361 and 1367.
7. Leach, The Schools of Mediaeval England p. 208.
8. Leach, Educational Charters Statutes of New College, Oxford p. 363.
9. Leach, The Schools of Mediaeval England, p. 235
10. Leach, Educational Charters, pp. 415–7.
11. J H Lupton, John Colet, pp 166–7 (cited in G G Coulton's "Mediaeval Panorama").

habundant grace hath sent and daily sendeth to the inhabitants there copyous plentie of children, to whose lernyng and bryngyng forth in conyng and vertue right fewe Techers and Scholemaisters be in that contre".[12] From the same period dates the foundation of the grammar school at Blackburn where in 1509 the church reeves and parochyens had bought land for an "honest, seculer prest and no reguler, suffyciently lerned in gramer and playn song, if any such can be gettyn, that shall kape continually a Free Gramer Schole".[13]

The statutes of Westminster School
10. After the Reformation and up to about 1620 the industry and commerce of the country were greatly expanded and many new schools were founded by men who had prospered from this expansion. School statutes, too, became much more detailed. Thus those of Westminster, refounded by Elizabeth I in 1560 after the second disolution of the monastery there, prescribed the regime for the entire school day, beginning at 5 am when the boys, who slept two in a bed, were roused by the cry of "Surgite" till 8 pm when they went to bed.[14] The statutes of the schools at Bangor Friars (1560) and Ruthin (1564) were modelled on those of Westminster; they even prescribed the same number of pupils (120)[15].

11. The qualifications and duties of the Head Master and the Under Master, who were to be elected in turn by the Dean of Christ Church and the Master of Trinity, with the consent of the Dean of Westminster, were prescribed in no less detail.

" . . . " . . . Their duty shall be not only to teach Latin, Greek and Hebrew grammar, and the humanities, poets and orators, and diligently to examine in them, but also to build up and correct the boys' conduct, to see that they behave themselves properly in church, school, hall and chamber, as well as in all walks and games, that their faces and hands are washed, their heads combed, their hair and nails cut, their clothes both linen and woollen, gowns, stockings and shoes kept clean, neat, and like a gentleman's and so that lice and other dirt may not infect or offend themselves or their companions and that they never go out of the college precinct without leave. They shall further appoint various monitors from the gravest scholars to oversee and note the behaviour of the rest everywhere and prevent anything improper or dirty being

---

12. Leach, Educational Charters p 436.
13. Leach, The Schools of Mediaeval England, p 284.
14. Lessons started after prayers at 6 am and, with an interval for dinner, continued until 6 pm when the boys had supper. After supper there was another half-hour's work and then, after prayers, they went to bed. Intentionally or not the statutes made no provision for breakfast but in practice, apparently, the hour from 8 to 9 am was not spent in school. The regime on Saints' day was somewhat less exacting. Then, in addition to spending at least one hour before mid-day "sometimes in learning the catechism, sometimes in learning "Scripture", the boys had in the afternoon to show up to the Headmaster, a summary of the sermon preached that morning in the collegiate church – the first and second forms in English, the third and fourth forms in Latin prose and the three highest forms in verse".
15. Fleming Report on Public Schools, paragraph 244.

done. If any monitor commits an offence or neglects to perform his duty he shall be severely flogged as an example to others."[16]

The Jacobean, Georgian and early Victorian Eras

12. Greek had been added to the curriculum in many schools in the fifteenth and sixteenth centuries and also, in a few schools, Hebrew. In the seventeenth century the growing demand for ships' captains and officers with a knowledge of mathematics led to the founding of a few schools with a mathematical bias.[17] The first such school was established in Sunderland in 1652 with the aid of a grant from the Commission responsible for implementing the Act of 1650 for the Propagation of the Gospel in the four Northern Counties. (There was a similar Commission for Wales.) There was in Sunderland "exceeding great want of a Schoolmaster . . . to teach children to write and instruct them in Arithmetique to fitt them for the sea or other necessary callings"[18]

13. But further progress on these lines and the liberalizing tendencies that emerged under the Commonwealth were checked at the Restoration. The tendency to revert to the status quo ante was aggravated by the policy of ecclesiastical uniformity adopted after 1660[19] and also in that and the following century by the torpid condition of the two ancient Universities, where, according to Gibbon, "decent, easy men . . . supinely enjoyed the gifts of the founder". And throughout there operated what Dr R F Young has called "that conservative and imitative tendency which is so salient a characteristic in the evolution of English political and social institutions"—and which yields to radical change only under some dire threat of national dimensions.[20]

14. The consequence was that by the nineteenth century the grammar schools were, for the most part, very little changed from what they had always been. With the secular fall in the value of money their incomes had declined, unless they happened to own property in the newly developing commercial and industrial areas; they were poorly staffed—often by indigent and inadequately educated parsons in search of a benefice[21]; and their curriculum was limited to Latin and Greek, which had no appeal for the emerging middle classes, who for the more practical and relevant education they sought for their sons turned to the Nonconformist dissenting academies, which had been established in increasing

---

16. In his Annals of Westminster Schools (1898) John Sergeaunt in outlining this statute thought it best to leave the reference to lice in the original Latin (pediculi). But in those days he could have been confident of the ability of his readers to penetrate "the decent obscurity of a learned language". In his "History of Winchester College" (p 302) A F Leach seized on the same reference and the fact of the pupils sleeping two in a bed to draw the conclusion that Westminster was intended for a "lower class of scholar" than Winchester.
17. Well-known examples are the Mathematical Division established in 1673 within Christ's Hospital (1552), Sir Joseph Williamson's Mathematical School at Rochester (1701) and Neale's Mathematical School in Fetter Lane, London (1722).
18. Leach, Educational Charters, pp xlvii and 538.
19. "The connection of education with religion", G M Trevelyan has written, "and of religion with politics, had the grave disadvantage of continual proscription in the Universities and the schools, first of Puritan teachers by Laud, then of Laudian teachers by the Puritans, and finally of all save Anglican teachers by the Restoration Parliament". History of England (1945) p 431.
20. Spens Report p 72.
21. Like Mr Partridge in Fielding's "Tom Jones".

numbers after 1670, and to the private schools, which after 1779[22] flourished in London and the large industrial towns. Further, though the public schools had had troubles of their own and were the subject of much criticism in the press and elsewhere, some of them under energetic and enlightened headmasters were beginning to reform themselves. The development of the railways made access to them and also to the new boarding schools that were founded from 1840 onwards much easier. But, above all, the shifts of population consequent upon the industrial revolution (and in rural areas the coincident enclosure of the commons and open fields) and the growth of population due to the decline in the infant mortality rate meant that in a great many places there were schools with too little population to support them and, in the new industrial and urban areas, too few schools, or even no schools at all, to meet the needs of their greatly increased populations. These deficiencies, and others in other aspects of life, were to be emphasized, despite the nation's outward seeming prosperity, by the threat increasingly posed by its competitors overseas and by the revealing light cast on its administrative competence by the Crimean War (1852).[23]

15. The action taken set a pattern that has endured to this day. A succession of Commissions were set up to probe into different facets of the overall problem.

The Clarendon Commission

16. This Commission was set up in 1861 "to inquire into the Revenue and Management of Certain Colleges and Schools and the studies pursued and instruction given there".[24] It reported in 1864 and the subsequent Public Schools Act set up new governing bodies for these schools (with the exception of St Paul's and Merchant Taylors') and laid on them the duty of revising the statutes, which had to be submitted for the approval of the Queen in Council.

17. There were some common features which the Commission considered these governing bodies should have:—

"Such a body should be permanent in itself, being the guardian and trustee of the permanent interests of the school; though not unduly large, it should be protected by its numbers and by the position and character of the individual members from the domination of personal or local interests, or professional influences or prejudices; and we should wish to see it include men

---

22. An Act passed in that year (19 Geo III c 44) allowed Nonconformists to follow the teaching profession. A similar Act passed in 1791 (31 Geo III c 32) extended a like measure of liberty to the Roman Catholics, and made possible the establishment of the Teaching Orders in this Country.

23. "From the frozen and blood-stained trenches before Sebastopol", G M Trevelyan has written "and from the horrors of the first Scutari hospitals have sprung . . . many things in our modern life that at first sight seem far removed from scenes of war and the sufferings of our bearded heroes on the winter-bound plateau". One of these was "a new conception of the potentiality and place in society of the trained and educated woman". History of England p 653.

24. The nine schools were Eton, Winchester, Westminster, Charterhouse, St Paul's, Merchant Taylors', Harrow, Rugby and Shrewsbury.

conversant with the world, with the requirements of active life and with the progress of literature and science".25

18. The Commission also thought it important that the headmaster's responsibility should be clear and plain, and the powers of the governing body well understood and "duly exerted whenever the exercise of them is well called for". They saw no difficulty in tracing out the limits within which these powers should be confined.26

19. The Governors' powers should include, at the least:—

"The management of the property of the school and of its revenues, from whatever source derived, the control of its expenditure, the appointment and dismissal of the Head Master, the regulation of the boarding houses, of fees and charges, of Masters' stipends, of the terms of admission to the school, and of the times and length of the vacations; the supervision of the general treatment of the boys, and all arrangements bearing on the sanitary condition of the school".27

20. As regards discipline and teaching, "the Head Master should be as far as possible unfettered. Details. . . such as the division of classes, the school hours and school books, the holidays and half-holidays during the school terms, belong properly to him . . .; and the appointment and dismissal of Assistant Masters, the measures necessary for maintaining discipline, and the general direction of the course and methods, which it is his duty to conduct and his business to understand thoroughly, had better be left in his hands".28

21. But to this statement of the headmaster's responsibilities the Commission added an important qualification.

"The introduction of a new branch of study, or the suppression of one already established, and the relative degrees of weight to be assigned to different branches, are matters respecting which a better judgement is likely to be formed by such a body of Governors as we have suggested, men conversant with the requirements of public and professional life and acquainted with the general progress of science and literature, than by a single person, however able and accomplished, whose views may be more circumscribed and whose mind is liable to be unduly pressed by difficulties of detail. What should be taught, and what importance should be given to each subject are therefore questions for the Governing Body; how to teach is a question for the Head Master."29

---

25. Clarendon p 5. In reproducing this passage in "the Government and Management of Schools" (page 12) Baron and Howell by a strange aberration make it conclude ". . . progress of literature and letters", notwithstanding that so worded it would be incompatible with the passage about the control of the curriculum which they reproduce on p 13. They also omit from the passage about discipline and teaching the words 'as far as possible' and reproduce 'school terms' as "school time".
26. Clarendon p 5.
27. Clarendon p 6.
28. Clarendon p 6.
29. Clarendon p 6.

22. At the same time the Commission emphasised that it was important that, before coming to any decision affecting in any way the management or instruction of the school, the Governors should:—

"not only . . . consider attentively any representations which the Head Master may address to them, but of their own accord . . . consult him in such a manner as to give ample opportunity for the expression of his views".[30]

23. The Commission were also impressed by the practice introduced by Dr Arnold at Rugby, and followed by Dr Butler at Harrow, but not at Eton, of meeting all his assistants for consultation at frequent intervals. They therefore recommend the establishment of a school council, consisting of the Head Master, in the chair, and the assistants (or some of them), which should consider any matters which might be brought before them by the Head Master or other member of the council, affecting the instruction or discipline of the school; which should be entitled to advise the Head Master, "but not to bind or control him in any way"; and which should have the right of addressing the Governing Body whenever a majority of the whole Council thought fit.[31]

24. Finally it may be noted that the Commission were not oblivious of the part that parents could play. If, they said, the parents' real object in sending a boy to a public school:—

"is merely or chiefly that he should make advantageous acquaintances and gain knowledge of the world, this is likely to be no secret to him, and the home influence which ought to be the Master's most efficacious auxiliary becomes in such cases the greatest obstacle to progress."[32]

The Taunton Commission

25. This Commission was appointed in 1864 to inquire into those schools which did not fall within the remit of the Clarendon Commission or the Newcastle Commission on Popular Education of 1858. They considered 782 grammar schools, as well as proprietary and private schools, and also the secondary education of girls, to which, in the event, they gave a considerable impetus. Their recommendations for the setting up of Provincial Authorities were not accepted but others formed the basis of the Endowed Schools Act of 1869 which set up an Endowed Schools Commission to approve new schemes for the schools.[33]

26. The Commission found that the country was "in some places thickly dotted with grammar schools, which have fallen into decay because they give undue prominence to what no parents within their reach desire their children to learn". The first requisite they concluded was:—

"to adapt the schools to the work which is now required of them, by prescribing such a course of study as is demanded by the needs of the country. ."[34]

---

30. Clarendon p 6.
31. Clarendon p 6.
32. Clarendon p 40.
33. The Commission's powers were subsequently transferred to the Charity Commission and in 1899 to the Board of Education.
34. Taunton p 576.

27. They were equally convinced of the need for the different duties and powers of the various authorities in charge of schools to be precisely defined. It is unnecessary to set out in full their recommendations about the responsibilities of the governors and of the headmaster since in all essentials they followed those of the Clarendon Commission.[35]

28. What is of interest are the failings which the Commission's Assistant Commissioners found when they investigated the government of individual schools. Some of these were, of course, peculiar to the time; others were ordinary human failings, which could recur.

29. The grammar schools which the Commission investigated fell into three main classes, according to whether the patrons or trustees or governors were:—

   i. One or two (rarely more) persons, representatives of the founders, either as heirs or proprietors of certain manors or lands.

   ii. A society of persons already associated for other purposes, such as a municipal corporation, livery company, an Oxford or a Cambridge College, and the dean and chapter of a cathedral.

   iii. A body specially created and continued for the administration of the school or of the charity or charities of which it formed a part.

30. It is unnecessary to say much about the schools in class i, which were relatively few in number. It included a few which were well-known, such as the schools at Bromsgrove, Newcastle-under-Lyme and Wotton-under-Edge.[36] It also included one, at Bosworth, which had been famous for its mismanagement in former times (1787), the property having been misappropriated and a "waiter in a public house" having been appointed master.

31. Of the schools in class ii the Commission found that the fears of danger to grammar schools from government by municipal corporations found no confirmation in the state of the 20 which were so governed.

32. It was a different matter with the schools whose trustees were City Companies or Colleges. Of the 27 under City Companies 10 or 12 were described as being really useful. The rest were not all bad but some appeared to involve a great waste of money, while others would have not been missed if they had not existed. It was much the same with the 17 schools which had Colleges as trustees. Three[37] were described as being in a miserable condition, the others needed much help, encouragement and oversight. A fourth, the grammar school at Thame (now part of a flourishing comprehensive school), which had been founded in 1574 by Lord Williams, on the model of Winchester but with the Warden and Fellows of New College as its trustees, was described as "one of the greatest scandals in the country". It had two masters receiving £300 between them, one of whom also had a good house. When the Assistant Commissioner visited

---

35. There was, however, one new issue to which they addressed their minds – whether in a day school the headmaster ought to be allowed to expel a boy without reference to the governors. On the whole, it seemed to them best to allow a master to expel a day scholar till the end of the term or half year, but not finally to expel him without the governor's sanction. Taunton p 617.
36. See para 5.
37. Portsmouth, Middleton (in Lancashire) and Childrey.

the school he found one boy in it.[38] There were in all four boys on the books, two of them sons of the Master. The registrations were entered in an old buttery book of New College, in which the headings for "cheese", "butter" etc were occasionally erased and the names of boys entered. Yet within a short distance of the school there was a private school with 80 boarders and 40 day boys and fees higher than those of the Grammar School.

33. The lessons that the Commission drew from their review of these schools were, first, the serious disadvantage of non-resident trustees and, in the case of the College schools, the serious risk of a conflicting pecuniary interest. This risk also affected the cathedral schools.

34. But it was class iii that was by far the most numerous, about three quarters of the schools investigated. Among the governing bodies of these schools the commonest failing was neglect.[39] It is hardly surprising that undue interference was rare, though the Commission did note that at 'Bath a reporter was present at the quarterly meeting of the trustees and the pettiest details are circulated in the local paper'. Other failings noted were defects in the constitution of governing bodies—the requirement of residence within a small area;[40] the fact that those appointed tended to be of a different social class from the pupils;[41] the tendency for co-option to result in the appointment of like by like; the exclusion of dissenters;[42] and the tendency of ex-officio members to be non-resident and inactive.

35. There were also defects in the size of governing bodies. Some were too small, others too large. At Blackburn, for example, there were 50 on the governing body of the grammar school. At Normanton a revenue of £10 was entrusted

---

38. The boy was aged 11 years 9 months and was the son of a farmer; his reading and arithmetic were bad, his spelling very bad.

39. At Lewes, the then trustees, who had been appointed in 1852 had not met since 1859 – five years before the Commission was appointed. At Burtonwood the full number of trustees was 15. Of the three surviving when the Assistant Commissioner made his visit, two were paralytic and one an imbecile.

40. The Commission were really in a dilemma. "Trustees who are non-resident, as many county gentlemen often are non-resident for all practical purposes, are often little better than no trustees at all; trustees who are chosen from a narrow area, and perpetually on the spot, if they have not a tendency to be meddlesome, are least likely to take wise and enlightened views." But they did cite the Heath Grammar School at Halifax as an exception to the disadvantages usually attendant on the appointment of governing bodies from within parochial limits. Because the parish of Halifax was one of the most extensive in England, the range of choice open to the governors when they filled up vacancies was very large. "They watch over the interests of the school with much more care and judgment and evince the greatest desire to increase its usefulness."

41. Though the Commission accepted that the class of the parents should be well represented, they thought it very undesirable that the parents themselves should have much power of interference. They cited, with evident approval, the dictum of one of their Assistant Commissioners, that "judicious parents, when they have once reposed confidence in a school master, never do interfere. They are nevertheless subject to all the evils resulting from the interference of other parents more ignorant than themselves".

42. Governing bodies were usually composed exclusively of Anglicans, the law often requiring such a restriction, and the power of self selection supplying the deficiencies of the law. It was reported to the Commission that in Birmingham, where at least half the population were dissenters, the governing body of King Edward VI School had once had a majority of governors who were non-conformists, "but accident having given the opportunity to the churchmen, none but churchmen were ever afterwards elected".

to a body composed of various ex-officio persons "who can hardly have been thought likely to be less than 20, and might be almost any number". When the Assistant Commissioner visited the school he found the master "leisurely reading 'Bell's Life in London', and eleven children following their own devices". And, of course, there were instances of incompetence or indifference—on the part of masters and trustees together. Thus at Whitgift's Hospital, Croydon, the Assistant Commissioner was informed that the late master found no pupils attending the school when he came, and never had any at all during the 30 odd years that he was master.

36. In the Commission's view the greatest danger to be apprehended was neglect. They therefore recommended that bodies of trustees for grammar schools should be specially appointed for the purpose, or at least be resident within a moderate distance, and have a natural interest in the school; they should have no pecuniary interest in the estates; and if the schools were not to suffer, they should be controlled in their selection of free scholars and exhibitions by a test of intellectual qualification.

The Bryce Commission

37. This Commission, the first to include women,[43] was set up in March 1894 "to consider what are the best methods of establishing a well organised system of Secondary Education in England, taking into account existing deficiencies, and having regard to such local sources of revenue from endowments or otherwise as are available or may be made available for this purpose and to make recommendations accordingly". Its report, which was submitted in 1895, led directly to the establishment, in 1899, of the Board of Education.[44] The Commission had also recommended the establishment of local authorities for secondary education. In the event this precise recommendation was not adopted. Instead the Education Act 1902 made the recently created county councils and county borough councils authorities for higher, as well as for elementary education, with power to "supply or aid the supply of higher education. . . to provide or assist in providing scholarships. . . and to pay or assist in paying the fees of students at schools or colleges or hostels within or without that area". (It also made some 169 borough and urban district councils the authorities, under Part III, for elementary education in their areas.)

38. The Commission accepted that in many boroughs, and even in the smaller counties, there would be advantage in the local authorities performing the functions of a governing body. "But in the larger areas such a course would overburden them and interfere with their more important functions. On this ground, and from a desire to preserve continuity as far as possible in the management of schools, most of those who addressed us on the subject were in favour of governing bodies independent within their own spheres of the Local Authority

---

43. They were Lady Caroline Cavendish, Dr Sophie Bryant and Mrs E M Sidgwick.
44. The Board of Education Act, 1899, merged the powers of the Education Department and the Science and Art Department; the powers of the Charity Commissioners in respect of educational charities were transferred to the Board, which was also authorised to inspect "any school supplying secondary education and desiring to be so inspected" (Section 3(1)).

. . . As a rule, no doubt, these would, in the case of endowed schools, continue to be constituted separately for each school, but where there are a considerable number of schools fairly close to another, a suggestion made to us with regard to London, for placing groups of schools under a single governing body deserves consideration . . . "

39. The Commission further recommended that the local authority should be represented on the governing bodies of endowed schools which it aided and should have a majority on the governing bodies of unendowed public schools. They also recommended that in a school wholly or partially for girls the governing body should include women. "The proportion must vary according to circumstances but there should be no obstacle in the way of a body composed mainly or even exclusively of women".[45]

40. As to the functions of governing bodies the Commission took the view that, subject to any general rules made by the local authority, the governing body should be entrusted with the general supervision of the school and with the exercise of such supervision over the management, teaching and curriculum as was usually conferred on governing bodies by schemes under the Endowed Schools Act.[46]

41. The relation between the governing body and the headteacher on questions of internal management was seen by the Commission as being more one of co-operation than of employer and employed. They considered it essential that they should be brought together as closely as their respective duties permitted. But because, in their view, a headteacher could not be an ordinary governor and might be more embarrassed than helped by being treated as such, they recommended that every headteacher of a public secondary school should be entitled to sit, but not to vote, on the governing body of his or her school, except when the governing body for special reasons considered that that would be inexpedient.[47]

1902-1939   Action under the 1902 Act

42. "The organisation and the development of the education given in secondary schools is the most important educational question of the present day" said the Board in their report for 1903/4 in reviewing progress since the enactment of the 1902 Act. "As soon as we pass beyond the sphere of Elementary Education proper (or what may conveniently be called by the almost disused name of Primary Education) . . . we plunge into chaos".[48] "The object of the first importance . . . is to establish a standard of quality rather than to hasten an increase in quantity." The latter was considered to be mainly a matter for the Local Education Authorities. The Board sought to achieve the objective they

---

45. Bryce, paras 110, 111.
46. Bryce, para 114.
47. Bryce, para 115.
48. Annual Report 1905/6 p 45.

had set themselves by the processes of inspection and through the medium of the Regulations for Secondary Schools, which were issued annually.[49]

43. This is not the place to examine the soundness of the Board's conception of secondary education or to go into the question whether Sir Robert Morant sought to shape the schools in the image of the public schools. It must suffice to make two points. The first is that in the following half century there was to be a very considerable expansion of secondary education[50] and that, in the opinion of an eminent historian, the 1902 Act went a long way to remedying England's most obvious weakness—her dearth of higher educated personnel.[51] The second is that, though as Permanent Secretary Morant[52] occupied the dominant position among officials and was, obviously, a dominating as well as dynamic personality, who provided the drive and much of the guidance, the planning of the new system of secondary education was not just the work of himself. In particular the formulation of the Regulations was very largely a team effort.[53]

44. In the very first body of Regulations for Secondary Schools, those for 1902/3, it was laid down that "every school must be under the superintendence of a body of Managers responsible to the Board" and that the managers should appoint a person to act as correspondent with the Board. Specific provision was also made for a local authority to be the managing body of a school or group of schools.[54]

45. The next year the term "governors" appeared as an alternative to "managers", and superseded it altogether in the regulations for the following year (1904/5). The regulations for that year, which were framed with the express purpose of "promoting the provision and organisation of Secondary Schools, each . . . [with] a clearly defined purpose, and a well-considered scheme of

---

49. Among the first steps taken by the Board were the establishment at South Kensington of a Secondary Branch and the strengthening of the Inspectorate. The first head of the Secondary Branch was W N Bruce, a former Charity Commissioner, who had been the Bryce Commission's secretary. Up to the middle of 1904 the Board conducted its inspections through the Inspectors previously employed by the Science and Art Department, with the assistance of men and women of established reputation in the educational world who were engaged for particular inspections. During 1904/5 a permanent staff was built up specifically for the inspection of Secondary Schools. Annual Report. 1913–14. Chapter I. Inspection of Secondary Schools by the State. Its History and Character.
50. In 1904/5 the number of secondary schools recognised for grant was 491 with 85,358 pupils. The corresponding figures for 1925 were 1,161 and 334,194, nearly half the latter girls. Over the same period the number of schools provided or controlled by Local Education Authorities rose from less than 200 in 1906 to 624 in 1925.
51. Sir Robert Ensor. "England 1870–1914".
52. It is a pity that there is no adequate full scale biography of Morant. The best short account of him is by his successor, Sir Amherst Selby-Bigge, in the Dictionary of National Biography. A penetrating and informative assessment of his work was contributed, on the centenary of his birth, by Professor Eaglesham to the British Journal of Educational Studies, Vol XII, No 1 November 1963.
53. At that time, and indeed up to the end of the 1914–18 War, the Board recruited its office staff directly and not, like other Departments, through the Civil Service Commission. Many of those so recruited had already earned, or were to earn, distinction in other walks of life, such as E K Chambers, J W Mackail, and C S Schuster, all of whom were involved in one way or another in work on the Regulations for Secondary Schools.
54. See Regulation VII and its side note.

instruction, suiting it to take its proper place in an organised system of National Education", stipulated that:—

"The school must be conducted by a body of governors. The constitution and functions of the Governing Body, and their relation to the teaching staff, must be such as the Board can approve . . . "

46. In the Prefatory Memorandum to those regulations, after an expression of the Board's desire to work in harmony with the Local Education Authorities, it was stated that:—

"the Board regard it as of great importance both that local interest in the management of schools should be preserved and developed, and that the Head Master or Head Mistress should not be liable to any unnecessary interference in matters of school administration for which he or she is primarily responsible. The immediate relations of the Head Master or Head Mistress will be with the Governing Body; and the control of the Local Education Authority over the school, and its relations with the school staff, should be exercised through the Governing Body.

In order to secure the best local knowledge and the best educational experience, the functions of the Governors, and their discretion in exercising them, must therefore both be considerable. Nothing should be done to discourage the best men and women available from serving as Governors of schools, or to weaken their sense of responsibility for the effective discharge of their functions; and control exercised too closely or too minutely by the Local Education Authority would leave insufficient scope in these respects to the Governors, except by their encroaching in turn on the sphere of the Head Master or Head Mistress, a result which would be no less undesirable."

47. The 1904/5 Regulations continued substantially unchanged until a fresh body of regulations was made for 1907/8. The primary purpose of these Regulations was to secure for the schools freedom from denominational restrictions or requirements, representative local control and accessibility to all classes of the people. They also stipulated that:—

"the system on which the School is conducted and managed must be such as the Board can approve. It must define clearly both the ultimate responsibility for general control, and also the immediate responsibility for the details of management, including that of the Head Master or Head Mistress and the teaching staff for carrying on the School within the lines laid down for its work.

Where the school is not provided by a Local Education Authority, it must be conducted by a body of Governors acting under and in accordance with . . . [an instrument] which defines the constitution and functions of the governing body and their relations to the teaching staff. . . "

The Governing Body had to include a majority of representative governors, "appointed or constituted by local representative authorities, or elected by popular local constituencies". With it rested the appointment and dismissal of the head master or head mistress, which were not to be subject to any further approval except that of a local representative authority or combination of local representative authorities.

48. It was still possible for a Local Education Authority (or one of its committees) to be the governing body of a school. That was made clear in the Regulations for 1909/10 which stated that "the Governing Body of the School, where it is not a Local Education Authority or a Committee of a Local Education Authority, must contain a majority of representative Governors. . . . "

49. Towards the end of 1908 the Board had issued a model form of Articles of Government for schools provided by a Local Education Authority (Form 245). In the Prefatory Memorandum to the 1909/10 Regulations it was stated that:—

"This form is not prescribed, but may be adopted when desired with such adaptations as may be suitable for the particular School. It will in any case be useful as showing the points on which the Board lay stress. Any alternative form of instrument may be proposed for acceptance which makes satisfactory provision for (a) the composition of the Governing Body; (b) the appointment and dismissal of assistant teachers; (c) the powers and responsibilities of the Head Master or Head Mistress; and (d) the relations of the Governing Body to the Local Education Authority in respect of finance. The Governing Body should be so constituted as to ensure that it shall be in full personal touch with the School, that it shall have time and interest for the effective discharge of its duties, and that it shall not be overloaded with other functions. There should be secured to the Head Master or Head Mistress a voice in appointment and dismissal of the assistant staff, and a right to submit proposals to, and be consulted by, the Governing Body."

50. The Board's subsequent efforts to secure compliance with this model brought it into conflict with Leeds and some other Local Education Authorities, principally those in the industrial belt running from Birmingham through Yorkshire to the north-east. It is unnecessary to go into the details of the conflict.[55] Its nature and its outcome were colourfully summarized by Professor Eaglesham when in his article about Morant he wrote:—

"He had envisaged the state secondary school of the future as mirroring the great public school as he knew it—with a responsible governing body, a self-respecting headmaster and a life and soul of its own. He found that many local officials had very different ideas. They planned to run all the secondary schools of their area under one higher education sub-committee, on one uniform pattern, with the headmasters in a subordinate position and without direct access to any responsible body of governors.

Morant fumed and stormed against these petty bureaucrats, as he called them, 'who would technicalize every school in the place'; he cajoled them and he threatened; he even withdrew grants to recalcitrant authorities; but he only partially succeeded (and to this day his plans for locally maintained secondary schools with real status have not come to full fruition).

His partial failure doubtless reflected the strength of local bureaucracy, but it was also in some measure a result of his greatest weakness as an administrator—the tendency, which we have already noticed, to personify opposition."

---

55. There is an account of it in Baron and Howell's "The Government and Management of Schools" (pp 17–23).

51. There is another point to be made. Annex I sets out the more important provisions of a scheme made in 1871 by the Endowed Schools' Commission for the Grammar School of King Charles I in Bradford, of the 1909/10 Model and of the 1945 Model. As will be seen, the 1909/10 Model derived a great deal from the work of the Endowed Schools' Commission, just as it, in turn, influenced the 1945 Model.

52. After Morant left the Board, in 1911, the 1909/10 Regulations continued in force up to 1917 and the new Regulations which were made in that year repeated word for word the management provisions of the 1909/10 Regulations. These provisions indeed continued substantially unchanged until they were superseded by an entirely fresh body of regulations made under a different Act.

The types of Grant Aided Grammar School

53. At this point it may be helpful to describe the different types of secondary grammar school that came into being under the 1902 Act since they were described by terms that were also used in the 1944 Act but with a different connotation. Authorities could exercise their powers under the 1902 Act by building new schools; by aiding schools provided by others and by paying the fees of pupils not under their control. When the Act came into operation a number of schools were already receiving a capitation grant from the Board—a survival from the old grants to Science and Art classes; others were recognised for the first time. Some of these also received aid from the local education authority. This was of no consequence until 1919 when, following the introduction of percentage grants to local education authorities, it was considered that the Board should not pay direct grant to a school and percentage grant to the local education authority on its expenditure in aiding that same school. Accordingly schools were given the option to decide by 1926 whether they would receive grant direct from the Board or indirectly through the local education authority.

54. There were, therefore, three main types of school:

i. Provided and Maintained schools (usually referred to as "maintained schools"). This category included all schools provided or fully maintained by local education authorities. It also included a certain number of former endowed schools which, owing to the depletion of their resources, had been "municipalised". A scheme had been framed placing them virtually under the control of the local education authority.

ii. Aided schools, ie all other schools which received their grant solely through the local education authority. They were usually regulated by schemes or similar instruments.

iii. Direct grant schools, ie those schools which received grant direct from the Board.

The Welsh Intermediate Schools

55. In Wales events had taken a somewhat different course. Following the report of the Committee on Intermediate and Higher Education in Wales (1881),

156

the Aberdare report, the Welsh Intermediate and Technical Education Act of 1889 provided for the establishment for each county and county borough of a joint education committee. It was the duty of these committees to prepare and submit, through the Charity Commissioners, for the approval of the Education Department in Whitehall, schemes for the provision of intermediate and technical education in their areas. The Act also provided for the establishment of a Central Welsh Board to co-ordinate the system, inspect the schools and examine their pupils.

56. The schemes provided for a county governing body, who acted mainly as trustees, and a local, undenominational and representative, governing body for each school. Many of the provisions of these schemes are like those in English schemes. It is, however, noteworthy that the appointment (and dismissal) of the headmaster was vested in the county governing body, which had first to consider a written report by a specially constituted committee. This committee consisted of not less than seven persons, of whom three were to be local governors and four county governors. The latter were not appointed until it was known who the local governors were to be.

57. The purpose of the Act of 1889 was to bring secondary education within the reach of the whole population. The county committees, therefore, followed a policy of establishing several day schools in each county rather than a few large schools with hostel provision or to which pupils could be conveyed. By the end of 1903 there were no less than 96 intermediate schools, of which 17 were old foundations and 79 new schools. If they did not wholly achieve the expectations of their founders, it was because the Central Welsh Board, established in 1896, tended to over-emphasise its examination responsibilities and the parents were vociferous in their demands for certificates. The local governors had discretion to arrange a suitable curriculum[56] and some of them sought to influence their headmasters towards a less academic bias. In general, however, they had little real influence over the curriculum[57]. The consequence was that notwithstanding the clear intentions of the Act and of the schemes made under it that the instruction should be suited to the needs of each district, the schools tended to be forced into a uniform mould and their curricula concentrated on standard examinable subjects.

1939-45

58. In the inter-war years there had been no significant developments though there was no lack of ideas about what needed to be done. Once more in the history of this country it was to be a major war that was to be the catalyst which

---

56. The earlier schemes, such as that of Caernarvonshire (1893), prescribed a core curriculum and a number of optional extra subjects. This common core was not the same in all the early schemes and from 1912 onwards such detailed prescription was abandoned.

57. Owen M Edwards, the Chief Inspector for Wales, discovered to his surprise that "in one school the Governors admitted that they had never regarded the drawing up of school courses as part of their duties, and had left this in the hands of the Headmaster, whose natural tendency was to disregard the adaptation of education in favour of the demands of examinations, and a good haul of certificates". Leslie Wynne Evans, Studies in Welsh Education, p 294.

precipitated a real advance. At the beginning of the war the conditions and habits of many of the evacuees from the more densely populated urban areas had appalled the rest of the country. Thereafter the crumbling of the evacuation scheme, the persistence of half-time schooling and the delay in starting up school medical and meals services for the returning evacuees gave rise to increasing criticism of the education services and of the Board for what was considered to be the weakness of its authority.

The Green Book

59. On the 19 October 1940 while Mr. Ramsbotham (later Lord Soulbury) was still President, the Board's main office was established in the Branksome Dene Hotel at Bournemouth.[58] There, in the pine-laden atmosphere and within sight of the gently swelling sea and even though disturbed from time to time by an air raid,[59] the Board's senior officers had ample opportunity to reflect on the measures needed in the field of education to achieve the Prime Minister's ideal of "establishing a state of society where the advantages and privileges which hitherto have been enjoyed only by the few, shall be far more widely shared by the men and youth of the nation as a whole".

60. The proposals of the Board's officials were set out in "Education After the War", the Green Book which was circulated, on a strictly confidential basis, to selected recipients in June 1941.[60] These proposals were the basis of much (though by no means all) of what was subsequently to be enacted in the Education Act 1944. The fundamental aim was to secure a greater unification of the educational system and a wider spread of its benefits. With this in mind, it was proposed, among many other things, that the existing differentiation between elementary and secondary education should be abolished and that, instead, there should be three stages of education, primary, secondary and further; the provision of secondary education should be a duty and not just a power of local education authorities; all schools at the secondary stage should be subject to a single Code of Regulations "providing for equality of treatment in such matters as accommodation, size of classes, etc"; and all secondary schools provided, maintained or aided by local education authoties should be free. Fees, it was suggested, should continue to be charged in the direct grant grammar schools.

61. Inevitably the Green Book had a great deal to say about the dual system (of provided, or council, and non-provided, or voluntary, schools), and it was predominantly in that context that the position of managing and governing bodies was considered. It was believed that, instead of ending the dual system, public opinion would look for some measure of extended financial assistance

---

[58.] The staff were billeted in nearby hotels and a variety of boarding houses, with names like "Linga Longa". The Bournemouth contingent and the small cadre which, with the Minister and their private offices, had remained at Alexandra House, Kingsway, were reunited in London at Belgrave Square on the 5th November, 1942, much to the relief of all concerned.

[59.] In one of these raids several members of the staff were seriously injured.

[60.] In response to Parliamentary and other pressures, a very brief summary was published on 24th October 1941. The whole book has now been published as an Appendix to Middleton and Weitzman's "A Place for Everyone" (Gollancz 1976). It deserved a better setting.

to the non-provided schools, "accompanied, as it must be, by such extended public control as is necessary, not simply to secure a quid pro quo, but to ensure the effective and economical organisation and development of both primary and secondary education".

62. It is unnecessary to go into the details of the Green Book proposals in this particular sphere since they were, in the event, superseded. It is, however, of interest that whereas it was proposed that a local education authority should have the duty to maintain a non-provided secondary modern school, it was not considered necessary to impose a similar obligation on local education authorities in the case of aided secondary grammar schools. It was thought that it could be left to Authorities to decide whether in the altered circumstances brought about by the abolition of fees they would continue to aid the school on the existing basis, or demand, as a condition of continued aid, a greater measure of control in the governance of the school. It was also proposed that the management of non-provided modern schools should be in the hands of governing bodies constituted in accordance with the regulations applicable to secondary schools generally. Aided secondary schools already had such governing bodies.

63. Mr. Butler had succeeded Mr. Ramsbotham as President in July 1941 and it was he who conducted the ensuing discussions with interested organizations, which lasted, on and off, from November 1941 to April 1943. In these discussions attention was largely concentrated on the proposals for the reform of the dual system and such issues as the redefinition of the stages of education and the recasting of the units of administration. The local education authority Associations thought that all post-primary schools, including the direct grant schools, should be governed and administered on similar lines; they objected to the continuance of the direct grant schools because they had too little control over the appointment and actions of the governors.[61] The Headmasters' Conference naturally took a contrary line; they agreed that in many areas financial dependence on the local education authorities would be no handicap, but elsewhere they had reason to fear a rigid control by the Education Committee and, still more, by the Director of Education.

64. At first the position of the aided secondary schools attracted little attention but the implications of the proposals for the recasting of the dual system had not escaped the notice of Canon Spencer Leeson.[62] In a letter to Sir Maurice

---

61. At that time Dr Percival Sharp (formerly of Sheffield) was secretary of the AEC. The CCA and the AMC's principal advisers were directors of education of the "old guard", such as J L Holland (Northants), F A Hughes (Staffordshire), W G Briggs (Derbyshire) and P D Innes (Birmingham). A less authoritarian breed of chief education officers was not to emerge in any significant numbers or in positions of influence until later.

62. Canon Spencer Leeson was born in 1892 and educated at Winchester and New College. After serving in the 1914–18 War he was an Assistant Principal at the Board of Education from 1919 to 1924. He left to become a schoolmaster and was Headmaster of Winchester from 1935 to 1946, when he became Rector of St Mary's, Southampton. Appointed Bishop of Peterborough in 1949 he died on the 27 January 1956.

He was Chairman of the Headmasters' Conference from 1939 to 1945 and with A B Emden, Principal of St Edmund's Hall and G G Williams, the head of the Board's Secondary Branch, he was a member of the unofficial "Committee of Three" which produced a report on the prospects, which at the time seemed gloomy, of the public

Holmes on the 16 December 1942 he said:—

". . . the Grant Aided Schools are full of suspicion . . . they have got the impression that the local education authorities are trying to circumvent their freedom, first, by proposing the abolition of fees, and, secondary, by manipulating the Dual System in ways with which the Headmasters are not familiar; and many of the Headmasters suspect that the Board are with the local education authorities in this matter."[63]

65. This was followed by a meeting, on 18 December 1942, between the President and representatives of the two Governing Bodies' Associations, led respectively by the Bishop of London and the Earl of Besborough, the Headmasters' Conference, and the four associations which constituted the "Joint Four".[64]

66. At this meeting it was represented by Canon Leeson and others that the abolition of fees in "aided" schools was an indirect attempt to destroy their independence; continuation under an independent governing body was life to them and headmasters would resist the destruction of their freedom to the limit of their power. They did not wish to see the life of the schools subject to the ebb and flow of local politics. Examples were cited of interference by local education authorities over such matters as the teaching of Greek and the continuation of contingents of the Officers' Training Corps; such interference was said to be specially serious in the north of England and in the county boroughs. If only the President could contrive to smooth out the administrative difficulties without infringing the independence of the school he would find he had their support. Mr. Butler told the deputation that it was unthinkable that the secondary schools should be left in isolation, untouched by reform. They must shortly face the day when tuition fees would be abolished and he put it to them that, as well as benefiting financially, they would be better off under the arrangements he was now proposing. (These were the new proposals for the reform of the dual system which had superseded the Green Book proposals, and were to be announced in the White Paper on Educational Reconstruction (Cmnd 6458).) Under these proposals their relationships with the local education authorities would be clearly defined, instead of their being left to be subjected to whatever conditions of aid the local education authority chose to impose, or even municipalised. He cited the severe conditions for grant to aided schools laid down by the Birmingham local education authority as an indication of what they could expect. No definite conclusions were reached

<hr />

schools. The activities of this committee led directly to the passing of the Public and Other Schools War Conditions Act, 1941, and indirectly, when representative governors decided it was time they took charge, to the establishment in 1940 of the Association of Governing Bodies of Public Schools (GBA) and in 1942 of its feminine counterpart (GBGSA). The sequel to that was the establishment in July 1942 of the Fleming Committee on "The Public Schools and the General Educational System". Canon Leeson had a slight stammer which was most noticeable when his feelings were deeply moved. At one meeting at Belgrave Square he advanced from the back of the conference room where he had been sitting within a few feet of the President, not, as some though to attack him but to overcome the difficulty he was having in uttering the words "But, Minister!".

63. PRO File Ed 136/261.
64. PRO File Ed 136/224

beyond Mr. Butler's undertaking to write to the associations setting out his proposals, of which he had given a detailed account at the beginning of the meeting.

The Fleming Committee's special report on the abolition of fees

67. Prior to this meeting Mr Butler had, on 7th November, 1942, invited the Fleming Committee to make known to him their views, about the suggestion, on which "a good deal of discussion has taken place", that tuition fees should be abolished in grant-aided secondary schools. His reason for seeking the Committee's views was that a number of these schools were public schools as defined in the Committee's terms of reference.

68. The Committee's report, which was submitted in April 1943, has by now passed into oblivion.[65] Mr Butler was disquieted by the majority's recommendation that fees should be abolished in direct grant, as well as in maintained schools[66]. Mr Chuter Ede while accepting the conclusion of the majority was unimpressed by either its arguments or those of the minority.[67] Nevertheless the views expressed in the report about the respective responsibilities of local education authorities, governing bodies and headteachers both reflected and influenced the trend of thinking within the Department[68] and outside it and also affected subsequent developments. Because it still merits study there is reproduced in Annex II the passage in which the Committee described their basic approach.

69. The Committee saw themselves faced with two problems—defining and safeguarding the functions and duties of the governors and teachers in the internal organization of secondary schools of all types; and preserving within the grant-aided system a type of school in which the governors and teachers should enjoy the fullest autonomy compatible with the general responsibilities of local education authorities for their areas.

70. Basing themselves upon the experience of forty years of secondary education administered by local authorities, the Committee's answer was to propose that suitable instruments or articles of government should be adopted by the local education authorities and governors on the lines of a model prepared by the Board of Education, after due consideration of the views of the parties involved. They further recommended that these instruments or articles should be given statutory sanction and that the principles on which they should be based should be included in the Bill. They did not, of course, think that the same instruments or articles would necessarily be suitable for all types of schools but they did believe that the principles they advocated should apply to maintained no less than to aided schools.

---

65. There is, for example, no reference to it in Baron and Howell's "The Government and Management of Schools".
66. Personal knowledge.
67. Copy of minute dated 27.4.43 PRO file Ed 136/622.
68. G G Williams, and the Chief Inspector for secondary education, F R G Duckworth, were assessors to the Committee.

71. They further suggested that the points with which the instruments or articles should deal should include:

i. The institution of a separate governing body for each school and its composition and method of appointment.

ii. The functions of the governing body, which should include the appointment of the headmasters or headmistresses in consultation with the local education authority, and the general financial administration of the school within the limits of the financial provision made by the local education authority.

iii. The relationships between headmasters and headmistresses and their governing bodies, in particular their right of direct access to the governing body and of attendance at its meetings, and their functions, which should include control of the general organisation, curriculum and discipline of the school and of its incidental minor finance, and the appointment of the assistant staff with the approval of the governing bodies.

72. A minority[69] of the Committee held that the case for abolishing tuition fees had not been made out. They agreed with the majority in holding that full provision must be made for independence and for the possibility of variety in all types of secondary schools. They were, however, less sanguine than their colleagues about the reliance to be placed upon current and past experience—"administrative practice varies greatly"—and said that the majority's proposals about the contents of the instruments and articles were just as consistent with an excessive measure of control by the local education authority as with a proper degree of freedom. "It will still be possible" they suggested "for the Governing Body to be wholly appointed by the Local Education Authority or to be identical with one of its sub-committees". They concluded by saying that because "the abolition of fees in Maintained and Aided Schools involves . . . , at least potentially, an increase of control by the adminstrative authority . . . these Instruments or Articles should secure to the fullest degree the freedom not only of the Governing Body in the general administration of the School, but of the headmaster or headmistress under the Governing Body in regard to the curriculum, discipline, appointment of staff and other matters."

The discussions continued

73. Following the meeting with the governing bodies and other associations on 18 December 1942 Mr Butler had another meeting with Canon Leeson on 21 December before the annual meeting of the HMC in the New Year. As well as making Canon Leeson read in front of him the Birmingham local education authority's conditions of aid, Mr Butler warned him that he should not attempt to form a block of all the secondary school system in opposition to the alterations in the secondary school world which must be regarded as inevitable. If his whole attitude of mind were dominated by fear he would be neither a good politician nor a good headmaster. He did not feel, however, that fear or "mighty

---

69. It included, in addition to the Chairman, the Bishop of London (Dr Geoffrey Fisher) and Dr A W Pickard-Cambridge, formerly Vice-Chancellor of Sheffield University.

dread" need overwhelm him. Schemes of management could be drawn up which would define the relationships of the governing body and the headmaster with the local education authority and its Director.[70]

74. The message evidently got through. Reporting on the HMC's meeting Canon Leeson indicated (19 January 1943)[71] that, while they still disputed on educational grounds the wisdom of abolishing tuition fees, their apprehensions would be allayed if there were full statutory guarantees (for which, if necessary, they would have to fight "tooth and claw"), to be administered by the Board, for the maintenance of spiritual, educational and administrative freedom and independence, and their extension to all schools. He went on to state what these guarantees should cover—a separate governing body for each school; the headmaster and staff to be represented on the governing body and the head-master to have a right to be present at their meetings, with full opportunity to state his views; appointments to the staff to rest with the governors, in the case of assistant masters on the recommendation of the headmaster; the school premises and endowments to be vested in the governing body; the annual grant to the school to be assessed in relation to the needs of the school and the govern-ing body to have the financial responsibility on the basis of that assessment once it had been approved; and a right in the school authorities, in consultation with others interested, to receive applications for admission and to make a selection from them.

75. In the subsequent letter (4 March 1943) Canon Leeson, while attempting to refute the charge that the Conference were opposing reform, on the ground that what was under consideration was "not educational reform but administrative change", expressed his Committee's willingness to help in the negotiation of model articles of government.[72]

76. Canon Leeson, who was not lacking in either resilience or dog-collared persistence, continued to reiterate these and similar points both at subsequent meetings and in a succession of letters. Even Mr Butler's patience was sorely tested when on 25 May 1943[73] there was communicated to him a resolution (which Canon Leeson subsequently said he had done his best to avoid) in which the Conference

"while reaffirming their opposition on educational grounds to the abolition of tuition fees in grant-aided schools, desire to co-operate to the full in the advancement of English education by any means in their power. They regard themselves as charged especially to uphold the principle of spiritual and educational freedom in all post primary schools; and they must, therefore, press for the establishment of Model Articles of Government for all these schools to preserve those essential freedoms".

77. This provoked from Mr Butler the comment:—

"I am by temperament for these schools, but this sort of resolution calls I feel for a short answer indicating that we see through this unwise cant."

---

70. PRO file Ed 136/224.
71. PRO file Ed 136/224.
72. PRO file Ed 136/224.
73. PRO file Ed 136/423.

It got one. The fact was that the Conference were in a dilemma. If they advocated the retention of fees in all secondary schools they were logically driven to ask for the re-imposition of fees in the secondary modern schools, which was patently out of the question. If on the other hand they advocated the retention of fees in a section of the secondary schools they were open to the charge that they were splitting the ranks of the secondary schools. Even within the grammar school sphere, though the IAHM supported them, the Association of Headmistresses and the Associations of Assistant Masters and of Assistant Mistresses wished to see fees abolished in grant-aided schools. But all the associations were agreed on wanting to see a governing body in every secondary school.[74]

78. But from now on the problem became one of identifying the best means of achieving the desired ends. The White Paper on Educational Reconstruction (Cmnd 6458), which was published in July 1943[75], was warmly welcomed, both in and out of Parliament, and there was a general desire to see the reforms it outlined speedily enacted. Within the circles of HMC, for whom Canon Leeson had laboured so unceasingly since 1939, other voices were beginning to come into prominence, including those of some who were members of the Fleming Committee and had, perhaps, a better understanding of the role of the local education authorities and were not obsessed by the fear that the coincidence of the proposals to abolish fees in maintained schools and to reform the dual system was the outward manifestation of a plot to undo the older grammar schools. The IAHM, too, were beginning to play a more prominent part. There was a real desire to co-operate. All the outside organisations concerned wanted model articles and wanted to see them produced quickly. The questions to be settled were two. First, would it be feasible to produce a model which would be applicable to schools of such varying types and no less varying in the degree of financial responsibility which would rest on the local education authority? Second, assuming that such a model could be produced, should it, by some means or other, be given statutory backing?

79. The general feeling within the Department was against laying a White Paper on articles of government during the passage of the Bill through Parliament. Articles ought to be negotiated between the parties concerned; it would hardly be possible to produce typical articles since there was no typical school and by the time the Bill received the Royal Assent any model articles laid during its passage might no longer be appropriate.[76] This view was strongly held by Sir Maurice Holmes[77] and in large measure adopted by Mr Butler in a letter he sent on 24 December 1943 to Mr Henry Brooke, who had mooted the possibility of laying model articles. He did not, however, exclude the possibility of evolving "sets of Articles which would *prima facie* be appropriate. But such sets of articles,

---

74. Note of meeting with GBA etc on 19 May 1943. PRO file Ed 136/224.
75. The original intention had been to publish the White Paper and the Bill simultaneously but, because of its complications, the Bill could not be got ready in time. Mr Butler turned this to advantage by presenting the prior publication of the White Paper as a thoroughly democratic way of proceeding, because it provided a renewed opportunity for views to be expressed. There was another round of intensive discussion with the interests concerned.
76. Note of meeting with Ministers on 22.xii.43. PRO file 136/529.
77. Minute dated 23.xii.43 PRO file Ed 136/529.

before being imposed by order, would need examination in the case of each school, in the light of the views of the individual Local Education Authority (not of some body representative of Local Education Authorities in general), the circumstances of the school and the manner in which the school, if an existing one, had previously been conducted."[78]

80. One obstacle was removed when, early in 1944, a joint submission was made by the Incorporated Association of Head Masters and the Headmasters' Conference specifying the principles which they wished to see included in the Bill or, if that should be impossible, embodied either in a White Paper sent round to local education authorities as a guide or in a statement by the President in the House. In a covering letter L W Taylor, the joint secretary of the two organisations, said "I think everyone realises that inclusion in the Bill is impossible—hence the suggested alternative methods of establishing basic principles for all Model Articles or rather all articles".[79]

81. The points to which the two organisations attached importance were developed by their representatives at a meeting on 26 January 1944[80] (attended also by representatives of the Association of Headmistresses). In summary form they were:

1. Every secondary school should have its own governing body.

2. Such governing bodies should have their own clearly defined spheres of responsibility, including (subject to clause 23 of the Bill) the appointment of the headmaster and, on his recommendation, of the staff.

3. Every governing body should include persons of educational experience who need not be members of the local education authority or any of its committees.

4. Subject to clause 22 of the Bill, the headmaster should have control of the internal organisation, management and discipline of the school.

5. The headmaster should have direct access to the chairman of the governing body and the right to be present at its meetings, save when otherwise determined at any particular meeting.

6. The articles should include legitimate safeguards for the position of the headmaster and the staff.

82. In his reply to the deputation Mr Butler said that he did not consider it possible to amend the Bill further than had already been done to meet their wishes. Neither did he consider it possible to regulate the detailed lives of their schools in a Bill. It would be politically useful if he could issue model articles but the difficulty about doing that was that the Bill had been so drafted as to retain local characteristics. A model might have a straight-jacketing effect. As to calling a conference of the interested organisations he questioned the wisdom of bringing together people with such divergent views. He thought that it would be better to wait until the Bill was through the Commons and concentrate on getting its structure right.

---

78. PRO file Ed 136/529.
79. Letter of 17 January 1944. PRO file Ed 136/470.
80. PRO file Ed 136/470.

83. In reply to suggestions from the Headmaster of Nottingham High School, one of the Fleming minority, he said that he could hold out no hope of the Bill's being amended by the Government to enable the Board, as a long term policy, to insist on a separate governing body for every school and in the meantime to require separate governing bodies for grammar schools or, where joint governing bodies were proposed, to set a time limit to their existence. Many senior public elementary schools would be entering the secondary sphere and some large urban local education authorities took the view that there was no practicable alternative to grouping.

The Genesis of the White Paper (*Cmnd 6523*)

84. In the event, the divergence of views apprehended by Mr Butler did not prove to be so great. By the middle of February both the IAHM and the Association of Directors and Secretaries of Education (ADS) had produced tentative draft models and an examination of them within the Department disclosed a considerable measure of agreement, as may be seen from the following tabular summary.[81]

---

[81]. Minute of 19 February 1944 (PRO file Ed 136/529). It is not apparent from the available Departmental records whether the two associations took this action on their own initiative or whether they were prompted to do so.

Subject	IAHM proposals	ADS proposals
Constitution of governing body (GB)	GB to include 1. adequate representation of local education authority. 2. representative of university or other form of higher education. 3. others with special qualifications. 4. limited number of co-opts.	GB for every school (not merely a sub-committee acting as GB) Different types of secondary schools to be grouped in appropirate cases under "multilateral" GB. GB to include persons representing academic, industrial, commercial and social interests.
Finance	GB to submit estimate of income and expenditure for approval of local education authority. No expenditure beyond approved estimate without local education authority's approval (Cf Form 24S, the existing model).	Responsibility to rest with local education authority but GB to have discretion within approved estimates, subject to any over-riding regulations of local education authority.
Appointment and dismissal of teaching staff	Headteacher to be appointed by GB, and dimissed by GB, subject to right to appear before two meetings of GB. Assistant teachers to be appointed, and dismissed by GB, in consultation with headteacher.	Headteacher to be appointed by Education Committee in consultation with GB, and dismissed by local education authority on recommendation of GB. Assistant teachers to be appointed by GB subject to local education authority's right to transfer teachers in consultation with GB. Teachers to be dismissed by GB subject to right of appeal to local education authority.
Internal organisation & curriculum	GB prescribe general subjects of instruction. Headteacher controls choice of books, methods of teaching, internal organisation, management and discipline. Headteacher normally to be present at GB meetings.	GB responsible for curriculum, subject to general direction and general approval of local education authority. Headteacher to have control of general organisation, curriculum, discipline and internal management. Headteacher normally to be present at GB meetings. CEO (or his representative) to have right to be present.
Admission of pupils	Applications for admission to be made to headteacher (or other person approved by GB) according to a form to be approved by them.	Pupils to be placed according to their abilities and aptitudes. Local education authority to be responsible for determining these points and for advising parents.

85. The way was, therefore, clear for discussions to take place. The talks with the ADS and the IAHM (on 29 February 1944 and 2 January 1944) proceeded on the basis of a document headed "Points for Interview". No copy of this document seems to have survived but it seems likely that it posed three general issues and then the five specific topics listed in the summary of the two bodies' proposals. Both bodies accepted the general propositions that a memorandum setting out agreed principles, with detailed suggestions where appropriate, would be appropriate; that there was no reason why the same broad principles should not apply to all types of secondary schools; and that the same principles might apply to county, controlled and aided schools, subject to certain differences in matters of detail. There was also ready acceptance of the proposition that schools should be governed by properly constituted governing bodies, though the ADS considered that the governing bodies of county schools should be made sub-committees of the local education authorities. The IAHM for their part agreed that the authority should settle the broad type of education to be given in a school and its place in the local system, subject to changes in its organisation and character being made in consultation with the governing body and to directions about the organisation and curriculum being communicated to the governors by the local education authority and not given individually by the Director of Education. They also recognised the need for grouping governing bodies in some cases, though they did not favour combining different types of school under the same governing body.

86. Such few differences as emerged—and they were not serious—concerned such matters as:

1. The appointment of the head teacher—the IAHM favoured appointment by the governing body, subject to confirmation or consent by the local education authority, but agreed that the joint committee procedure in force in Surrey merited further consideration; for county and controlled schools the ADS preferred the practice, analogous to that in London, of the short list being drawn up by the governors, with the help of a local education authority representative, and the final appointment being made by the appropriate committee of the local education authority, with a governor present but not voting.

2. The suggestion, favoured by the IAHM, that the governors and head-teacher should have a proportion of the vacancies at their disposal. The ADS were opposed to this but were inclined to agree that, if possible, some means should be found of associating the governors and headteacher with the process of admissions.

87. In reporting on these discussions G G Williams, who with W C Cleary (the head of the Elementary Branch) led for the Board, said in a minute dated 4 March 1944[82] that the NUT were to be seen within the next fortnight. "After that probably the Bishop[83] and other Governors, followed by the women. That should be the whole story". No records appear to have survived of these further

---

82. PRO file Ed 136/529.
83. ie the Bishop of London.

discussions, if indeed any were made. According to the White Paper[84], those consulted included representatives of the various associations of local education authorities, the LCC, the ADS, the NUT, the Governing Bodies Associations, the London Aided Schools Association, the Aided Schools Committee and the Joint Four Secondary Associations.

88. The draft of the White Paper was submitted to Mr Butler on 21 April 1944. It was published on 4 May 1944, twelve days before the Education Bill had its first reading in the House of Lords.

The Bill in Parliament

89. For the secondary schools the significant features of clause 16 (Constitution of managers and governors and conduct of county and [voluntary] schools) in the Bill presented to Parliament were two. First, whereas all grammar schools had had instruments or articles, which varied a great deal and did not in many cases require the approval of the Department, in future all secondary schools were to have instruments and articles, the voluntary school instruments and articles being made by an Order of the Minister and county school articles requiring the approval of the Minister. This last requirement was a change from past practice. The second innovation was the stipulation that the position of the headteacher in relation to the governing body should be settled in the articles.

90. The fact that discussions were proceeding with the interested parties and the knowledge that there was a good prospect of reaching agreement undoubtedly facilitated the passage of clause 16 and the related clauses. So also did the fact that on the day, 9 March 1944, on which the House of Commons in Committee considered these clauses they were for the first time working to a voluntary time-table which had been devised to speed up the examination of the Bill.[85] There was, therefore, little disposition to be long-winded or to press amendments.[86] The only amendment pressed to a division was one moved by Mr Clement Davies (Carmarthen, Lib) to reduce the number of foundation members on managing bodies. It was essentially a demonstration of Welsh nonconformist sentiment and as such both brief and calm.[87]

91. Mr Butler had, therefore, little difficulty in dealing with amendments to ensure that articles would be in general conformity with articles set out in a schedule to the Bill. He promised to lay the results of the discussions before the

---

84. See footnote 81 page 166. According to a minute by G G Williams dated 20 April 1944 there had been discussions with the LEA Advisory Committee (a consultative body of representatives of the Associations of LEAs and Education Committees and the LCC), the ADS, the NUT, the GBA and the Joint Four Associations (separately). The two statements can be reconciled if one assumes that G G Williams forgot to mention the London Aided Schools Association and the Aided Schools Committee and that GBA should have read GBAs.
85. The House of Commons had spent three days on clauses 1-8 and another three on clauses 8-15.
86. The House had yet to learn the unwisdom, in war-time, of carrying amendments against the wishes of the Government. They learned that lesson on 29 March 1944.
87. Personal knowledge.

end of the passage of the Bill "either here or in another place". He was equally successful in resisting amendments moved by spokesmen for the schools designed to extend the Minister's power of approval or control and amendments moved by local authority spokesmen aimed at limiting it. He based himself on the proposition that the object of the clause was to preserve a proper, individual life for the school but equally to preserve the proper position of those who had the responsibility for education in their own areas.[88]

92. As to the remaining clauses in this group, an amendment to clause 17 (Managers of primary schools), by Mr Harvey (Combined English Universities, Independent), a Quaker, to secure the inclusion of at least one parent on managing bodies met with a sympathetic response. Even so Mr Kenneth Lindsay (Kilmarnock, Nat Lab), a former Parliamentary Secretary to the Board, and Captain Cobb (Preston, Conservative), a former chairman of the LCC Education Committee, were worried by the problem of selecting a parent. So also was Mr Chuter Ede. He confessed to being a little suspicious of the nominees of parents' associations, "because it is not always the best person who is put forward, but the most thrusting person who thinks he has to justify his existence by making as much trouble as he can".[89] A similar amendment, to clause 18 (Governors of secondary schools), moved by Mr Lindsay to secure the inclusion of parents and persons of educational experience on the governing bodies of secondary schools also met with a sympathetic response,[90] though the consideration of it was overlaid by the discussion of another (unrelated) amendment which the Deputy Chairman had selected for discussion with it.

93. Clause 19 (Grouping of schools under one management) provoked amendments designed either to limit to four the number of schools that could be grouped (Mr Harvey) or to restrict the operation of the clause to county boroughs (Professor Gruffyd, University of Wales, Lib) or to primary schools (Captain Cobb). In his reply Mr Butler reminded the House that the clause re-enacted existing legislation and went on to say that, in the light of discussion with those responsible for education in the great cities, he had concluded that it was essential to have a power to amalgamate certain schools which would fall within the secondary sphere—"partly because, in a compact city, you will get overlapping of personnel and problems". He also questioned the wisdom of embodying in the statute a precise numerical limitation. He frankly admitted the weakness in his argument but said that he would rather have the clause with its general powers, on the understanding that it would not be misused. From the information he had he could say that there was no intention on the part of the important authorities to misuse the clause.[91]

94. By the time the Bill reached the House of Lords (16 May 1944) the White Paper on the Principles of Government had been published. It is a measure of its general acceptability that only two amendments were put down to this group of clauses. If it had been otherwise, there would have been no shortage of speakers

88. Hansard, 9 March 1944—Col 2251.
89. Hansard, 9 March 1944—Cols 2303/4.
90. Hansard, 9 March 1944—Col 2313.
91. Hansard, 9 March 1944—Cols 2328-2331.

in that House to put the schools' point of view with conviction and force. Of the two amendments put down one, moved by Earl Stanhope, a former President of the Board, proposed to substitute "articles of association" for "rules of management" and "articles of government". Like Mr Gallacher (West Fife, Communist) and his Left wing supporters who in the House of Commons had sought to substitute "school council" for both managing and governing body, Earl Stanhope's aim, though he stood at the opposite end of the political spectrum, was to remove the distinction in the Bill between managers and governors. The Earl of Selborne, who was in charge of the Bill, easily persuaded the House that "articles of association" had commercial associations that made it inappropriate.[92]

95. The major relevant change made in the House of Lords was the replacement of clause 8(2) (b), which had been added in the House of Commons,[93] by the insertion of what is now Section 76 (General Principle to be observed by Minister and Local Education Authorities: Pupils to be educated in accordance with wishes of parents).[94]

The 1945 model

96. A model instrument and articles for county secondary schools were issued on 26 January 1945. It was known that local education authorities would welcome the issue of such a model.

It was thought, too, that it would reduce the load of work on the Department's Legal Branch who were responsible for approving or making the necessary Orders. No inconsistency was seen with Mr Butler's remarks during the Parliamentary proceedings since the model was designed for county secondary schools only and its issue as an administrative action was very different from incorporating a model in an Act of Parliament.[95]

The last word

97. The last word in this section may be left with Canon Leeson. In his book "The Public Schools Question"[96] he included an essay on "The Education Act, 1944, and The Grammar Schools". He considered the question how, if the hold of the State over secondary education were to be extended and strengthened, could essential freedoms be maintained in the day-to-day administration of the schools. He passed in review the relevant provisions of the 1944 Act and also the White Paper on the Principles of Government in Maintained Secondary Schools.

---

92. Hansard, 21 June 1944—Cols 323/4.
93. Hansard, 15 February 1944—Cols 138-143 and 16 February 1944—Cols 197-9.
94. Hansard, 12 July 1944—Col 864. See also 20 June 1944—Cols 285-9 and 11 July 1944—Col 774.
95. Personal knowledge. Later in 1948 there was a proposal by three of the LEA Associations to issue model instruments and articles for aided and controlled secondary schools. The Ministry made a number of suggestions for improving the models but declined to give them their imprimatur unless and until they commanded the assent of the other interests concerned. Subsequently one of the Associations withdrew and no more was heard of the proposal.
96. Longmans Green & Co, 1948. It is not mentioned in the appendix entitled "The Literature on School Government" in Baron and Howell.

On the latter his verdict was that its authors were to be congratulated on the courage and resourcefulness with which they had tackled a difficult problem, and had worked out something which on paper at any rate was fair and reasonable. Then in a passage, which is too long to be quoted in extenso, but which, perhaps especially in this day and age, merits careful study, he specified what he considered to be the essentials for the different parties concerned. He concluded by saying:

"What counts perhaps most of all is mutual confidence and the individual care of the governing bodies for the individual school."

Elementary (or primary) schools

98. The first schools to provide instruction in reading, and possibly also in writing were the song schools. Such a school was described by Chaucer in the Prioress's Tale:—

"A litel scole of Cristen folk ther stood
Doun at the ferther ende, in which ther were
Children an heep, y-comen of Cristen blood,
That lerned in that scole yere by yere
Swich manner doctrine as men used there
This is to seyn, to singen and to rede,
As smale children doon in hir childhede."

The teaching was largely by rote and the little boy who continued to sing "Alma redemptoris" as his corpse was carried to his funeral service had learned the hymn from an older boy, who had explained:—

"I lerne song, I can but smal gramere"

Sometimes a grammar school might have an elementary (or petty) school attached to it, or a writing school, as at Rotherham where Archbishop Thomas Rotherham of York included such a school in his foundation of Jesus College (1483).[97] There were also a few separately endowed elementary schools. But at least up to the time of the Commonwealth the provision of elementary schools was sparse and sporadic.

99. Under the Commonwealth some advance was made, notably in Wales, where under the "Act for the Better Propagation of the Gospel in Wales" over sixty free schools were established.[98] An even more far-reaching development in that period was the increasing acceptance of English as the proper medium of instruction. This paved the way for the remarkable expansion of elementary education which took place in the following century. There was at the time a great sense of philanthropy which manifested itself in a variety of ways. Of these the most popular was the establishment of charity schools. A great many schools

---

97. He did so because "that county produces many youths endowed with the light and sharpness of ability, who do not all wish to attain the dignity and elevation of priesthood, that these may be better fitted for the mechanical arts and other concerns of this world, we have ordained a third fellow, learned and skilled in the art of writing and accounts". Leach, Educational Charters, pp 423-5.
98. Miss M G Jones, "The Charity School Movement" p 16.

were established either by endowment[99] or by private subscribers, who also contributed to the schools' maintenance. "Instruction in Bible and catechism during the formative years of childhood", the historian of the charity school movement has written,[100] "before the infant population was ready for apprenticeship or service, would build up a God-fearing population and, at the same time, would innoculate the children against the habits of sloth, debauchery and beggary, which characterised the lower orders of society"—especially in the slums of London and Westminster. It would also help to protect the Protestant succession against the machinations of Rome. Children who had learned the Anglican catechism, the psalms and prayers, said the Archdeacon of Huntingdon in a charity school sermon in 1706, "would never stoop to beads and Latin charms, nor bow their neck to the dark slavery of Rome".[101]

100. Of special interest for present purposes is the Grey Coat Hospital School, Westminster, which was established by six tradesmen of the parish of St Margaret's. As well as contributing generously themselves, they persuaded others to do so, and they called a meeting of subscribers to discuss a scheme for the charity. A house was taken for the school, a master appointed and a statement of what would now be called "aims and objectives" drawn up for his guidance. "The principall designe of this Schoole" was the education of poor children in the principles of piety and virtue. The master was instructed "to study to endeavour to win the love and affection of the children, thereby to invite and encourage them, rather than by correction to force them to learne . . . reason as well as experience having plainly shown that too great severity does rather dull than sharpen the wits and memory".

101. Nor was that all. The trustees, records Miss Jones, "met every week to supervise the charity they had set up. They ordered the new grey coats for the children, and were present when the tailor tried them on. They supplied the mothers with grey yarn to make stockings for the children and prevailed upon their own wives and daughters to make the caps and stitch the bands which constituted the boys' uniform. Convinced believers in the value of inspection, they evolved schemes for testing the children's progress in learning, at first making themselves each responsible for the examination of five of the children, and later arranging on every quarter day a general examination by the whole body of governors, putting on a file specimens of the children's writing 'to judge, from time to time, of their progress in learning' ".[102]

102. The charity school movement petered out towards the end of the century partly because of defective administration and the misappropriation and mismanagement of so much of the monies left for the education of the poor and partly because it got caught up in the struggles between high and low churchmen early in the eighteenth century. Nevertheless it had laid a foundation on which

---

99. One such was the school at Lamport and Hanging Houghton, founded in 1772 by Sir Edmund Isham, from which came the first president of the NUT, Mr I J Graves (1832-03.)
100. Miss M G Jones, p 4.
101. Miss M G Jones, p 35. The Archdeacon of Huntingdon was White Kennet, who later became Bishop of Peterborough.
102. Miss M G Jones, loc cit pp 53, 54.

the National and the British and Foreign Schools Societies were able to build when they entered the field in 1811 and in 1814. Though his figures must be treated with reserve, Lord Brougham estimated that there were in 1818 about 18,500 schools in England and Wales, of which about 4,100 were endowed schools; the remaining 14,500 were financed by fees or by voluntary subscriptions.

103. The National Society provided building grants—its aim was the establishment of a church school in every parish; applications for help towards the teachers' salaries were refused. The British and Foreign Schools Society supplied its schools with teachers trained at its expense. As a result of both societies' efforts the number of children attending day schools in 1828 was double that of 1818. But there were still a great many children who were not attending school at all and it was becoming ever more clear that the needs could not be met by unaided voluntary effort. In 1833, the year after the passing of the first Reform Act, Parliament made its first grant (£20,000) for education. Six years later the Committee of the Privy Council on Education was established, with Dr James Kay-Shuttleworth (as he became known) as its first secretary, to administer the increased grants then made available by Parliament.

104. The Committee made it a condition of aiding a school that it should be open to inspection and that it should be conducted in accordance with a suitable scheme of management. Their reasons for insisting upon the latter were explained in a letter sent to the Diocesan Board of the Deanery of Bristol on 7 October 1847:—

"The provision for school management in the trust deed comprised every form of negligent or discordant arrangements. Often there was no management clause, in which case the government of the school devolved on the individual trustees, and their heirs, who might be non-resident, minors, lunatics or otherwise incapable. When a management clause was inserted there was seldom any provision for the supply of vacancies or re-election, nor any qualifications for the office of management.

Consequently in the majority of these schools, the seeds were sown of future parochial disputes or litigation; of uncontested usurpation, of alienations of the trust property to other public uses, or of absorption of the property into the estate of the proprietors. Time and opportunity alone were wanting to ripen this harvest of discord, confusion or plunder."[103]

105. The Committee devised for Church of England schools four model management clauses which varied according to the size of the population of the district served by the school and the extent to which it included wealthy and well educated people. Model C, for very small parishes, provided for the parson to be the sole manager, unless and until the Bishop directed the election of a committee of subscribers. Under model A the managers were elected annually; under B new managers were elected only to fill vacancies due to death, resignation or incapacity; while under D the managerial committee filled its own vacancies unless and until the Bishop directed an election by the subscribers.

---

103. Committee of Council on Education. Minutes and correspondence 1848-9.

106. Taking model A as a sample, the principal officiating Minister had the superintendence of the religious and moral instruction of the scholars. In all other respects the management, direction, control and government of the school, its premises, funds and endowments . . . . . and the selection, appointment and dismissal of the school master and school mistress and their assistants were vested in and exercised by a committee of management. This committee consisted of the principal officiating Minister, his licensed Curate(s), the Wardens (if so desired), and an unspecified number of other persons who were members of the Church of England and who had at least a life interest in property in the parish or were resident in it, and who contributed twenty shillings a year to the funds of the school. They were elected annually by contributors of at least ten shillings a year who were members of the Church of England and qualified by residence or estate. The officiating Minister was chairman and another member of the committee was deputed to act as secretary. Decisions were reached by a majority of votes.

107. Differences within the managing body about religious education were determined by the Bishop. Other differences were referred for determination by a panel consisting of HMI and a beneficed clergyman nominated by the Bishop and an Anglican JP selected by HMI and the clergyman.

108. The managing body was also authorised to appoint a committee of Anglican ladies to assist them in the visitation and management of the girls' and infants' school.

109. Somewhat similar models were evolved for the Wesleyans and the Roman Catholics. The principal differences were that in the case of the Wesleyans, the chairman was the (circuit) Superintendent (or his nominee); in the case of the Roman Catholics the managing body consisted of the priest and six other members nominated by him, unless and until the Bishop directed that they should be elected by contributors to the funds of the school. The associated ladies' committee was also limited to six.

110. It was the aim of the Committee of Council in framing these models "to secure for the clergy their rightful influence in the management and to provide for a proper representation of those of the laity who, as members of the Church, by their subscriptions, exertions and influence, promote the prosperity of the Parochial schools".[104]

111. The models did not pass unchallenged. The Roman Catholic Poor Schools Committee pressed for a provision which would give the Bishop the power to decide whether any particular matter or dispute did or did not involve or affect religion or morals. To their Lordships that savoured of absolutism. "It would not be consistent with their view of the civil interests of education . . . . . to provide for the absolute supremacy of the spiritual power . . . . . The only tribunal they could sanction would be one in which all the parties would be adequately represented".[105]

[104.] Committee of Council on Education. Letter to Bishop of Ripon dated 7 November 1947.
[105.] Committee of Council on Education. Letter to the Hon C Langdale, Chairman of the Catholic Poor School Committee.

112. A more serious and sustained challenge came from the National Society and in particular from Archdeacon Denison[106] and his supporters. For the Archdeacon, it has been written, there were two principles which were above question. First, there must be no state interference in the internal affairs of schools; this meant no State-Management Clauses whatsoever. Second, school promoters must be at liberty to give to the parish priest absolute control and no representation of the laity must be enforced.[107]

113. If the moderates in the National Society had had their way they would in all probability have reached an accommodation with the Committee of Council. But the turbulent Archdeacon and his supporters were too strong for them and since neither the Society nor the Committee could or would give way, negotiations were broken off. But this did not prevent the Committee of Council from enforcing the clauses on promoters who sought aid. And brought into operation they were, in Wales to begin with.[108]

The Newcastle Commission 1858–1861

114. The report of this Commission, which was set up to inquire into complaints[109] against the existing system is relevant in the present context only insofar as its outcome, Lowe's Revised Code of 1861, put more responsibility on voluntary school managers and changed their relationship with the teachers. From then on grants were no longer paid, as some had been, to teachers and pupil teachers, but to the managers. All payments to a school were merged into a single capitation grant and the payment of this grant, which was limited to pupils under 12, was dependent on a certain number of attendances being made by the children and to the examination by HMI of each child in reading, writing and arithmetic. To stimulate local co-operation the amount of grant was related to the school's income from fees and subscriptions. "If the new system will not be cheap" said Lowe, "it will be efficient, and if it will not be efficient, it will be cheap".

---

106. G A Denison (1805-96) a high churchman of the old school, "dignified, kindly and paternally despotic, with a keen eye to the temporal as well as the spiritual needs of his flock", was successively vicar of Broadwinsor and East Brent. Appointed Archdeacon of Taunton in 1851 he was prosecuted in the ecclesiastical courts in 1856 for breaches of the 28th and 29th Articles of Religion and deprived. The decision was reversed in 1857. He was one of those who opposed the election of Frederick Temple as Bishop of Exeter in 1869 because he had been a contributor to "Essays and Reviews" (1860) which included essays denying the inspiration of scripture and the eternity of punishment. From 1862-5 he edited the "Church and State Review". In 1885 he published a violent political diatribe against Gladstone. (DNB (1975) p 2404).

107. H J Burgess and P A Welsby. "A Short History of the National Society 1811-1961". Chapter V. Controversy.

108. Kay-Shuttleworth had by that time been succeeded by R R Lingen, one of the three Commissioners appointed in 1846 to inquire into the state of education in Wales, "especially into the means afforded to the labouring classes of acquiring a knowledge of the English language." It is said that having on one occasion been told by Kay-Shuttleworth "Get it done, let the objectors howl" he made that his maxim for the conduct of affairs. According to the Saturday Review he was quite as powerful as Mr Lowe "and a good deal more offensive. It is from Mr Lingen that all the sharp snubbing replies proceed". In 1869, fittingly enough, he was made Permanent Secretary of the Treasury. On his retirement in 1885 he was made a peer (DNB (1975) p 2754).

109. The principal subjects of complaint were the excessive cost of education, the inadequacy of the instruction even in the best schools, the insufficiency of the provision in rural areas, the undue shortness of school life and the great irregularity of attendance.

115. The new arrangements aroused widespread criticism and in 1864 Lowe was driven from office. In any case it was by then becoming increasingly clear that more fundamental measures were required if the country's educational needs were to be met. This was what Forster's Education Act of 1870 sought to do. It had two objects—to cover the country with good schools and to get the parents to send their children to them. As a first step the country was mapped out into school districts, each separately chargeable with the duty of providing elementary education within its borders. These districts were boroughs and parishes or groups of parishes; the metropolis was made a district by itself. A school board was to be established in every school district which required more schools. A school fund was also to be established, made up of income from fees, grants and money raised by rate. The Board were empowered to delegate to local managers any of their powers except that of raising money.

The Cross Commission 1886–1888

116. This Commission was set up to review the working of the Elementary Education Acts in England and Wales.[110] In chapter 3 of its Final Report it considered school management.

"If we regard the school as a place of education in which the character is to be formed as well as the intelligence cultivated and the success of which is to be estimated not so much by the scholars passing examinations or gaining prizes, or even by the amount of knowledge acquired, as by their conduct in after life, then much more than oversight is demanded from the managers as well as the teachers, inasmuch by their active sympathy with, and kindly influence over, individual scholars, they may do much to mould their character, and help to make them good and useful members of society."

117. The Commission distinguished two branches of management, on the one hand duties such as the appointment and removal of teachers, the proper equipment of the school, the regulation and remission of fees and such other matters as were more or less capable of being settled in committee and, on the other, frequent visitation and personal superintendence of the schools. From this analysis they deduced the qualities which they considered school managers should have.

"A general zeal for education being presupposed as a necessary condition for both branches of management, breadth of view, business habits, administrative ability and the power of working harmoniously with others, are important qualifications for the work of the school management committee. For the personal oversight of schools, some amount of education, tact, interest in school work, a sympathy with the teachers and the scholars, to which may be

---

110. The Chairman, Sir R Assheton Cross, was Home Secretary. Other members included Cardinal Manning and the Bishop of London, Dr Frederick Temple. The latter on leaving Oxford had been for a short time an Examiner in the office of the Committee of Council on Education. He subsequently became a school master and was Headmaster of Rugby from 1859 to 1869 when he was appointed Bishop of Exeter. See also footnotes 106 and 62.

added residence in reasonable proximity to the school, together with leisure time during school hours are desirable qualifications; and it is hardly necessary to say that personal oversight of the religious and moral instruction implies religious character in those who are to exercise it."[111]

118. In London the functions of management were divided between the school management committee, composed of members of the school board, and bodies of local managers, totalling not more than twelve or fifteen, for every two or three schools. The local managers were nominated by the management committee members who were elected for the division in which the schools were situated. In Liverpool the entire management of each school was, subject to the general rules of the Board, remitted to local bodies of managers. These were initially selected by the Board but subsequent vacancies were filled by the local managers by co-option. There was also in Liverpool a conference of managers which formulated a common policy for such matters as the dates of holidays, hours of attendance, the reception of new pupils and the measures needed to check capricious migration from school to school. Co-operation of this kind was welcomed by the Commission, as was also the growing practice of managers of voluntary schools combining to effect what could not be done by the schools individually.[112]

119. Some of the other larger School Boards chose not to delegate powers of management to local managers, thus instituting a practice which in some cases has persisted to this day. These Boards included Manchester, Bradford, Leeds and Hull. At Salford a committee of the Board undertook the whole management. At Stoke-on-Trent the elected members of the Board superintended the schools in the township which they represented. Birmingham was another Board which took a similar line and the Commission regarded the evidence of Dr Crosskey, the chairman of the school management committee, as of such significance that they reproduced it in the main body of their report. Since it is of contemporary interest extracts from it are reproduced here.

31,238   Q. How do you get on without managers?

A. By a system of inspectors and by hard work on the part of the committee . . . the school management committee have to make themselves acquainted with the state of their schools.

31,243   Q. Then they act as managers, do they not?

A. No . . . We have inspectors who examine the schools, child by child precisely on the lines of HMIs; we have another inspector who goes through and sees the general condition of the school. Reports from these inspectors [and from HMIs] come regularly before the committee with a very perfect and systematic analysis of the work of the teachers and of the condition of the schools . . .

---

111. Cross Report ch 3 p 65.
112. Cross, p 70. There is a more detailed account of the London arrangements in P Gordon's "The Victorian School Manager" (Woburn Press 1974). There is in that book a great deal of detailed information about school management in the period 1800-1902.

[The committee] form their opinion of what is going on in the schools; they take the measures to appoint the teachers or to add to the staff, or what not, as may be necessary, based upon these reports and upon personal examination of the schools.

31,244 Q. Do . . . these inspectors take a personal interest in the children?

A. No . . . personal interest is being developed in another and . . . better direction. Our great object is to make the teachers come into such a relationship with the parents and children that the parents and children group themselves around the school as they do their home; the personal interest of the headteacher and the staff goes into the homes of the children, and in that direction we are very anxious to extend the influence of the school.

31,245 Q. I do not quite see how you secure such interest in the homes of the scholars as you desire?

A. They frequently have entertainments; the teachers will go to the homes of the children very often; they visit them if they are irregular . . . We think that if the children and the parents feel it to be their school, and take a pride and interest in it, if you get a personal interest between the staff and the parents, that is the best thing; we think that no committee of managers dropping in, or any work in visiting that they can do, will equal that.

31,246 Q. Then you trust in fact . . . to this co-operation between the parents and the teachers?

A. We try to cherish it largely.[113]

120. The Commission were unimpressed. Their view was that it would be very advantageous if school boards, and especially the larger boards, were in the supervision of their schools, always to associate with themselves local managers; local inspectors could only very imperfectly discharge the function of managers.

121. The Commission went on to draw a comparison between the management of board schools and that of voluntary schools. Their verdict was that in that branch of administration which could be conducted outside the school it was impossible to deny the superiority of the management of the school board dispensing the money of the rate payers. If, however, they looked for the closest supervision of the school and the most effective sympathy between managers and teachers, or between managers and scholars, they felt, on the whole, bound to pronounce in favour of the efficiency of voluntary management. It was in the combination of the advantages of both systems that they looked for progress in the future.[114]

[113.] Cross. pp 67, 68.
[114.] Cross. p 69.

122. Managing bodies and especially those of the voluntary schools tended to be drawn from the leisured and moneyed classes. As evidence of the extent to which it was possible to interest various classes of a community in elementary education the Cross Commission cited the fact that the chairmen of local managing bodies in Liverpool included eight merchants, two medical men, a county court judge, a journalist and two "extensive" clothiers.[115] In London an analysis by P Gordon of the composition of managing bodies shows that the leisured classes accounted for 31 per cent., the professions for 10½ per cent., the churches for 21 per cent., merchants and managers for 8½ per cent., sub-managers for 22 per cent., skilled workers for only 4½ per cent and teachers for 2½ per cent. The workers were mostly higher-paid workers in such trades as printing, ship-building and building, together with a few less well paid workers, such as bootmakers. The teachers were headmasters or principals of independent or endowed grammar schools or training colleges.[116] Teachers serving in the board's schools were not allowed to be members.

123. The position of women was in some doubt up to the passing of the 1902 Act. There was no shortage of capable women. The London School Board numbered among its members such women as Miss Susan Lawrence, Mrs Pankhurst, Mrs Annie Besant, and Miss Bayliss, who headed the poll one year. Of the members of local managing bodies in 1884, 19½ per cent. were women. But though Section (1) (a) of the Interpretation Act, 1889 specifically provided that unless the contrary intention appeared, words importing the masculine gender should include females, the Courts in that same year had decided that where a statute dealt with the exercise of public functions, unless that statute expressly gave power to women to exercise them, the exercise of the powers was confined to men.[117] The thinking underlying this decision, as it was explained in the 1902 debates, was that, legally, a married woman was not a personality; she was merged in the personality of her husband, and therefore disqualified both by sex and couverture.[118]

---

[115]. There were several reasons for the paucity of working class representation, among them the fact that managers' meetings were usually held in the day time, the cost of travel and the fact that not many workers were (direct) ratepayers. Nor were they likely to be able to qualify as voluntary school subscribers. During the Parliamentary proceedings on the 1902 Act an amendment to permit the payment of travelling expenses was resisted on grounds which have a marked affinity with the reasons for rejecting the "equal pay" amendment in 1944 (See note 84). The reply of the President of the Local Government Board provoked from Mr Winston Churchill the comment that there was no great question in which the thin edge of the wedge had not already been inserted. He held that if there was any board upon which the working classes ought to be represented it was the education authority. (Hansard 13.xi.02. Cols. 891 and 894).

[116]. P Gordon, loc cit pp 161-3.

[117]. Beresford Hope v Lady Sandhurst 23 QB, 16.5.89. p 91 (cited by P Gordon).

[118]. Section 23(6) of the 1902 Act dealt with the immediate problem by declaring that a woman should not be disqualified either by sex or marriage from being on a body of managers. The Education (London) Act of 1903 provided that due regard should be had to the inclusion of women in the proportion of not less than one third of the whole body of managers. The wider problem was not resolved until the enactment of the Sex Disqualification (Removal) Act, 1919.

124. The Cross Commission had said that they would be glad to see parents represented on the committee of management, so long as they were not a preponderating element.[119] Though, however, the idea of parental representation was widely debated, there was no great support for it. A committee set up by the London School Board in 1887 "to investigate the Mode of Election and the Powers of Managers" found that opinion was almost unanimously against it. Bills in 1890 and 1891 to permit the representation of parents on the managing bodies of voluntary schools made no progress. An amendment to secure the inclusion of parents on the governing bodies of diocesan associations of voluntary schools, for which the Voluntary Schools Act, 1897 provided, was defeated. So was an amendment to the 1902 Bill to make provision for parent managers.[120]

The Education Act, 1902

125. This Act effected a transformation. The local education authorities which it established were made responsible for secular education in both the old board schools, which they took over, and in the voluntary schools. They were also made responsible for the maintenance of the voluntary schools (apart from the cost of repairs, other than those necessitated by fair wear and tear, and of improvements to the buildings) and, in particular, for the payment of the salaries of the teachers serving in them. Teachers in voluntary schools continued to be appointed by the managers (subject to the veto of the authority on educational grounds) nor could they be dismissed without the consent of the authority except on grounds connected with the giving of religious instruction.

126. Changes were also made in the management of the schools. Under Section 6[121] (largely re-enacted in Section 30 of the 1921 Act) all public elementary schools provided by a county local education authority had to have a body of managers, of whom four were appointed by the local education authority, two by the minor authority. It was left to the discretion of a local education authority which was the council of a borough or urban district whether or not they appointed managing bodies for provided schools. Under Schedule I B (4) (=Section 35 of the 1921 Act) the managers of a provided school dealt with "such matters relating to the management of the school, and subject to such conditions and restrictions as the local education authority may determine".

127. Every non-provided school had to have a managing body consisting, usually, as to two-thirds of foundation managers and as to one-third of public popular representatives. In county areas, assuming a managing body of six, one of the popular representatives had to be appointed by the local education authority, one by the minor authority.[122] Under Section 11(1) (=Section 31(1) of the 1921 Act) foundation managers were managers appointed under the provisions of the trust deed or of an order made under the Act. If the trust deed were defective the Board could make an order under Section 11 (=Section 32

---

119. Cross, p 67.
120. P Gordon pp 173-81.
121. The House of Commons spent no less than seven days in Committee on this section, largely because of its denominational implications.
122. 'Minor' authority was defined as the council of any borough, including a metropolitan borough, an urban district, or the parish council (or parish meeting).

of the 1921 Act). In making it they had to have regard to the ownership of the school building, and to the principles on which the education given in the school has been conducted in the past.[123]

128. Under Section 12 (=Section 33 of the 1921 Act) provided schools could be grouped for purposes of management and so also, if the managers agreed, could non-provided schools. The groups had to consist entirely of provided schools or entirely of non-provided schools. This section was added by the Government in Committee in response to strong expressions of opinion in favour of grouping from MPs representing urban constituencies.

129. Under Section 2 of the Education (London) Act, 1903 every public elementary school in London had to have a body of managers but the number of managers and "the manner in which schools, in cases where it is desirable" should be grouped under one body of managers was determined by the council of each borough, after consultation with the local education authority, and subject to the approval of the Board.

The Education Act, 1944

130. The terms of the 1902 Act aroused strong opposition at the time and subsequently. Though they lasted for over forty years, the legal safeguards and the divided responsibilities of the dual system gave rise to endless complications in administration which, in the words of the 1943 White Paper, retarded educational progress, engendered friction and consumed time and energies which could have been spent to much better purpose. An even more serious problem was that most non-provided schools were conducted in old buildings, nearly 92 per cent. of them dating from 1902 or earlier.

131. The basic aims of the 1944 Act have already been outlined. Here it is necessary to do no more than summarize the changes it made in the management of primary schools. They are as follows:—

(i) Under Section 17 every primary school, county as well as voluntary, has to have an instrument providing for the constitution of the whole body of managers, made in the case of county schools by the LEA and by the Minister in the case of voluntary schools. Both county and voluntary schools are to be conducted in accordance with rules of management made by the local education authority.

(ii) In aided schools, assuming a managing body of six, there are four foundation and two local authority managers. In controlled schools, where the whole financial responsibility rests with the local education authority, the proportions are reversed.

[123.] This wording may be compared with that of Section 16(5) of the 1944 Act. Parliamentary Counsel who drafted the 1944 Act considered that the 1921 Act, which had been drafted within the Board, was one of the worst drafted Acts on the Statute Book. It was his ambition that the Education Act of 1944 should be one of the best. (Letter of 24 February 1943 on PRO file Ed 136/293).

(iii) Under Section 18 in county primary schools the managing body consists of such number, not less than six, as the local education authority may determine.

(iv) Section 20 permits the grouping of schools for purposes of management. It differs from Section 12 of the 1902 Act in that it covers secondary as well as primary schools; it also permits the grouping of county with voluntary schools, provided that the managers of the latter agree.

General conclusion

132. What has this look into the past shown? There are several conclusions that might be drawn but two points stand out.

133. The first is the shift in the balance of control. For many years the Church had exclusive control. Then, after the Reformation, even though the Bishops' right to licence teachers lasted, at least formally, until 1869, laymen came more and more into the picture. The State, too, intervened by requiring the teaching of the doctrines and formularies of the Established Church and the use of such text books as "the Grammar set forth by King Henry VIII of noble memory"[124] and also, especially after the Restoration, by imposing religious tests on teachers. But the provision and maintenance of schools continued to be a wholly voluntary effort until well into the nineteenth century. Then, as it became increasingly evident that the burden was too great for voluntary effort to bear unaided, the State had to step in, first by making grants and then by transferring to newly created public authorities an increasing share of the responsibility for school provision and maintenance. This transfer of responsibility was accompanied by an increasing measure of control by those authorities. Today when the responsible public authorities are fewer in number and, it is said, more "remote", when the teachers are no longer the "poor ushers" of by-gone days when, largely as a result of the reforms of 1944, there is a much larger body of better educated and articulate parents, many of them anxious to "participate" and when, in terms both of beliefs and of ethnic origins, the nation is of a more heterogeneous character then it has been for a very long time, other voices are to be heard claiming that they too should have a share in this control.

134. The second point is the persistence of ideas and practices. The concept of school governing bodies has a long history and it would be expected that over the years ideas about their composition and functions should change. There have been changes but what is noticeable is, first, how comparatively little change there was before the middle of the nineteenth century and, second, how the changes that were then effected by the Public Schools Commission and the Endowed Schools Commission have endured. Many of the ideas that they evolved and, in some instances even the language in which they expressed those ideas, have survived to this day. Also noticeable is the persistence in certain of the larger urban areas[125] of the scepticism about the need for managing bodies in provided elementary or primary schools that first emerged in 1870.

---

124. The injunctions of Elizabeth, 1559. Gee and Hardy, Documents Illustrative of the History of the English Church (cited by D W Sylvester, Educational Documents, 800-1816).
125. But no longer in Sheffield.

183

135. A body to look after the interests of the foundation will, obviously, continue to be needed in the voluntary schools. But so far as the rest of the maintained school system is concerned, the greater part, the question inevitably arises whether in the circumstances of today, managing and governing bodies are still needed. Should they be abolished? Or, if the new demands for a share in the control are thought to be justified, should they be replaced by an entirely different kind of body?—Governing bodies were after all evolved to meet the administrative needs of a type of school, the grammar school, that is now in process of being eliminated from the public system of education. Or can they, with such changes in their composition and functions as may be considered necessary, be given a further period of useful and worthwhile life? These are questions which are considered in the main body of the report.

ANNEX I*

Bradford (1871)

Governing Body

Part II—Constitution of Governing Body and Management

2. The Governing Body, hereafter called the Governors, shall, from and after the date of this Scheme, consist of not more than 16 persons, nor less than 13, as hereinafter provided. Of these, four shall be ex officio Governors, four representative or elective, and the remainder co-optative.

3. The ex officio Governors shall be:—

The Vicar of Bradford
The Mayor of Bradford
The Chairman of the School Board of Bradford
And the President of the Bradford Mechanics' Institute, if they will respectively undertake to act in the Trusts of this Scheme.

4. Of the Representative Governors two shall be elected by the Town Council of Bradford, and two by the School Board of Bradford. The first elections shall take place as soon after the date of this Scheme as can conveniently be managed.

5. The Representative Governors shall be elected to hold office for the term of five years, and shall then retire, but be re-eligible.

Clauses dealing with
    46. Headmasters' stipend
    47. Payments for entrance and tuition
    48. Payments to be made in advance
    62–
    64. School exhibitions and other awards
    65. Repair and improvement fund
    66–
    68. Pensions
    69. Use of residue

Head Master Appointment

34. The Head Master, who shall have control over both departments, and shall be responsible for the whole work of the boys' school, shall be appointed by the Governors at some meeting to be called for that purpose, as soon as conveniently may be after the occurrence of a vacancy, or after notice of an intended vacancy. The Master shall be a graduate of some University within the British Empire. In order to obtain the best candidates the Governors shall, for a sufficient time before making any appointment, give public notice of the vacancy, and invite competition by advertisements in newspapers or by such other methods as they may judge best calculated to secure the object.

---

*The purpose of this Annex is explained in Appendix B paragraph 51.

Dismissal

35. The Governors may dismiss the Head Master without assigning cause, after six calendar months' written notice, given to him in pursuance of a resolution passed at two consecutive meetings held at an interval of at least 14 days, and duly convened for that express purpose, such resolution being affirmed at each meeting by not less than two-thirds of the Governors present.

36. For urgent cause the Governors may by resolution passed at a special meeting duly convened for that express purpose, and affirmed by not less than two-thirds of the whole existing number of Governors, declare that the Head Master ought to be dismissed from his office, and in that case they may appoint another special meeting to be held within not less than a week of the former one, and may then by a similar resolution affirmed by as large a proportion of Governors, wholly and finally dismiss him. And if the Governors assembled at the first of such meetings think fit at once to suspend the Head Master from his office until the next meeting, they may do so by resolution affirmed by as large a proportion of Governors. Full notice and opportunity of defence at both meetings shall be given to the Head Master.

Head Master to appoint and dismiss Assistant Masters, and to distribute fund assigned to Assistant Masters and plant.

44. The Head Master shall have the sole power of appointing and dismissing all Assistant Masters, and shall determine in what proportions the sum assigned by the Governors for the maintenance of Assistant Masters and of plant or apparatus shall be divided among the various persons and objects for the aggregate of which it is assigned. And the Governors shall pay the same accordingly, either through the hands of the Head Master or directly, as they think best. In the case of the Senior Master of the Junior Department his appointment or dismissal shall not be valid until it has been confirmed by the Governors.

45. The Head Master may from time to time submit proposals to the Governors for making or altering regulations as to any matter within their province, and the Governors shall consider such proposals and decide upon them.

Jurisdiction of Governors over Scholastic arrangements

41. Within the limits fixed by this Scheme the Governors shall prescribe the general subjects of instruction, the relative prominence and value to be assigned to each group of subjects, the division of the year into term and vacation, the payments of the scholars, and the number of holidays to be given in term. They shall take general supervision of the sanitary condition of the school buildings and arrangements. They shall determine what number of Assistant Masters shall be employed. They shall every year assign the amount which they think proper to be paid out of the income of the Trust for the purpose of maintaining Assistant Masters and a proper plant or apparatus for carrying on the instruction given in the School.

Governors to consult the Head Master

42. Before making or altering any regulations under the last preceding clause the Governors shall consult the Head Master in such a manner as to give him full opportunity for the expression of his views.

Jurisdiction of Head Master over Scholastic arrangements

43. Subject to the rules prescribed by or under the authority of this Scheme the Head Master shall have under his control the choice of books, the methods of teaching, the arrangement of classes and school hours, and generally the whole internal organisation, management and discipline of the School: Provided that if he expels a boy from the School, he shall forthwith make a full report of the case to the Governors.

1908 Model

Governing Body

3. (a) There shall be a Governing Body of the School (in these Articles called the Governors) which shall be constituted as a Sub-Committee of the Committee, and shall, when complete, consist of   persons to be appointed by the [Committee] [Council] of whom   shall be appointed on the recommendation of the [Borough] [Urban District] Council of   [and one shall be appointed on the recommendation of the University of   .]

(b) There shall always be amongst the Governors:—

i. [at least   women and]*

ii. at least   members of the Committee,
but the Council, the Committee, and any other body upon whose recommendation members of the Governing Body are to be appointed, may appoint or recommend for appointment persons who are not members of their own body.

(c) All Governors shall be appointed for a term of three years, provided that any Governor who, at the date of his appointment, is a member of the Council or of the Committee or of the recommending body, shall on ceasing to be a member thereof, cease also to be a Governor.

FINANCE

Estimate

10. (a) The Governors shall [when required by the Committee] [in the month of   in each year] submit for the consideration of the Committee an estimate of the income and expenditure required for the purposes of the School [for the 12 months ending   in the following year] in such form and for such period as the Committee require; the estimate shall show in particular the salary to be paid to each master and the estimated amount to be received in fees under the Rules for Payments made in accordance with these Articles.

(b) The Committee shall consider the estimate and make any variation in it which they think fit and shall then submit it [to the Finance Committee for recommendation] to the Council.

(c) The School shall be conducted in accordance with the estimate as approved by the Council, and no expenditure on any object beyond the amount of the estimate so approved shall be incurred by or on behalf of the Governors in any year without the previous consent of the [Committee] [Council].

---

*Only to be inserted where the school provides education for girls.

Receipts and Payments

11. (a) All moneys received by the Governors (except as in this Article mentioned), shall be carried to the [County]* Fund in such manner as the Committee, subject to any directions of the Council, prescribe [and shall be carried to a separate account to the credit of the School].

(b) The funds necessary for the maintenance of the School shall be provided by the Council and paid to the Governors by†   instalments in each year, and the Governors shall thereupon discharge all liabilities incurred by them on behalf of the Committee.

ALTERNATIVE

Receipts and Payments

[11A. (a) All moneys received by the Governors shall be carried to the [County]‡ Fund in such manner as the Committee, subject to any directions of the Council, prescribe [and shall be carried to a separate account to the credit of the School].

(b) The funds necessary for the maintenance of the School shall be provided by the Council, and all liabilities incurred by the Governors on behalf of the Committee shall be referred for payment to the   § Committee and discharged by them.]

Head Master

13. (a) The Head Master of the School shall be a graduate of a University in the United Kingdom or have such other equivalent qualification as may be approved by the Board of Education.

(b) He shall be appointed by [the Governors] [after due public advertisement of a vacancy or intended vacancy in newspapers and otherwise so as to secure the best candidates.

(c) The Head Master shall be employed under a contract of service in writing determinable only (except in the case of dismissal for misconduct or any other urgent cause) upon six months' written notice taking effect at the end of a School Term, which may be given by either side. The notice of determination or dismissal may be given by the Governors either on their own motion or after having been requested by the Committee to consider the matter.

(d) The resolution of the Governors to dismiss the Head Master for misconduct or any other urgent cause shall not take effect until it has been confirmed at a meeting of the Governors held not less than a week after the date of the meeting at which the resolution was passed. But the Governors may by resolution passed at the first of those meetings suspend the Head Master from his office until the second meeting.

---

*If the Authority providing the School is not a County Council, substitute the name of the fund out of which the expenses of the Council under the Education Act 1902, are payable.
†Insert number.
‡See note * above.
§Insert name of Committee referred to.

Assistant Masters

16*

Jurisdiction of Governors over School Arrangements

17. Within the limits fixed by these Articles, the Governors shall prescribe the general subjects of instruction, the relative prominence and value to be assigned to each group of subjects, what reports shall be required to be made to them by the Head Master, the arrangements respecting the school terms, vacations and holidays, [and the number of boarders]†. They shall take general supervision of the sanitary conditions of the school buildings and arrangements. Subject to the provisions of these Articles with respect to the submission and approval of estimates, they shall fix the number of Assistant Masters to be employed, and the amount to be paid for the purpose of providing and maintaining proper school plant or apparatus, and awarding prizes.

Views and Proposals of Head Master

18. Before making any rules under the last foregoing clause, the Governors shall consult the Head Master in such a manner as to give him full opportunity for the expression of his views, and he shall be entitled to be present at all meetings of the Governors, save when otherwise determined by them at any particular meeting. The Head Master may also from time to time submit proposals to the Governors for making or altering rules concerning any matter within the province of the Governors. The Governors shall fully consider any such expression of views or proposals and shall decide upon them.

Jurisdiction of Head Master over School Arrangements

19. (a) Subject to any rules prescribed by or under the authority of these Articles, the Head Master shall have under his control the choice of books, the method of teaching, the arrangement of classes and school hours, and generally the whole internal organisation, management, and discipline of the School, including the power of expelling pupils from the School or suspending them from attendance for any adequate cause to be judged of by him, but on expelling or suspending any pupil he shall forthwith report the case to the Governors.

(b) If an aggregate sum is fixed in the estimate for the maintenance of school plant and apparatus and prizes, the Head Master shall determine, subject to the approval of the Governors, in what proportions that sum shall be divided among the various objects, for which it is fixed in the aggregate.

---

*Note.—An Article should be inserted in this place dealing with the terms of employment of Assistant Masters, and the Authority or person in whose hands their appointment or dismissal is to rest. The Board of Education will require that all Assistant Masters and Mistresses should be employed either by, or upon the nomination of, or after consultation with, the Head Master or Head Mistress, under a contract determinable by a notice specified in the contract, and suggest, as the most appropriate term, two months ending at the end of any School Term. The Board will also require that the contract shall only be determinable by, or after consultation with, the Head Master or Head Mistress. Details as to these matters should be contained in the Article, which can also comprise provisions for the employment of Assistant Masters or Mistresses on probation.

†In the case of Boarding Schools only.

189

GENERAL

Copies of Reports and Returns

28. Copies of all reports, whether of the Head Master or of examiners or inspectors, and of all returns for the Board of Education, shall be forwarded to the Committee.

Questions under Articles

29. Any question as to the construction of these Articles, or as to the regularity or the validity of any acts done or about to be done under them by the Committee or the Governors, shall be determined conclusively by the Council.

Copies of Articles

30. A copy of these Articles shall be given to every Governor, Head Master and other Teacher, upon entry into office.

1945 Model

FINANCE

3. (a) The Governors shall in the month of   in each year submit for the consideration of the Local Education Authority an estimate of the income and expenditure required for the purposes of the school for the 12 months ending   in the following year, in such form as the Local Education Authority may require.

(b) The Local Education Authority shall consider the estimate and make such variation in it as they think fit.

(c) Where the Governors are empowered by the Local Education Authority to incur expenditure they shall not exceed the amount approved by the Local Education Authority under each head of the estimate in any year without the previous consent of the Local Education Authority.

Appointment and Dismissal of Head Master

5. (a) The appointment and dismissal of the Headmaster shall conform to the following procedure:—

Either The vacant post shall be advertised by the Local Education Authority and a short list of three names shall be drawn up from the applications for the post by the Governors, a representative of the Local Education Authority being present. The final appointment shall be made by the Local Education Authority, a representative of the Governing Body being present.

One or other of the alternatives to be inserted.

or The vacant post shall be advertised by the Local Education Authority and a short list shall be drawn up from the applications for the post by a Joint Committee consisting of an [equal number] of Governors and representatives of the Local Education Authority under the chairmanship of a person nominated by the Local Education Authority. The said Joint Committee shall also meet to interview the persons on the short list and shall recommend one person on the list for appointment by the Local Education Authority.

(b) The Head Master shall be employed under a contract of service in writing, determinable only (except in the case of dismissal for misconduct or any other urgent cause) upon [six/three] months written notice, taking effect at the end of a school term, which may be given by either side. Except when otherwise determined by the Local Education Authority he shall not be dismissed except on the recommendation of the Governors.

(c) A resolution of the governors to recommend the dismissal of the Head Master shall not take effect until it has been confirmed at a meeting of the Governors, held not less than 14 days after the date of the meeting at which the resolution was passed. The Governors may by a resolution suspend for misconduct or any other urgent cause the Head Master from his office pending the decision of the Local Education Authority.

(d) The Head Master shall be entitled to appear, accompanied by a friend, at any meeting of the Governors or the Local Education Authority at which his dismissal is to be considered, and shall be given at least [three] days notice of such meeting.

Assistant Masters

6. The appointment and dismissal of assistant masters shall be subject to the following procedure:—

(a) On the occurrence of a vacancy for an assistant master the Governors shall notify the Local Education Authority, who shall if they think fit, advertise the post and shall transmit to the Governors the names of candidates. Provided that the Local Education Authority may, if they think fit, and after giving full consideration to the views of the Governors and the Head Master, require the Governors to appoint a master to be transferred from another school or from any pool of new entrants to the teaching profession.

(b) The appointment of assistant masters shall be made to the service of the Local Education Authority by the Governors in consultation with the Headmaster within the limits of the establishment of staff laid down for the current year by the Local Education Authority, and such appointments shall, except where made under the proviso to paragraph (a) of this Article, be subject to confirmation by the Local Education Authority.

(c) Appointments of assistant masters shall in all cases be determinable upon [   ] months notice in writing.

(d) The procedure for the dismissal or suspension of assistant masters shall be similar to that specified for Headmasters, except that two meetings of the Governors shall not be required.

Organisation and Curriculum

8. (a) The Local Education Authority shall determine the general educational character of the school and its place in the local educational system. Subject thereto the Governors shall have the general direction of the conduct and curriculum of the school.

(b) Subject to the provisions of these Articles the Head Master shall control the internal organisation, management and discipline of the school, shall exercise supervision over the teaching and non-teaching staff, and shall have the power of suspending pupils from attendance for any cause which he considers adequate but on suspending any pupil he shall forthwith report the case to the Governor, who shall consult the Local Education Authority.

   (c) (i) There shall be full consultation at all times between the Head Master and the Chairman of the Governors.

       (ii) All proposals and reports affecting the conduct and curriculum of the school shall be submitted formally to the Governors. [The Chief Education Officer or his representative shall be informed of such reports and proposals and be furnished with a copy thereof at least [7] days before they are considered].

       (iii) The Head Master shall be entitled to attend throughout every meeting of the Governors, except on such occasions and for such time as the Governors may for good cause otherwise determine.

       (iv) There shall be full consultation and co-operation between the Head Master and the Chief Education Officer on matters affecting the welfare of the school.

       (v) Suitable arrangements shall be made for enabling the teaching staff to submit their views or proposals to the Governors through the Head Master.

Returns

11. The Governors shall furnish to the Local Education Authority such returns and reports as the Authority may require.

Copies of Articles

12. A copy of these Articles shall be given to every Governor, the Head Master, and every Assistant Master on entry into office.

ANNEX II

Extract from Fleming Committee's Report on
abolition of tuition fees in grant-aided secondary schools

"It is an established principle of our public life that when public money is provided, whether by Parliament or Local Authorities, it is the duty of the elected representatives of the people to ensure that it is wisely and prudently expended. It would be generally agreed that this would not necessarily entail a rigorous or exact examination of every detail in the expenditure. In practice a system of mutual trust between the representatives and their officers on the one hand and those actually engaged in a special field of social activity on the other makes possible a wise latitude. Nor is it generally held that this principle entails that in all the varied services provided for the people the precise lines of policy must always be laid down and controlled by these representatives and their officers. The same atmosphere of trust allows the people to use the services of experts in their own fields, relying on their integrity and sense of duty to ensure that, to the best of their ability, they will act wisely in the public interest.

The question of the extent of such freedom which should be allowed to those engaged in the service of the community as teachers is one of particular difficulty. Education is an Art and can never be regarded only as a branch of administration. But it is a subject in which all are interested and in which all feel concern. In the most profound sense of the word it is a political question. Every community has been forced to recognise the truth of Aristotle's words, that 'children must be trained by education with an eye to the State, if their virtues are supposed to make any difference to the virtues of the State'.

Regard, however, should be paid to another educational principle laid down by the same writer. 'To have been educated in the spirit of the constitution is to perform not the actions in which oligarchs or democrats delight, but those by which the existence of an oligarchy or democracy is made possible'. England is a democracy and its children should be educated in the spirit of a democratic constitution. This does not mean that it is necessary for the education of children to reflect each change in the minds of the electorate. It does mean that it is necessary for the children to be trained for citizenship in a democratic community, imbued with those qualities which alone can make democracy a successful form of government—a sense of loyalty to the community, a readiness to work unselfishly with others in its service, and the courage and independence of judgment which are needed when the men and women of the community are themselves its rulers.

As a means of training future citizens the school must be itself a community. It must command the loyalty of its members, the pupils and the teachers. This can only be obtained if it has its own individuality, which they themselves build up, preserve and develop. Any action on the part of national or local representatives or those acting on their behalf, which would have the effect of destroying this individuality or corporate sense, would be educationally disastrous. Individuality could be destroyed or seriously endangered if schools were compelled to adopt a uniform line of policy, and the result might be the same if the public representatives or their officers felt they should give minute consideration to the administrative details of the school. We appreciate that the public representatives must ensure a prudent expenditure of public money. That is a duty they cannot

193

abandon. But methods of fulfilling it in the educational field need not be precisely similar to those employed in others.

We wish to make it clear that we do not believe that among those engaged in the administration of Education in this country there is any desire to deny to the schools a real variety. But it will be appreciated that the administrative control of schools may, in itself, tend to produce uniformity. If a single committee or their officer undertakes the supervision of several schools, there is a danger that they may be treated alike. Often a sense of fairness, a scrupulous feeling that no one school should receive any different, or what appears to them to be preferential, treatment, will lead to this. But if schools are to preserve their individuality, they must preserve also their variety. This variety is not only a sign of health; it is essential for an effective educational system, designed to meet the needs of different children and the views of different parents. In practice it is immensely difficult, if not impossible, for one man, or one body of men, acting on the principle of majority rule, consciously to effect this variety. We can only hope for this to be secured and developed by allowing those who control the schools, the Governing Bodies, and those who serve in them, the headmasters and headmistresses and assistant teachers, the greatest possible measure of independence. The aim of our educational system should be that expressed by Milton: 'The perfection consists in this, that out of many moderate varieties and brotherly dissimilitudes that are not vastly disproportional, arises the goodly and graceful symmetry that commends the whole pile and structure'."

APPENDIX C

Visits

Members of the Committee discussed school management and government with representatives of a wide range of interests drawn from the areas covered by the following local education authorities:

Bedfordshire
Birmingham
Calderdale
Clwyd
Devon
Ealing
Gwent
Gwynedd
Harrow
Humberside
ILEA
Isle of Wight
Lancashire
Northumberland
Nottinghamshire
Richmond
Sheffield
Solihull
Staffordshire

Committee members also attended the following courses and conferences:

a seminar for managers and governors in the Warrington district of Cheshire,
the 1975 annual conference of the British Educational Administration Society,
the 1975 annual conference of the National Association of Governors and Managers,
a conference on the government of secondary schools at Cumberland Lodge, Windsor,
a conference for school governors and managers at Nottingham University School of Education,
an induction course for managers, governors and clerks in the London Borough of Ealing.

APPENDIX D

The Education Act, 1944: Selected Extracts

SECTIONS 17-21 AND THE FOURTH SCHEDULE

Management of Primary Schools and Government of Secondary Schools.

17.—(1) For every county school and for every voluntary school there shall be an instrument providing for the constitution of the body of managers or governors of the school in accordance with the provisions of this Act, and the instrument providing for the constitution of the body of managers of a primary school is in this Act referred to as an instrument of management, and the instrument providing for the constitution of the body of governors of a secondary school is in this Act referred to as an instrument of government.

Constitution of managers and governors and conduct of county schools and voluntary schools.

(2) The instrument of management or the instrument of government, as the case may be, shall be made in the case of a county school by an order of the local education authority and in the case of a voluntary school by an order of the Secretary of State.

(3) Subject to the provisions of this Act and of any trust deed relating to the school:—

(a) every county primary school and every voluntary primary school shall be conducted in accordance with rules of management made by an order of the local education authority; and

(b) every county secondary school and every voluntary secondary school shall be conducted in accordance with articles of government made in the case of a county school by an order of the local education authority and approved by the Secretary of State, and in the case of a voluntary school by an order of the Secretary of State; and such articles shall in particular determine the functions to be exercised in relation to the school by the local education authority, the body of governors, and the head teacher respectively.

(4) Where it appears to the Secretary of State that any provision included or proposed to be included in the instrument of management, rules of management, instrument of government, or articles of government, for a county school or a voluntary school is in any respect inconsistent with the provisions of any trust deed relating to the school, and that it is expedient in the interests of the school that the provisions of the trust deed

197

should be modified for the purpose of removing the inconsistency, he may by order make such modifications in the provisions of the trust deed as appear to him to be just and expedient for that purpose.

(5) Before making any order under this section in respect of any school, the Secretary of State shall afford to the local education authority and to any other persons appearing to him to be concerned with the management or government of the school an opportunity of making representations to him with respect thereto, and in making any such order the Secretary of State shall have regard to all the circumstances of the school, and in particular to the question whether the school is, or is to be, a primary or secondary school, and, in the case of an existing school, shall have regard to the manner in which the school has been conducted theretofore.

(6) Where proposals for a significant change in the character of a voluntary school are approved under section 13 of this Act, then, without prejudice to the power to vary orders conferred by section III the Secretary of State may by order make such variations of the articles of government (if the school is a secondary school). . . as appear to him to be required in consequence of the proposed change in the character of the school; and so much of sub-section (5) of this section as relates to the making of representations with respect to orders under this section shall not apply to an order made in pursuance only of the power conferred by this subsection.

18.—(1) The instrument of management for every county primary school serving an area in which there is a minor authority shall provide for the constitution of a body of managers consisting of such number of persons, not being less than six, as the local education authority may determine:

Provided that two-thirds of the managers shall be appointed by the local education authority and one-third shall be appointed by the minor authority.

(2) The instrument of management for every county primary school serving an area in which there is no minor authority shall provide for the constitution of a body of managers constituted in such manner as the local education authority may determine.

(3) The instrument of management for every voluntary primary school shall provide for the constitution of a body of managers consisting of such number of persons not being less than six as the Secretary of State may, after consultation with the local education authority, determine:

Provided that:—

    (a) if the school is an aided school or a special agreement school, two-thirds of the managers shall be foundation managers, and, if the school is a controlled school, one-third of the managers shall be foundation managers;

(*b*) where the school serves an area in which there is a minor authority, then of the managers who are not foundation managers not less than one-third nor more than one-half shall be appointed by the minor authority and the remainder shall be appointed by the local education authority; and

(*c*) where the school serves an area in which there is no minor authority, all the managers who are not foundation managers shall be appointed by the local education authority.

19.—(1) The instrument of government for every county secondary school shall provide for the constitution of a body of governors consisting of such number of persons appointed in such manner as the local education authority may determine.

(2) The instrument of government for every voluntary secondary school shall provide for the constitution of a body of governors of the school consisting of such number of persons as the Secretary of State may after consultation with the local education authority determine:

Provided that—

(*a*) where the school is a controlled school, one-third of the governors shall be foundation governors and two-thirds of the governors shall be appointed by the local education authority;

(*b*) where the school is an aided school or a special agreement school, two-thirds of the governors shall be foundation governors and one-third of the governors shall be appointed by the local education authority.

20.—(1) A local education authority may make an arrangement for the constitution of a single governing body for any two or more county schools or voluntary schools maintained by them, and any such arrangement may relate exclusively to primary schools, or exclusively to secondary schools or partly to primary schools and partly to secondary schools:

Provided that an authority shall not make any such arrangement with respect to a voluntary school except with the consent of the managers or governors thereof.

(2) The governing body constituted in pursuance of any such arrangement as aforesaid shall, if all the schools to which the arrangement relates are county schools, consist of such number of persons appointed in such manner as the local education authority may determine.

(3) Where all or any of the schools to which any such arrangement relates are voluntary schools, the governing body constituted in pursuance of the arrangement shall consist of such number of persons appointed in such manner as may be determined by agreement between the local education authority and the managers or governors of those schools, or, in default of such agreement, by the Secretary of State.

(4) The local education authority, in making any such arrangement as aforesaid which relates to a primary school serving an area in which there is a minor authority, shall make provision for securing that the minor authority is adequately represented upon the governing body constituted in pursuance of the arrangement.

(5) Every arrangement made under this section may, if it does not relate to any voluntary school, be terminated at any time by the local education authority by which it was made, and any such arrangement which relates to such a school may be terminated by agreement between the local education authority and the governing body constituted in pursuance of the arrangement, or, in default of such agreement, by one year's notice served by the local education authority on the said governing body or by one year's notice served by the said governing body on the local education authority.

(6) While an arrangement under this section is in force with respect to any schools, the provisions of the last three foregoing sections as to the constitution of the body of managers or governors shall not apply to the schools, and for the purposes of any enactment the governing body constituted in accordance with the arrangement shall be deemed to be the body of managers or governors of each of those schools, and references to a manager or governor in any enactment shall, in relation to every such school, be construed accordingly.

Proceedings of managers and governors of county and voluntary schools.

21.—(1) Any manager or governor of a county school or of a voluntary school may resign his office, and any such manager or governor appointed by a local education authority or by a minor authority shall be removable by the authority by whom he was appointed.

(2) The provisions of the Fourth Schedule to this Act shall have effect with respect to the meetings and proceedings of the managers or governors of any county school or voluntary school.

(3) The minutes of the proceedings of the managers or governors of any county school or voluntary school shall be open to inspection by the local education authority.

MEETINGS AND PROCEEDINGS OF MANAGERS AND GOVERNORS.

1. The quorum of the managers or governors shall not be less than three, or one third of the whole number of managers or governors, whichever is the greater.

2. The proceedings of the managers or governors shall not be invalidated by any vacancy in their number or by any defect in the election, appointment or qualification of any manager or governor.

3. Every question to be determined at a meeting of the managers or governors shall be determined by a majority of the votes of the managers or governors present and voting on the question, and where there is an equal division of votes the chairman of the meeting shall have a second or casting vote.

4. The managers or governors shall hold a meeting at least once in every term.

5. A meeting of the managers or governors may be convened by any two of their number.

6. The minutes of the proceedings of the managers or governors shall be kept in a book provided for the purpose.

Section 36.   Duty of parents to secure the education of their children

36. It shall be the duty of the parent of every child of compulsory school age to cause him to receive efficient full-time education suitable to his age, ability, and aptitude, either by regular attendance at school or otherwise.

Section 114.   Interpretation of expressions "Foundation Managers" and "Foundation Governors"   Interpretation.

114—(1) In this Act, unless the context otherwise requires, the following expressions have the meanings hereby respectively assigned to them, that is to say:

"Foundation managers" and "foundation governors" mean, in relation to any voluntary school, managers and governors appointed otherwise than by a local education authority or a minor authority for the purpose of securing, so far as is practicable, that the character of the school as a voluntary school is preserved and developed, and, in particular, that the school is conducted in accordance with the provisions of any trust deed relating thereto; and, unless the context otherwise requires, references in this Act to "managers" or "governors" shall, in relation to any function thereby conferred or imposed exclusively on foundation managers or foundation governors, be construed as references to such managers or governors;

201

APPENDIX E

Administrative Memorandum No. 25 and Model Instrument, Articles of Government and Rules of Management

To Local Education Authorities for   Administrative Memorandum No. 25
Higher Education and (for information)   (26th January, 1945)
to Local Education Authorities for
Elementary Education

MINISTRY OF EDUCATION

Instruments, Articles of Government and Rules of Management

I. COUNTY AND VOLUNTARY SECONDARY SCHOOLS

1. Under Section 17 of the Education Act, 1944; every county secondary school is required as from 1st April 1945 to have an instrument of government made by order of the Local Education Authority and articles of government made by order of the Local Education Authority and approved by the Minister of Education. Voluntary secondary schools are similarly required to have instruments and articles of government made by order of the Minister. The Minister has already issued a memorandum on "principles of government in maintained secondary schools", and he has now decided to circulate a model instrument and articles of government applicable to county secondary schools for the assistance of Local Education Authorities.

2. Under Section 32(1) (b) of the Act voluntary schools which, prior to 1st April, 1945, were maintained as non-provided Public Elementary Schools are not required to have instruments and articles of government until the question whether the school is to be a controlled, aided or special agreement school is settled. During the transitional period they are to be managed and conducted in like manner as they were immediately before 1st April, 1945. Grammar schools which, prior to 1st April, 1945 were recognised for grant under the Regulations for Secondary Schools but which do not become County Schools under Section 9(2) of the Act, are not required under the Act to have instruments and articles, until they become voluntary schools by virtue of the Minister's approval of proposals under Section 13 of the Act; meantime, as one of the conditions of assistance by the Authority under Section 9(1) of the Act, they will be governed and conducted in like manner as they were immediately before 1st April, 1945.

3. In making instruments and articles for voluntary secondary schools the Minister will have regard, subject to the provisions of the Education Act, 1944, to existing Schemes or other

instruments and to the model instrument and articles for county secondary schools, in so far as they are applicable. School authorities are, however, at liberty to submit their views after consultation with the Local Education Authority on such matters as the composition of the Governing Body and the procedure for appointment of teaching or other staff. Such views should be expressed when proposals or applications are made under Sections 13 and 15 of the Act.

II. COUNTY AND VOLUNTARY PRIMARY SCHOOLS

4. Under Section 17 of the Act every county primary school is required, as from 1st April, 1945, to have an instrument and rules of management made by order of the Local Education Authority.

Voluntary primary schools are required to have instruments of management made by order of the Minister, and rules of management made, as in the case of county schools, by order of the Local Education Authority. Voluntary primary schools are not required to have instruments and rules of management until the question whether the school is to be controlled or aided is settled; during the transitional period they are to be managed and conducted in like manner as they were immediately prior to the 1st April, 1945.

Certain provisions as to the constitution of the body of managers of county primary schools are contained in Section 18 of the Education Act, 1944. The Minister does not propose to issue model rules of management, but Authorities may find that the model articles of government for county secondary schools will assist them in drawing up such rules of management. Authorities may find it convenient to compile the rules of management for county and voluntary primary schools in a handbook with a list of the schools, to which the rules apply, appended.

III. GROUPING OF GOVERNING BODIES

5. Local education authorities should inform the Minister in due course of any arrangements, which they propose to make, with the consent of the managers or governors, for grouping voluntary primary or secondary schools under Section 20 of the Act.

Schedule to Administrative Memorandum No. 25
issued 26th January, 1945

MINISTRY OF EDUCATION
EDUCATION ACT 1944

Model Instrument and Articles of Government for a County Secondary School

NOTES

I. The following suggestions are intended for the use of Local Education Authorities in drawing up Instruments and Articles of Government for County Secondary Schools. Authorities will find it generally convenient to include the Instrument and Articles in one document, but, inasmuch as the Instrument does not require the approval of the Minister of Education, it should be shown separately from the Articles in the manner indicated below.

II. Attention is directed to the Fourth Schedule to the Education Act, 1944, which contains additional provisions relating to meetings and proceedings of Governing Bodies.

III. Adequate representation should be given to women in the constitution of Governing Bodies and particularly in the case of Girls' and Mixed Schools.

IV. In accordance with the Interpretation Act, 1889, references to Headmaster and Master include also in appropriate cases Headmistress and Mistress.

V. In cases where several schools are grouped under one Governing Body it may be found convenient to set out the individual schools in a schedule both to the Instrument and Articles of Government. A separate Instrument and Articles must however be made for every School which is not grouped.

VI. Where a County Local Education Authority have made a Scheme of Divisional Administration it will be appreciated that some of the functions of the Local Education Authority under the Instrument and Articles of Government will be delegated to the Divisional Executive and, where this is the case, the true interpretation of the Instrument and Articles of Government will be obtained only when they are read in conjunction with that Scheme.

COUNTY [BOROUGH] COUNCIL
A. *INSTRUMENT OF GOVERNMENT*

The County (Borough) Council of
acting as the Local Education Authority hereby orders as follows:—

Governing Body

1. The Governing Body, hereinafter called "the Governors"

of the   School shall, when complete,
consist of   persons, that is to say:—
(   ) Representative Governors, to be appointed as follows:—
(   ) by the Local Education Authority
N.B. here add any other categories of Representative Governors
(   ) Co-optative Governors, to be appointed,
except as hereinafter provided in the case of the first such
Governors, by resolution of the Governors.

The Representative Governors shall be appointed for a term
of   years; and the Co-optative Governors, except as hereinafter provided, each for a term of   years.

A Representative Governor need not be a member of the
appointing body.

First Governors and Meeting

2. (i) The following persons shall be deemed to be the first
Co-optative Governors, and, subject to the provisions of this
Instrument as to the termination of Governorship, shall be
entitled to hold office for   years.

N.B. Here insert names of first Co-optative Governors

(ii) The First Representative Governors shall be appointed
as soon as possible after the date of this Instrument, and their
names shall be notified to the Clerk of the Governors on behalf
of the Governors.

(iii) The first meeting of the Governors under this Instrument
shall be summoned by the said Clerk not later than the
day of   1945, or, if he fails to summon a meeting
for two months after that date, by any two Governors or by the
Chief Education Officer.

Governors not to be financially Interested in the School

3. Except with the approval in writing of the Local Education
Authority no Governor shall take or hold any interest in any
property held or used for the purposes of the school or receive
any remuneration for his services, or be interested in the supply
of work or goods to or for the purposes of the School.

Masters not to be Governors

4. No master or other person employed for the purposes of
the School shall be a Governor.

Determination of Governorship

5. Any Governor who is absent from all meetings of the
Governors during a period of one year, or who is adjudicated
a bankrupt, or who is incapacitated from acting, or who com-
municates in writing to the Clerk of the Governors a wish to
resign, shall thereupon cease to be a Governor.

Vacancies

6. Every vacancy in the office of Representative or Co-optative Governor shall as soon as possible be notified to the proper appointing body or person or filled by the Governors as the case requires. Any competent Governors may be re-appointed.

Casual Vacancies

7. A Governor appointed to fill a casual vacancy shall hold office only for the unexpired term of office of the Governor in whose place he is appointed.

Chairman

8. The Governors shall, at their first ordinary or stated meeting in each year, elect two of their number to be respectively Chairman and Vice-Chairman of their meetings for the year. If both the Chairman and the Vice-Chairman are absent from any meeting the members present shall choose one of their number to preside at that meeting before any other business is transacted. The Chairman and Vice-Chairman shall always be re-eligible.

Rescinding Resolutions

9. Any resolution of the Governors may be rescinded or varied at a subsequent meeting if due notice of the intention to rescind or vary the same has been given to all the Governors.

Adjournment of Meetings

10. If at the time appointed for a meeting a sufficient number of Governors to form a quorum is not present, or if at any meeting the business is not completed, the meeting shall stand adjourned sine-die, and a special meeting shall be summoned as soon as conveniently may be. Any meeting may be adjourned by resolution.

[Application of Scheme of Divisional Administration

11. Where the Local Education Authority have delegated under a Scheme of Divisional Administration to a Divisional Executive for the area in which the school is situated any of the powers and duties of the Local Education Authority under this Instrument the expression "Local Education Authority" in this Instrument shall, where necessary, be deemed to refer to or to include, as the case may be, the Divisional Executive.] *To be inserted in appropriate cases*

Interpretation Act

12. The Interpretation Act, 1889, shall apply to the interpretation of this Instrument as it applies to an Act of Parliament.

Date of Instrument

13. The date of this Instrument shall be   .

B. ARTICLES OF GOVERNMENT

The County (Borough) Council of   acting as
the Local Education Authority hereby orders as follows:—

Conduct of School

1. The   School shall be conducted in accordance
with the provisions of the Education Act, 1944, with the provisions of any Regulations made by the Minister of Education
relating to County Secondary Schools and with these Articles.

Date of Articles

2. The date of these Articles shall be the 1st day of April, 1945,
or the day on which the Minister of Education signifies his
approval of these Articles, whichever is the later.

Finance

3. (a) The Governors shall in the month of   in
each year submit for the consideration of the Local Education
Authority an estimate of the income and expenditure required
for the purposes of the school for the 12 months ending
                    in the following year, in such form as the Local
Education Authority may require.

(b) The Local Education Authority shall consider the estimate
and make such variation in it as they think fit.

(c) Where the Governors are empowered by the Local
Education Authority to incur expenditure they shall not exceed
the amount approved by the Local Education Authority under
each head of the estimate in any year without the previous
consent of the Local Education Authority.

School Premises

4. (a) The Governors shall from time to time inspect, and keep
the Local Education Authority informed as to, the condition
and state of repair of the school premises, and, where the Local
Education Authority so permit, the Governors shall have power
to carry out urgent repairs up to such an amount as may be
approved by the Local Education Authority.

(b) The Governors shall, subject to any direction of the Local
Education Authority, determine the use to which the school
premises, or any part thereof, may be put out of school hours.

208

Appointment and Dismissal of Head Master

5. (a) The appointment and dismissal of the Headmaster shall conform to the following procedure:—

EITHER   The vacant post shall be advertised by the Local Education Authority and a short list of three names shall be drawn up from the applications for the post by the Governors, a representative of the Local Education Authority being present. The final appointment shall be made by the Local Education Authority, a representative of the Governing Body being present.

OR   The vacant post shall be advertised by the Local Education Authority and a short list shall be drawn up from the applications for the post by a Joint Committee consisting of an [equal number] of Governors and representatives of the Local Education Authority under the chairmanship of a person nominated by the Local Education Authority. The said Joint Committee shall also meet to interview the persons on the short list and shall recommend one person on the list for appointment by the Local Education Authority.

One or other of the alternatives to be inserted.

(b) The Head Master shall be employed under a contract of service in writing, determinable only (except in the case of dismissal for misconduct or any other urgent cause) upon [six/three] months written notice, taking effect at the end of a school term, which may be given by either side. Except when otherwise determined by the Local Education Authority he shall not be dismissed except on the recommendation of the Governors.

(c) A resolution of the governors to recommend the dismissal of the Headmaster shall not take effect until it has been confirmed at a meeting of the Governors, held not less than 14 days after the date of the meeting at which the resolution was passed. The Governors may by a resolution suspend for misconduct or any other urgent cause the Headmaster from his office pending the decision of the Local Education Authority.

(d) The Headmaster shall be entitled to appear, accompanied by a friend, at any meeting of the Governors or the Local Education Authority at which his dismissal is to be considered, and shall be given at least [three] days notice of such meeting.

Assistant Masters

6. The appointment and dismissal of assistant masters shall be subject to the following procedure:—

(a) On the occurrence of a vacancy for an assistant master the Governors shall notify the Local Education Authority, who shall if they think fit, advertise the post and shall transmit to the Governors the names of candidates. Provided that the Local Education Authority may, if they think fit, and after

209

giving full consideration to the views of the Governors and the Headmaster, require the Governors to appoint a master to be transferred from another school or from any pool of new entrants to the teaching profession.

(b) The appointment of assistant masters shall be made to the service of the Local Education Authority by the Governors in consultation with the Headmaster within the limits of the establishment of staff laid down for the current year by the Local Education Authority, and such appointments shall, except where made under the proviso to paragraph (a) of this Article, be subject to confirmation by the Local Education Authority.

(c) Appointments of assistant masters shall in all cases be determinable upon [   ] months notice in writing.

(d) The procedure for the dismissal or suspension of assistant masters shall be similar to that specified for Headmasters, except that two meetings of the Governors shall not be required.

Non-teaching Staff

7. (a) The non-teaching staff shall, subject to any general directions of the Local Education Authority, be appointed by the Governors, after consultation with the Head Master, to the service of the Authority and shall be dismissed by the Local Education Authority upon the recommendation of the Governors.

(b) The Clerk of the Governors shall be the Chief Education Officer or such other person as may be appointed by the Local Education Authority.

Organisation and Curriculum

8. (a) The Local Education Authority shall determine the general educational character of the school and its place in the local educational system. Subject thereto the Governors shall have the general direction of the conduct and curriculum of the school.

(b) Subject to the provisions of these Articles the Headmaster shall control the internal organisation, management and discipline of the school, shall exercise supervision over the teaching and non-teaching staff, and shall have the power of suspending pupils from attendance for any cause which he considers adequate but on suspending any pupil he shall forthwith report the case to the Governors, who shall consult the Local Education Authority.

(c) (i) There shall be full consultation at all times between the Headmaster and the Chairman of the Governors.

(ii) All proposals and reports affecting the conduct and curriculum of the school shall be submitted formally to the Governors. [The Chief Education Officer or his representative shall be informed of such reports and proposals and be furnished with a copy thereof at least [7] days before they are considered]. *Sentence in square brackets to be omitted if circumstances make it unnecessary.*

(iii) The Headmaster shall be entitled to attend throughout every meeting of the Governors, except on such occasions and for such times as the Governors may for good cause otherwise determine.

(iv) There shall be full consultation and co-operation between the Headmaster and the Chief Education Officer on matters affecting the welfare of the school.

(v) Suitable arrangements shall be made for enabling the teaching staff to submit their views or proposals to the Governors through the Headmaster.

School Holidays

9. Holidays for the school shall be fixed by the Local Education Authority, but the Governors shall have power to grant mid-term or other occasional holidays not exceeding 10 days in any year.

Admission of Pupils

10. The admission of pupils to the school shall be in accordance with arrangements made by the Local Education Authority, which shall take into account the wishes of the parents, any school records and other information which may be available, the general type of education most suitable for the particular child and the views of the Governors and the Headmaster as to the admission of the child to the School.

Returns

11. The Governors shall furnish to the Local Education Authority such returns and reports as the Authority may require.

Copies of Articles

12. A copy of these Articles shall be given to every Governor, the Headmaster, and every Assistant master on entry into office.

211

[Application of Scheme of Divisional Administration

To be inserted in appropriate cases.
13. Where the Local Education Authority have delegated under a Scheme of Divisional Administration to a Divisional Executive for the area in which the school is situated any of the powers and duties of the Local Education Authority under these Articles the expression "Local Education Authority" in these Articles shall, where necessary, be deemed to refer to or to include, as the case may be, the Divisional Executive.]

Interpretation Act
14. The Interpretation Act, 1889, shall apply to the interpretation of these Articles as it applies to an Act of Parliament.

The governing body's letter to parents: idea of the letter which governing bodies might send to parents at the time of their formal acceptance of a place at school

To the Parents of ....

We understand that your child will be coming to this school and as governors we welcome him and hope he will be happy and successful here. He will be in the care of teachers who will do their best to see that he enjoys school and learns well, and we hope that the school will in every way earn your confidence.

We also welcome YOU, his parents. Your support for your child and your interest in the school are vital to his education. Because the part played by parents is so important, the school will always try to involve you in its life and work. You will be invited regularly to meet your child's teachers to hear how he is getting on and perhaps how you can help him. But we hope you will feel that the school is a friendly place where you are welcome at any time, and that you will not wait to be asked to come if you have any worries or questions. A member of staff will always see you by reasonable arrangement. We promise in turn that the school will contact you promptly if any problem arises with your child. You will be fully informed about the school's aims and methods, its rules and the reasons for them. You will see among our names and addresses given below those of governors representing parents. It is your right as parents to be represented, and you may be asked at some time while your child is here to take part in elections for the governing body. The school also recognises parents' rights to form their own organisations and we welcome you to our PTA/ Parents' Association/Friends of the School Association, which we encourage and support.

You will know that while your child is a pupil of the school it is your legal duty to see that he attends regularly and punctually; we hope that you will seek the help of the school if you have any difficulties in meeting this obligation. But this letter is not about legal matters: it is about the many ways in which schools and parents can work in willing partnership for the child's good. We have told you about the arrangements which the school makes to keep in close touch with you. You can best help your child if you take full advantage of these arrangements, joining in as often as possible in the consultations with teachers, meetings and activities for parents, and coming to discuss any problem which your advice and support may help the school to solve. You can help us by trying to make sure that any work set by the school is done and by supporting us in our efforts to encourage pleasant and considerate behaviour at school.

This is, in a very important sense, YOUR school, and your child's education is a responsibility we share with you. Please accept this letter of welcome as a promise that we will do our best to win your trust. No school is perfect, teachers are human and have a very difficult job. With parents' help and support they can do it a lot better. You will see that we enclose two copies of this letter. We

213

thought you might like to keep one as a reminder of a big occasion in your child's life. Perhaps you will kindly return the other after filling in the slip confirming that you have accepted the place at the school. We shall then know that an important message has reached you, and we too shall have a reminder of what we hope to achieve, with your help, for your child.

Names and addresses of governors

....

I confirm that I have accepted a place for my child at...

School in September.............................

Signature of Parent...

APPENDIX G

Translating the school's aims into practice: examples illustrating the part to be played by the new governing bodies

Note

These six examples have been chosen simply to illustrate a possible allocation of responsibilities and the procedures that might be followed. It is assumed that account will always be taken of any existing local education authority policies, and that where appropriate a headteacher before approaching the governing body about a particular proposal, will consult his staff. It should not be inferred that the procedures outlined will necessarily be followed in deciding such matters in individual schools, nor should it be assumed from the examples quoted that a particular method of teaching or of school organisation is considered to be better or worse than another.

Example A

Consideration of a proposal for the introduction of the initial teaching alphabet (ITA) as a means of teaching reading into the infants' department of a junior and infants' school.

1. Originator

The teacher in charge of the infants' department.

2. Action by headteacher

a. To ensure that it has been discussed at least by all the teachers in the infants' department and by those teachers in the junior department who may be involved.

b. To bring it before the next meeting of the governing body.

3. Action by governing body

To request the head to ascertain whether there was any LEA policy on the matter by discussion with the LEA adviser, to prepare a report on the merits of the proposal. The governing body might wish him to mention, in particular, such considerations as:

a. the place of reading in the school's aims and objectives;

b. the information available about the advantages of teaching reading through ITA rather than other methods;

c. the resource implications within the school (training of teachers in ITA, books, equipment);

d. the possible response of parents, and in particular access for them and their children to supplementary reading matter in ITA (e.g. from the public library);

e. the steps by which ITA might be introduced if the proposal were accepted;

f. if it were introduced, by what means progress could be monitored and the scheme evaluated.

[NB: The distribution of action between 2 and 3 above is arbitrary. The head might, for example, have prepared a report covering all the considerations listed in 3 before approaching the governing body.]

Governing body to consider the report and reach a decision to proceed or not to proceed with the proposal, or to require further information.

Conclusion

In general the choice of reading material to be used might be regarded as one for the teachers although the governing body could expect to be informed and its members would be free to raise questions about it. But the question of introducing ITA as a basic approach raises more general issues and might therefore be considered an appropriate matter for a decision by the governing body.

216

Example B

Consideration of a proposal to introduce the teaching of French into a primary school (ages 7-11)

1. Originator

A parent, in a letter to the headteacher.

2. Action by headteacher

   i. To acknowledge the proposal.

   ii. To hold preliminary consultations with the teaching staff.

   iii. To report to the next meeting of the governing body.

3. Action by governing body

Request to head, after further discussion with teachers, to consult local education authority adviser(s) and the appropriate secondary school(s) and to make a full report on:

   i. the educational merits of the proposal;

   ii. the implications for the overall aims and objectives of the school;

   iii. the resource implications (teachers, books, equipment etc.);

   iv. effects on existing timetable, including the steps by which the teaching of French might be introduced;

   v. the steps necessary to monitor progress and evaluate the scheme if it is introduced, including any resource implications of such measures;

   vi. implications for other primary schools feeding the same secondary school(s).

Again, the division of action between 2 and 3 above is made simply for the purposes of this example: some heads would probably have taken some at least of the steps in 3 before bringing the matter before the governing body.

The governing body might decide to convene a meeting with representatives of the local education authority and the appropriate secondary school(s) to discuss the proposal further. This is clearly not a matter which the governing body should decide in isolation. Only the local education authority can decide whether additional resources can be provided. If the school were to attempt to proceed without additional resources (eg of staff, of equipment) its ability to achieve its agreed aims and objectives might be impaired.

The governing body would reach a decision in the light of all the considerations mentioned. If they decided to go ahead, they would ask the headteacher to take the necessary steps and to propose arrangements for monitoring the effects and effectiveness of the teaching so that it could be evaluated in due course. If they decided not to go ahead, they would ask the head to convey and explain the decision to the parent. The matter would in due course be mentioned in the head's annual report.

Example C

Proposal to replace a system of streaming* by mixed ability† grouping in a secondary school

1. Originator

Members of the teaching staff.

2. Action by headteacher

Discussion with the proposers, then preparation for the governing body of statements of:

a. the educational and social reasons for considering the proposal;

b. particulars of the changes proposed (e.g. years affected, time scale envisaged by the proposers);

c. any consequential changes necessary, for example in remedial programme, in arrangements for preparation for public examinations, any other form of selective grouping of pupils proposed (e.g. "setting"‡);

d. the training implications for teaching staff and how they were envisaged for each department;

e. possible resource implications (e.g. changes or additional staff, books, equipment);

f. steps by which the change could be introduced, including comments on the time scale required.

3. Action by governing body

a. Request to head for information as to monitoring and assessment of standards of attainment under the new system, in order that their effects on the achievement of the school's aims and objectives could be estimated.

b. Suggestion that the local education authority advisers should be brought into the discussion.

c. To reach a decision.

4. Conclusion

Unless the local education authority has a policy within which this question would have to be decided, the governing body would reach their decision on the

---

*Streaming: Grouping children, usually for all their lessons, in classes within two or more parallel chronological strata (or streams) by reference to particular criteria (e.g. performance in tests described as of general, or verbal, ability). The intended result is to facilitate teaching by making classes more homogeneous in ability.

†Mixed ability grouping: Grouping in classes which each contain children of a wide range of ability. Selection is frequently random and not by reference to estimated ability or attainment.

‡Setting: Grouping by attainment in a particular subject with the object of rendering teaching more effective by making classes more homogeneous in respect of ability in that subject. A pupil may for example be in the top set for English and in the bottom set for Mathematics.

218

basis of their own views modified as necessary by their conclusions about the practicality and effectiveness of the arrangements proposed. By its nature, this question might be considered by the local education authority and the governing body to be appropriate for the latter to decide, whereas it might be considered that a question of setting for an individual subject should be decided by the headteacher after consultation with the staff concerned and reported to the governing body.

Proposal to organise pastoral care in a secondary school on a year group system instead of the existing house system

1. Originator

The headteacher, who suggests that a tutor should be appointed to each year group who would be responsible to heads of lower and upper school.

2. Action by headteacher

i. To consult teaching staff and LEA officers including advisers.

ii. To prepare for governing body statements of:

a. the general case for the proposal, including the results of the preliminary consultative referred to in i;

b. full particulars of the proposal;

c. the effects on form and departmental organisation;

d. the resource implications (distribution of scale posts etc.)

3. Action by governing body

i. To request the head to:

a. prepare a statement of the steps and time scale by which the scheme might be implemented;

b. prepare a plan to monitor and evaluate the scheme.

ii. On receipt of reports on 3 i.a. and 3 i.b. to decide whether or not to proceed, bearing in mind that the local education authority might require to be consulted formally.

4. Conclusion

The above assumes that at each stage the governing body will discuss the matter thoroughly in order to form a judgment about the usefulness and practicability of the proposal as a means of improving the existing situation.

Example E

Consideration of a proposal to improve careers teaching in a secondary school

1. Originator

Community representative members of the governing body who have criticised the scheme of careers teaching as being out of touch with the needs of local industry and employment opportunities.

2. Action by the governing body

a. To consider whether there appears to be a case for changes in the system, and if so;

b. after discussion to arrange a meeting of governors, teachers, parents, careers officers, and representatives of local industry to discuss the matter and attempt to define aims and objectives.

c. Thereafter to request the head to prepare plans to show how the objectives might be pursued.

3. Action by headteacher

After discussion with the teaching staff, careers officers and local education authority advisers, to prepare plans to show possible courses of action. For each alternative the plans would show:

a. details of the objectives to be pursued;

b. organisational changes involved;

c. staffing requirements, eg posts of responsibility, in-service training needs;

d. other resource implications;

e. steps by which the changes could be introduced, including the time scale, with an indication of the acceptability of the proposals to the staff concerned;

f. procedures suggested for evaluating the results.

4. Action by the governing body

To receive and discuss the report received from the head. If the plan, or one of the plans, is considered suitable with or without amendment, to consider what further steps must be taken to implement it.

Example F

Consideration of a proposal to introduce the teaching of Welsh as a second language/cease teaching of Welsh/to make second language Welsh an optional subject

1. Originator

A parent or an action group.

2. Action by headteacher

It is assumed that the local education authority has no established policy on the teaching of Welsh as a second language. This being so the head should prepare statements for the governing body on:

i. the general case for teaching Welsh in the light of the linguistic and cultural background of the school's catchment area;

ii. parental demand and attitudes towards the inclusion of Welsh in the curriculum as a compulsory or optional subject;

iii. the effect on the school timetable and the implications for the overall aims and objectives of the school;

iv. resource implications (availability in the school or local education authority of suitably qualified Welsh speaking teachers, books, equipment etc) including an assessment of the resource implications of providing alternative tuition for small groups of children wishing to opt out of Welsh;

v. the steps necessary to monitor progress and evaluation of Welsh teaching if it is introduced, including any resource implications of such measures.

3. Action by governing body

The governing body would reach a decision in the light of all the considerations mentioned but would, before implementation, have to refer their decision as a recommendation to the local education authority in cases where resource implications extended beyond the school or where additional resources would be required.

[NB: Questions concerning first language Welsh or Welsh as a medium of instruction will almost always fall to be considered in relation to a local education authority's language policy.]

INDEX

The references are to paragraphs except where otherwise indicated.

225

22 / 102

228

Printed in England for Her Majesty's Stationery Office by Burrup, Mathieson & Co. Ltd.,
Dd 586800 K80 9/77